THE
CAREER
GAME

Everyone must play the career game.

Those who understand the rules have the advantage.

THE CAREER GAME

*A Step-by-Step Guide
Up the Ladder of Success*

Charles Guy Moore, Ph.D.

Economist
Executive Director
National Institute of Career Planning

BALLANTINE BOOKS • NEW YORK

This book was set in Vega by
National ShareGraphics, Inc.
The editor was David Dunham;
the designer was Joan O'Connor;
and Barry Benjamin did the proofreading.
The drawings were done by Joan O'Connor;
and the cartoons were done by Anne Green
and Fred Haynes.

Library of Congress Catalog Card Number: 75-27335

ISBN 0-345-27618-3

This edition published by arrangement with the
National Institute of Career Planning

Manufactured in the United States of America

First Ballantine Books Edition: February 1978
Second Printing: April 1978

FOR THE MEN AND WOMEN
WHO MUST PLAY
THE CAREER GAME

There are two things to aim at in life:
first to get what you want;
and, after that, to enjoy it.
Only the wisest of mankind achieve the second.

Logan Pearsall Smith

ACKNOWLEDGEMENTS

In a very real sense, this book does not belong to me but to the several hundred individuals who shared the details of their career experiences with me. The principles expounded in this book represent the final precipitate from their career histories that served as the raw materials from which these principles were formulated. My former and present teachers, colleagues, friends, and the authors I have read constitute another large group of individuals to whom I am indebted. These people and their experiences have shaped my awareness and thinking, and these influences are consequently reflected in each of this book's pages.

I am also indebted to more than a score of college students who served as unpaid test readers of the manuscript during each stage in its development. Their unsparing criticisms have been instrumental in the selection of examples that are tangible and relevant to the experiences of the audience for which this book is designed. Because of their unselfish contributions, this book's message is clearer and more readily understandable. I am especially thankful for the comments and suggestions of: Ann Foster Hale (Skidmore College), Scot Maurer (Bloomsburg State College), Jessica Driansky (Brooklyn College), Peter H. Gebert (Lehigh University), Nancy Vader (Western Michigan University), Kenneth Guldner (Franklin and Marshall College), Jane Mossman (Smith College), Christopher Edris (Lebanon Valley College), Patricia Pailet (LaFayette College), Richard Peek (Brooklyn College), Dorothy Corcoran (College of New Rochelle), Stephen Mock, Jr. (Lehigh University), Racheal Orefice (Brooklyn College), Thomas Whitman (Lebanon Valley College), Ruth Pollack (Moravian College), Dixie Drybread (Lebanon Valley College), Jean Kruger (Brooklyn College), and Barbara Wattiker (New York University).

I am indebted to Carolyn Wuerch, Fern Pigott, Henrietta Farnan, and Susan Cikovic who assisted with the typing during the earlier stages of the research. A very special note of thanks is due Beverly Wengert, who did the bulk of the manuscript typing, and Marie Beard, who typed the final draft. Without these women, all of whom were underpaid in relation to their contributions, there could not have been a book. I am also very grateful to Patrick Clifford and Adam Jacobs for their help in producing this book.

Finally, I owe my greatest debts to Joan O'Connor, Bill McCormick, Dominic Riccio, and David Dunham. Their encouragement, unselfish assistance, companionship, concern, and love have sustained my spirit during the four years it has taken to research and write this book. Dominic was instrumental in connecting me with the people. Bill helped from the start with ideas and repositioned some of the pieces in the final puzzle. And David polished the final product that Joan tried to make beautiful. But there's even a limit to what a fine team like these people can do, and I accept full responsibility for all the knots that remain in this wood.

Charles Guy Moore

CONTENTS

THE CAREER GAME

THE CAREER EDUCATION BLINDSPOT
Career Liberation Through Knowledge of How the System Works

BORN 1946-1965 EQUALS TROUBLE CAREERWISE
Career Strategy Required by Today's Overcrowded Professional Markets

THE FIVE DECISION-MAKING STEPS
Decisions Cannot Be Postponed

CHAPTER ONE

WHO THIS BOOK IS FOR AND WHAT IT'S ABOUT

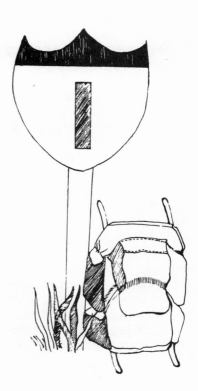

*The man who procrastinates is always
struggling with misfortunes.*

Hesiod

If you're pondering how to get ahead, floundering like so many young people and housewives do when they first try to enter or reenter the job market, trapped in work that isn't right for you, or a student wondering where there will be jobs when you graduate, then you too are suffering from our educational system's failure to provide us with effective career management courses. Students, business executives, career changers, housewives—virtually all of us make clumsy career decisions because we've never been taught how to manage our career affairs intelligently.

THE CAREER EDUCATION BLINDSPOT

While our colleges and universities have developed elaborate, specialized programs in such areas as business administration, hotel management, and even the administration of non-profit organizations—practically none of our schools offers a single course in career management and our guidance counselors alone can not fill this vacuum.

No one's ever systematically taught you how to: choose a career that's right for you; make yourself promotable; win in a job interview; and a score of other essential career management skills that could dramatically increase the control you exercise over your life and destiny. You probably aren't even familiar with essential facts about how the job market functions such as the fact that 80 percent of all jobs are never advertised or how to find out about these openings. Many of us get far better professional advice on how to play games like tennis than we ever get on how to play our career game.

Do you understand how to build flexibility into your career plans; when and how much to specialize; the special characteristics to look for in your first two or three career positions that you probably would not want in your later jobs? Probably not. Even the most successful professionals I've interviewed all admit they've made major, avoidable career blunders that have cost them dearly both in terms of foregone income and the frustrations associated with struggling with work that wasn't right for them.

200 professionals, 20 test readers and I have written this book to help people of all ages overcome handicaps like these that derive from our educational system's failure to provide us with effective career management courses. This book is based on five years of direct field research spent investigating and analyzing the career histories of those professionals coupled with my knowledge as a labor economist of how our job market system functions. Understanding certain key facts about how our economic system functions is another essential aspect of career decision-making that is overlooked by our educators.

No one's ever taught you: why jobs pay what they do; which jobs are recession-proof; what the tickets to the big money game are; and a host of other practical facts about our economic system that bear directly upon your ability to support yourself in your career both now and in the future. These are among the economic considerations we'll be getting into in Part II. And you need not worry that you won't be able to understand these sections.

The material I call "career economics"—the bare essentials everyone should know about how our economic system works in order to make intelligent career decisions—is explained clearly and simply in words and words alone. Moreover, the editors and I kept writing and rewriting these sections until our test readers' replies came back "interesting" as well as "relevant" and "clear." We went to all this trouble because we feel it's foolish for you to try to live and work in an economic system you don't understand. It's just exactly like trying to play the career game when you don't understand the rules. All you do is set yourself up to become victimized by the system and those who do understand how it works.

Career Liberation Through Knowledge of How the System Works

Knowledge is power and that's what this book is all about. Career Power. Career Liberation. Putting you in direct control of your career affairs on which you'll spend more of your life than on any other single activity.

The Career Game puts you in control by teaching you how our system works. Since you control the efforts you direct toward the system, you can also control what you get from the system once you understand how it works. After you've mastered *The Career Game* you'll know which efforts to apply in order to be most likely to get whatever it is you want out of your career.

Each of us is different and wants something different out of his or her career. Some want a lot of money. Others seek security. Some long for constant change and others crave power. What do you want? Part I will help you decide. Part II will show you where you can get it. Part III will teach you how to go after it.

This is a textbook in disguise. It's designed to provide you with the comprehensive career decision-making course you need to gain control over your vital career/life affairs. It's been illustrated with lots of examples so you will not need an instructor to help you interpret the points it makes. It focuses on two basic, interrelated topics: career choice and career advancement, and it provides *strategies* to help you:

1. Discover who you are and what type of work is most likely to make you happy. That is, help you find your career niche.
2. Discover how to predict the economic consequences of your career decisions.
3. Discover which jobs within your chosen career field will enable you to grow and advance at the rate you prefer.
4. Discover how to get current, comprehensive, career information that is tailored to your specific individual needs. The analytical tools you will learn

about in Part II will make this information meaningful and useful to you and thereby allow you to make much more intelligent, farsighted career decisions.

If you're not yet committed to a career field, you'll find this entire book germane to your needs. Those of you who are already settled in a field will probably be most interested in Parts II and III, however, you too should read Part I because it will help you decide in which direction you should plan to have your future promotions take you. The examples I've used reflect, in part, this dual readership and are designed more for a college audience especially in the earlier chapters.

I have deliberately kept the language in this book simple and couched many of its discussions in terms of a searching dialogue between myself and the reader. In most instances, however, I have used the pronoun "we" to reflect the views of the Institute as well as my own. In other cases, most of them obvious, the "we" refers to you the reader and me the author. Moreover, I have distinguished between my personal views and those of the Institute by using the pronoun "I" only when relating my personal experiences or expressing my personal convictions. In order to lend greater objectivity to the main body of the text, I have confined almost all such statements of my personal views and my interpretation of the facts reported throughout this book to Chapter Thirteen, which is written accordingly in the first person singular.

BORN 1946-1965 EQUALS TROUBLE CAREERWISE

A summary of the basic facts outlined in my recent report, *Baby Boom Equals Career Bust,* published in September 1977 by the Office of Career Education of HEW reveals why Americans born between these dates are in trouble careerwise. Basically, they're caught in an adverse "numbers game."

First of all, this generation is 1½ times as large as the generation that was born during the previous 20 years (79.5 million births 1946-1965 versus only 52.4 million births 1926-1945—an excess of 27 million plus babies in this baby boom generation). Second, the competition among college graduates is particularly severe because twice as high a percentage of this generation is finishing college. Consequently, the graduating college classes of the 70's are more than three times as large as those of the 50's. Third, the increased career consciousness of young women has also added significantly to the competitiveness of today's job market. Finally, the fact that the generation born after 1965 is much smaller has resulted in the elimination of many potential career opportunities in fields like teaching, the largest single employer of college graduates.

Moreover, the career difficulties of today's college graduates will not end once they find their first jobs. Since people are always in closest competition for advancement with others their own age, the competition among those in the baby boom generation will remain more intense throughout their careers because there will always be a relative abundance of competitors in this age group.

Career Strategy Required by Today's Overcrowded Professional Markets

The baby boom's effects on career opportunities is not limited, however, to the members of this generation. The competitive positions of older college graduates—especially those of housewives and others seeking to reenter the work force—are also being adversely affected by the availability of this large pool of newly trained, inexpensive college graduates.

Teachers and many other professionals are finding they can no longer afford to change jobs. Raises are becoming harder to come by. And professional fields like law have become glutted with new, would-be practitioners. We've entered a period of long term oversupply of college graduates. Having a college degree is no longer a more or less automatic ticket to a good job and the good life. Since surplus professionals are now present in most fields, it is becoming increasingly more important for professionals to get the competitive edge they can gain by knowing how to plan and strategically orchestrate their career moves.

THE FIVE DECISION-MAKING STEPS

The following five steps should be taken in order to rationally arrive at any decision:

Step 1   Identify exactly what it is you're deciding about.
Step 2   Define your preferred or ideal solution.
Step 3   Make an inventory of the resources you can use in working toward a solution.
Step 4   Identify and evaluate the alternative solutions.
Step 5   Rank the alternative solutions and choose the one that allows you to most closely approach your ideal solution with the least expenditure of your resources.

These are the steps around which the blueprint of this book was designed. In what follows, we shall refer to what we are deciding about as "the problem." Our discussion will be geared to career decision-making, and "the problem" will be your career decision.

Step 1, identifying and defining the problem, sounds much simpler than it typically is. Frequently what first appears to be the problem is merely a ramification of a broader, much more basic problem that still lies beneath the surface and remains to be discovered. Since all your effort will be for naught if you fail to correctly identify the problem, it may be wise to "put what you believe is the problem front and center on the stage." Then walk full circle around it and scrutinize it from every angle. There's a good chance you'll find it's just one side of a much larger problem—a problem or decision that interfaces with other decisions and has much broader implications.

For example, at this point you may believe that you must simply make a career decision. When we examine this problem, however, you'll soon discover that your career decision interfaces with and sets constraints on your future life-style, where you'll be able to live, and even the viability of any marriage you may make. Consequently, approaching career decision-making in this manner makes you aware that it must be considered an integrated part of a much broader set of life-planning decisions.

Once you've identified the problem, you must consider the solution you would prefer. To accomplish this you must define your preferences, rank your priorities, and imagine what you would consider to be the ideal solution to the problem you face. This is the goal-setting or objective-clarifying stage of the decision-making process. At this point you shouldn't be concerned with whether your goals are attainable. We ask you—in fact we encourage you—to dream during this goal-setting stage. Dreaming can be very productive, and dreams are often the buds from which tomorrow's possibilities unfold. Besides, as blind people like Helen Keller and others with handicaps have so often and so dramatically demonstrated, the truly impossible is a rather limited subset of the imaginable.

The third step constitutes making an inventory of the resources or means you have available to help you attain your preferred solution. It is at this point that you reintroduce realism into your evaluations. As regards career decision-making, step 3 consists of getting to know yourself and correctly identifying your strengths and shortcomings. Some people find this the most difficult task tackled in this book.

Step 4 involves the identification and evaluation of the alternative solutions to your problem. You begin by identifying all the alternative solutions that appear attractive. Then you contrast each alternative with the preferred solution you identified in step 2. Finally, you consider the "cost" of each alternative in terms of the resources you must use to attain it. That is, you compare the benefits of each solution with the resources you must sacrifice to achieve it.

The final step consists of ranking the alternative solutions and choosing the one that on balance, given your resources, allows you to most closely approach your preferred solution with the least expenditure of your resources. This is the "most efficient" solution as well as the attainable solution that your preferences indicate you prefer most.

There may be some degree of overlap among these five steps. It is often practical, for example, to give simultaneous consideration to the objectives, means, evaluation, and choice of the alternative solutions. Nevertheless, much can be gained in terms of clearer, sharper thinking by separating these issues and addressing each one in this recommended step-by-step procedure. That is why this book is structured around this logical step-by-step procedure. Finally, a word about the timing of decision-making.

Decisions Cannot Be Postponed

Decisions force us to commit ourselves. Since we are often hesitant to commit ourselves, it is only natural that we often want to avoid or postpone making decisions. But unlike going to the dentist, making decisions cannot be postponed. As time marches forward, events force us to make decisions. For example, the time we have to debate whether to catch the train is limited. If we don't decide, the train will "decide by default" for us when it pulls out of the station without us. Although frequently less obvious than this train example, the consequences of not deciding inevitably are "decisions by default."

Decisions are also intricately interconnected with each other. Every decision we make leads us along a path to new opportunities and to new decision-making situations. Likewise, by causing us not to proceed along other paths, every decision leads us away from the opportunities and decision-making siutations that lie along those other paths. Where you find yourself today is a direct reflection of your previous decision-making. The options you presently enjoy represent the net result of all the decisions made for or by you in the past.

For example, your going to college reflects the decision you made in eighth grade to pursue a college preparatory curriculum. That decision in turn was possible only because you had decided earlier to take grade school seriously. Are you an extrovert, athletic, knowledgeable about art, international affairs, birds, or butterflies? All of these attributes, developed skills, and the stock of knowledge you possess reflect how you have chosen to use your time and energy. Obviously, family circumstances and inherited traits also play a role. Nevertheless, it might be said that "we become our decisions"—that we become what our decisions allow us to become. This constitutes one of the major themes about which we will have a great deal more to say in Part I.

*Thales was asked what was most difficult to
man; he answered: "To know one's self."*

Diogenes Laertius

CHAPTER TWO

THE GROUND RULES OF THE CAREER GAME

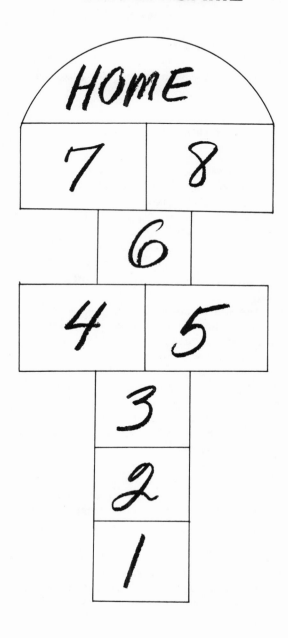

The first and most important rule of The Career Game is honesty. You simply must be honest with yourself about your strengths and weaknesses—and everything else about you—because the usefulness of your career plans and this book depends upon your being honest with yourself. We begin, therefore, by objectively evaluating the preparation of young people for the work they will be doing after graduation. We also make an honest appraisal of just exactly how this book can help you with your career planning, including what our approach cannot do for you. And finally, we speak frankly about the most common handicaps young people face in formulating career plans and suggest how they can be overcome.

PREPARING FOR THE FUNCTIONAL WORK ROLE OF COLLEGE GRADUATES

Although you and your classmates will work in widely diverse organizations, industries, and professions, your work will be similar in one important respect. Each of you will act as a decision-maker and/or as some type of problem-solver within an organization. Each of you will be one of the specialized players who contributes to your organization's team effort. Problems will be presented to you by your "teammates" or others outside your organization. You'll be expected to make decisions based on your analysis of these problems, and you'll have to communicate your decisions and proposed solutions to the others on your team.

Your college experience—outside as well as inside the classroom—should be preparing you to function as a decision-maker/problem-solver within an organization's chain of command. Figure 2–1 will help improve your understanding of the role you will be playing. You are functionally represented by the box with the rounded edges. Your mental activities take place in and are represented by the "mental wheel" inside the box. Information about the problems you are to work on is communicated to you through the tube on the left that leads into your mental wheel for processing. Resolution and decision-making take place inside the wheel. You must then communicate your solutions and decisions to your teammates and others through the off-loading tube that leads out to the right side of the box.

At the risk of being somewhat dehumanizing, Figure 2–1 does help pinpoint the importance of native intelligence and analytical, mathematical, and verbal skills, as these determine an individual's potential effectiveness in a decision-making/problem-solving role. IQ scores and our other imperfect measures of native intelligence might be·represented by the size of the mental wheel. The diagram reveals, however, that IQ is only partially responsible for the decision-maker/problem-solver's potential effectiveness.

An individual of genius-level intelligence who lacked developed verbal skills (which could be represented by blocked tubes leading into and/or out of the mental wheel) would nevertheless be of zero effectiveness as a decision-maker/problem-solver. Verbal skills must be developed if intelligence is to be useful. Porpoises, for example, are incredibly intelligent animals. Until we learn to communicate with them, however, their intelligence is of little functional value to us. Likewise, foreigners and "intelligent beings" from outer space cannot function within our organizations until they learn our language.

Your potential effectiveness in a decision-making/problem-solving role, therefore, is jointly determined by the quality of the mental machinery you inherit plus the verbal skills you develop. One's inherent mental ability is of little value unless one's verbal skills are developed. Whereas you can do nothing to augment the native intelligence you received from the lottery of birth, you can increase your potential effectiveness by developing your communicative skills and improving the efficiency with which you use your inherited mental machinery.

Thomas Edison claimed that people never fully use the mental machinery they inherit. He maintained that genius is 1 percent inspiration and 99 percent perspiration and that our limitations are self-imposed by our failure to fully develop and exploit the talents we do inherit. The next sections identify several of the limitations you are likely to have and suggest how you can increase your potential effectiveness by overcoming them.

Figure 2-1

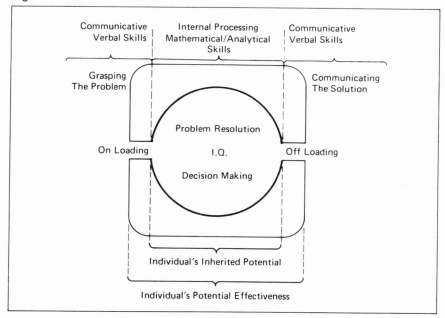

TV Child—How Well Can You Read? Write?

The introduction of television into our environment has significantly altered the way we communicate and how we spend our time. It has spawned an unpleasant reality that applies specifically to your generation and is glaringly revealed in these statistics. Almost half of the freshmen at the University of California at Berkeley must enroll in a remedial English course. Sixty percent of the freshmen at the University of Houston fail the first three essays they write.[1] It is painfully clear that television has had a devastating effect on verbal skill development among young people. You are likely to have been affected and may wish to overcome this television-induced handicap.

Although young people are receiving more schooling, they are reading less. And writing even less. Essay examinations and term papers have been caught in a pincer movement of larger class size and computerized scoring of "objective" multiple-choice exams. We were shocked to learn that some editors of college textbooks advise their authors to avoid three syllable words! Problems and opportunities, however, frequently come in sets like the two sides of a coin. Turn the coin with "problem" on it and you'll probably find "opportunity" stamped on its other face. You can profit from your generation's general lack of verbal skills by sharpening your own.

It may be relatively easy for you to become known as "a person who has a way with words" since so many in your generation use words poorly. Logic would suggest that it should be less difficult to become recognized as articulate when others are less so. Furthermore, when you enter the work force, you'll find that many of the top positions are still held by members of the pre-TV generation. These are the people with the authority to hire and promote you. Being articulate, which impresses nearly everyone, may leave an especially favorable impression with your older bosses.

How Well Can You Reason?

Unfortunately, there is strong evidence that, as a group, modern educators may place too much emphasis on *what* is rather than on *why* it is—that they emphasize the factual when they should rely primarily on an analytical or why approach. This contention is supported by the fact that national Scholastic Aptitude Test scores have dropped steadily in math as well as in English. This decline has been continuous since 1962, and it is acknowledged as real (that is, not a statistical quirk). The reason for the drop says Sam McCandless, Director of Admissions Testing for the College Entrance Examination Board: a decline in students' "developed reasoning ability." [2] The factual orientation of many educators reflects, in part, their reliance on "objective" (multiple choice, true and false, etc.) examinations. These types of examinations are naturally suited to factual questions and large classes.

The general permissiveness throughout our society has also left its mark on the educational establishment. It is reflected in phenomena like "gradeflation." At Yale in the spring of 1974, "42% of all undergraduate spring-term grades were A's and 46% of the senior class graduated with honors."[3] This too is wrong. School should prepare young people to cope with the circumstances they will face after graduation, and they are not easy. Making school easy is misleading. It ill prepares students for life, handicaps them, and is therefore very cruel in the end. If you were a gladiator, wouldn't you want to get the most rigorous training possible? Life, too, is a form of combat.

This, however, is not the place to delve into a general essay on the effectiveness of America's educational establishment and the causes thereof. Our educational establishment is vast and widely divergent in quality. Certainly some of you were fortunate enough to receive an analytically oriented education. We would like to persuade the rest of you to seek such training.

Courses with a factual orientation—courses that you can master by memorizing a string of facts—are an educational rip-off you cannot afford. They cannot possibly prepare you to shoulder the responsibilities you'll face after graduation. You're going to be a problem-solver and/or a decision-maker. True, you will be dealing with facts. But you yourself will be discovering many of these facts. And your most important task will be to analyze how these facts are interrelated and *why.* Life after graduation isn't anything like a multiple-choice exam. You'll be graded on your ability to think, to analyze fresh problems, and to communicate your solutions to others with whom you'll also have to get along.

Factual knowledge, which by itself has never been of much value to decision-makers and problem-solvers, is of even less value today. We are accumulating knowledge at a pace that was not thought possible a generation ago. No one knows exactly what the half-life of facts is today, but it is short and getting ever shorter. Many of the facts you memorize while in college will already be outdated before you enter the work force. Rapid change is a paramount characteristic of the twentieth century, and facts are among the first casualties of change. The modern computer with its capability for instant recall from a seemingly limitless memory is an impossible competitor for the memorizer. The market for the factually oriented is dead. Society needs and is only willing to pay for decision-makers and problem-solvers who can think, analyze, and make sound decisions based on their analysis of the constantly changing circumstances we face.

The Grade Trap

"But," you say, "I need good grades to get into graduate school and courses with a factual orientation—well, I know what I must do to get an A." A very seductive trap into which many of us have fallen. True, good grades may be instrumental in getting you into graduate school. But aren't you overlooking the fact that college and graduate school are preparing you for work in your career field? They represent perhaps half a dozen years whereas your career will occupy you for the subsequent 40. Getting into graduate school is an important consideration but hardly more important than functioning closer to your maximum potential during your career years.

While you're in school, you should be concerned with getting the mental exercise you need to stretch and develop your mind so that you'll be able to excel later as a problem-solver/decision-maker. When you're tempted to improve your academic record at the expense of your long-run career preparation, consider the fact that every compromise you make in favor of grades per se at the expense of your mental development will make you less of a mental giant, more like a mental midget. A decision in favor of higher grades may also leave you slightly handicapped for life.

Because of gradeflation, graduate schools have now been forced, in general, to ignore grades. They are relying increasingly instead on Graduate Record Examination test results to select their incoming classes.[4] How well will your gut courses prepare you for the thinking required on the Graduate Record Exams? Most shortcuts—and all educational shortcuts—end up cutting you off or down or out.

Seen from a long-range perspective, grades are of decidedly limited importance. They may help get you into graduate school and into your first job. After your first job, however, no one will care to study your transcript. Once you enter the work force, you'll be evaluated thereafter on your performance. At this point, I wouldn't consider working for an organization that was silly enough to ask for my transcript. If you take the tough, mind-stretching courses while you're in school, you'll gain confidence in yourself and you'll easily pass the grade grubbers when you meet them later in the real world of work.

Summarizing what we have learned from Figure 2–1, college prepares you for a role as a problem-solver/decision-maker. To function in this capacity you need to develop your analytical, mathematical, or problem-solving skills. In addition, you must develop your verbal skills in order to grasp the problems and communicate the solutions you propose. School is a training ground in which you ought to seek the maximum development of these general skills. Your performance in school as measured by the grades you earn is of secondary importance. The real test of your success in school will be reflected later in your performance in the world of work. No matter what you do in our rapidly changing world, it will require being able to think and communicate your ideas. Consequently, you should select courses that can develop these skills. Virtually any course can be taught from an analytical orientation, depending on the instructor. English composition, speech courses, and extensive reading will help you overcome any verbal handicaps you may have.

THE ASSUMPTIONS OF OUR APPROACH

During the next few years, circumstances will force you to make the most important set of decisions of your life. The decisions you make—either explicitly or by default—will shape your destiny. We at the National Institute of Career Planning would like to help you with your career decisions. But like the Wizard of Oz, we can act only as your catalyst. We can point out what you ought to consider and teach you how to analyze your alternatives. We can teach you how to think clearly and independently about your career decisions, but no more. We cannot find your answer for you.

The Why Approach

The why approach that is used throughout this book is designed to prepare you to independently make your own career decisions. It reflects our basic assumption that you will be best able to make sound, independent career decisions if you understand *why* circumstances in the world of work are as they are. This approach is consistent with the analytical, problem-solving/decision-making role that will be expected of you as a member of the college-trained labor force. Conditions are never exactly the same nor are they static. Our why approach is designed to prepare you to analyze and understand the particular and ever-changing circumstances you will encounter during your career. It would have been simpler and shorter to just state the whats. The why approach takes longer, but it teaches you to understand tomorrow as well as today. And without understanding tomorrow, there can be no enlightened career decision-making.

The Idealized Approach

There are good ways, bad ways, and a best way to do almost everything. This book teaches the idealized or "best" approach to career decision-making. It is the approach that might be taken by a perfectionist who is intensely concerned about every aspect and ramification of career decision-making. Since no one is so inhumanly perfectionistic, each of you will have to modify or abridge our idealized approach to fit your own interests, needs, and the amount of time you are willing to spend on your career plans.

You can better appreciate our "idealized" approach if you understand the parallel between it and the way you were taught physics. Physics is studied in the assumed context of a frictionless world. This assumption, though totally unrealistic, is nevertheless helpful because friction varies with local conditions. Consequently, it simplifies matters if the physicist accounts for friction in the frictionless model in accordance with local conditions. Similarly, career concerns vary with an individual's interests, needs, and conditions. We have chosen to present the comprehensive "idealized" approach and let you select from it in accordance with your preferences. Only you know what's most important to you, and, furthermore, what concerns you is likely to change over time. For example, Chapter Five, which discusses locational considerations, may become more relevant to you when you face job offers in several regions. In short, we present the unabridged approach and let you decide which aspects of it are most relevant to your individual needs.

There is another important sense in which our approach is "idealized." It assumes that the labor market is in "normal" balance or basic equilibrium. *The Career Game* is written to help you cope with the typical labor market conditions that you can expect to encounter during the vast majority of your career years. It is not specifically designed to help you deal with the difficult labor market conditions that occur periodically when our economy is dislocated and in search of a new basic equilibrium as, for example, in 1975–76. Explaining how to operate in dislocated labor markets is an extremely difficult, separate subject that exceeds the scope of this book and may indeed be an impossible task for any one book.

Trying to advise the economic novice how to navigate in dislocated labor markets would probably be even more confusing and misleading than it would be difficult. While mass unemployment is a typical symptom of most economic dislocations, the conditions of each dislocation are sufficiently different to require specific advice. Good advice on these matters cannot be prepared in advance because it must be geared to the specifics of each situation, and these, of course, are not known in advance.

Periods of economic dislocation and the mass unemployment that accompanies them can result from a bewildering array of causes. They may occur during the transition from war to peace; as a temporary adjustment to widespread technological change; as the economy downshifts to a slower rate of growth; during the period of economic shakeout that follows an inflationary price spiral; in response to resource shortages like the energy crisis; and combinations of these and many other factors—most notably inept and myopic governmental policies. They constitute periods during which a sizable segment of the economy's human and other resources are being reallocated to new and different uses.

For example, the energy crisis and the higher energy prices it has spawned represent a new economic reality to which our economy must ultimately adjust. Some unemployment is inevitable during this period of transition. Some jobs will be permanently lost in the automobile industry. Others will be created in factories that manufacture railroad equipment and building insulation. Similar shifts in resource usage have been made in the past. Icemen no longer make deliveries to homes; their jobs have "moved" to Indiana and other places where refrigerators are made.

While periods of economic dislocation can be expected, the time of their occurrence and their specific nature cannot be predicted. We can and do advise you as to the type of industries and career fields in which you can expect them. We can and do tell you how and at what price you can best insulate yourself from the most disadvantageous effects of these dislocations. And we suggest what types of "compromise bread-and-butter jobs" will nevertheless further your long-run career development if circumstances force you to temporarily seek work just to keep eating. But we cannot give advice on how you, with your specific qualifications and interests, can deal with the particular dislocations of 1975–76 or any other time. For that you need an ecomomic consultant who understands the specifics of your situation and the times.

Finally, there is yet another quite different and independent reason why we abstain from advising you on how to maneuver in dislocated labor markets. This book offers career advisement. Your career plans ought to be structured around the normal conditions you expect to encounter during the major part of your career years. The majority of employees in a good many fields never experience layoffs. But suppose you don't plan to work in one of these stable fields. In that case, while contingency planning to get you through a recession would be prudent, it would still hardly make sense to plan your career around such contingencies. If you enjoy engineering and your graduation is timed to coincide perfectly with a recession, you may face a very serious problem. However, you should not abandon engineering as a career simply because you are temporarily unable to find employment in your chosen field. Recessions, however unpleasant and bleak at the moment, will not last forever. You should be very reluctant to change your career direction based on such random, unpredictable, and transitory events. On the other hand, if you have several alternatives about which you are relatively indifferent, it might be sensible to allow a recession to "decide for you." You will simply have to let your best judgment guide you in modifying our "idealized" approach to fit prevailing economic conditions.

On Hedging and Qualifiers

Economists and sociologists, political scientists, and all other types of social scientists have at least one thing in common. They study the behavior and decision-making of people. Based on their observations and deductive reasoning, they do their best to formulate generalizations that accurately predict what human beings will do under a given set of circumstances. And they are always partially frustrated in their attempts—never 100 percent correct in their predictions.

Human nature itself is responsible for their frustration. People just refuse to be reduced to a set of generalizations, a set of rules. They will not cooperate with the social scientists' attempts to categorize them. For every generalization made, there are exceptions, some nonconformists. Social scientists—especially economists—are renowned for their mistakes, and even more renowned for their heated, sometimes bitter, professional disagreements with each other. These disputes are themselves a direct result of the variability of human nature.

Physicists and other natural scientists can formulate general laws that are 100 percent accurate. Consequently, they tend to engage in fewer disputes. It would be rather ridiculous to debate Newton's laws since they can be proved. The generalizations developed in this book predict the impact of human behavior on conditions in labor markets. These generalizations are helpful, but, unlike Newton's laws, they cannot be definitively proven; and there are exceptions to all of them. This is unavoidably the case because our subject is human behavior and decision-making. We wish to point this out now in order to avoid repetitiveness in the presentation of these generalizations. "It is practically always true that," "in the vast majority of cases," or similar words to this effect might have been prefixed to all the generalizations that appear throughout this book. These phrases have been omitted merely to streamline the presentation. You should "add" them to these generalizations in which they are *always* to be *implied.* We've simply tried to avoid boring you by repeatedly restating the same qualifier. Generalizations are very helpful. Without them it would be much more difficult to organize our thoughts. But we must understand their limitations.

Social scientists must also be prepared to make some informed judgments that cannot be "proven." Again, this reflects the nature of their subject matter. We can support our propositions and the generalizations we formulate with facts, observations, and logic; but we can prove very few of them. We are left with the alternatives of being right and saying very little or saying more and increasing the chances that we may occasionally be wrong. Those of us at the Institute have chosen the second option. But we've done our best to carefully support our generalizations with years of direct field research, including hundreds of personal interviews. We've tried to be helpful without being reckless. And since we've adopted the "why approach," our arguments are visible and you can scrutinize our logic.

One final word about our generalizations. If you encounter what you believe is an exception to one of them, double-check your facts and logic. You should be very reluctant to assume that your circumstances do indeed constitute an exception to the rule. They may, but this is unlikely. You should search for a good explanation for this discrepancy before you conclude that yours is an exceptional case. Then please drop us a line with your explanation. We'd like to learn from your experiences.

THE HANDICAPS OF YOUTH

We've already discussed some of the handicaps you're likely to have acquired from television and a factually orientated education. We feel we should point out a few more of your probable handicaps, not to bug or criticize you, but to offer you the opportunity to compensate for them. These handicaps are caused by your youthfulness. They appear on the problem side of the coin that has all the opportunities of youth on its other face.

When you're young you have all the advantages: health, energy, optimism, fewer responsibilities, and greater independence. All of the advantages except one—experience. If you can muster the humility to learn from the mistakes of those who have been buffeted and bruised by experience, you'll have all the advantages.

The Big Decisions Come at the Worst Possible Time

All of us have those days when our mental circuits are almost completely tied up with, for example, Excedrin headache number 113, the heartbreak of love a-wilting, or the advent of spring. A very poor time for decision-making. Yet it's the order of things that life's most important decisions are timed to coincide absolutely perfectly with the hallucinogenic glory of the springtime of our lives.

Right then when your body is seething with the imperative sexual juices of adolescence and you're leaving the confinement that your parents' home has become. Right then like millstones they come crashing down, trying to pin you down. Throwing mud on your spring. Career. Marriage. Location. The Commitments. The decisions that will constrain your future, mark the limits within which you'll act out most of the rest of your life.

You can't avoid these decisions. They can't be postponed. Trying to postpone them will merely alter the options you'll face later. Deciding or "deciding by default," either way what you do now will define and shape the possibilities you will face in your thirties, your forties, the rest of your life. What you do now will set off a chain reaction of events, a type of domino effect that will catapult you into the rest of your life.

Without frightening you, we would like to make you aware that you must make the most important decisions of your life at the worst possible time. You'll have to concentrate very hard in order to compensate for the unfortunate timing that nature and circumstances have put upon you. Even if you do not doubt the wisdom of these words, we would like you to ask this question of some people over thirty whose opinions you respect and trust. "If you had the opportunity of a fresh start in this whole game of life, what would you do differently?" Five will get you fifty that the decisions they will want to change will be those they made in their twenties.

When you're twenty, you've just left the dependency of your parents' home rule and in a sense your life as an individual has just started. You feel essentially immortal and you live in the eternal present. In the short space of ten years you'll be thirty. Your life will be nearly half spent, you'll have confronted some of the hard realities we've been discussing, and you'll be much better prepared to make farsighted career-life decisions. But for most of you, it will already be too costly to undo the consequences of your previous decade's decisions.

You'll have lost your mobility—a casualty of family, career, training. You'll be too much in debt paying off refrigerators, maternity bills, and your palace to take any big chances. You'll be embarrassed to admit your foolish mistakes. And you'll have lost some of your youthful energy. Now is the time to decide, to act. Now is the time to get serious about shaping your future because, whether

you realize it or not, your present actions are already shaping it for better or for worse.

Some Very Straight Talk

Finally, a little straight talk about how and why it's so difficult to get twenty-year-olds to listen and believe.

If we come at you preaching like some establishment type, you'll tune us out. If we season the message with your fad language and paste daisies on it, you'll reject it as a cheap, rip-off gimmick. If it's laid out like a textbook, you'll yawn. If it comes to you with your parents' recommendations, many of you will stamp "Poison: Do Not Read" all over it. Most colleges don't teach courses in career decision-making and most students don't buy books unless they have to. Conclusion: you've got to be a little crazy to write to an audience like that.

But you need good career advice, and you know it. The problem is, or rather a typical problem is, that you seek piecemeal advice. Most of you seek advice sporadically when a big decision comes up, but you fail to seek comprehensive, integrated career advice. You seek advice each time you find yourself at the chessboard, but you fail to integrate your moves into a consistent long-range game plan. You get uptight, seek advice, make your move, and then return to your delightful distractions until circumstances again force you to seek advice. At least that's what I did.

It's important that you get the message. We've tried to make it interesting. We've kept the language simple and used examples that the test readers have found relevant to their experiences. Making the message relevant or "tangible" is another Achilles' heel when it comes to giving young people career advice. After you've held a full-time job for several years, this message will become dramatically clearer and more relevant to you. But then it will be much

more costly to undo your mistakes. Please do your best to get the message now and spare yourself as much future grief as you can.

Much of what you will read may already be obvious to you. *Comprehensiveness,* however, is the key to formulating successful career plans. The *single* element you overlook can foul up your entire plan. It's like getting dressed for an interview. The single article of clothing you forget can drastically alter your entire appearance.

This whole book ought to be studied before you formulate your career plans. The chapters of Part I should be digested as one unit. Those in Part II can be read separately but in sequence. You should start picking the brains of those who are working in the career fields that interest you as soon as possible. Why? Because more than anything else, the perspective you will gain from interviewing them will help you relate to this book's messages.

Those are our suggestions, but feel free to reject them. The important thing is that you profit from reading this book and that it contributes to your future happiness. Reading it should be interesting as well as helpful. If you find that our recommended route drags you down, try a little hopscotch.

*I don't like work—no man does—but I like
what is in work—the chance to find yourself.
Your own reality—for yourself, not for
others—what no other man can ever know.*

Joseph Conrad

PART I

DECIDING WHAT YOU WANT MOST OUT OF LIFE

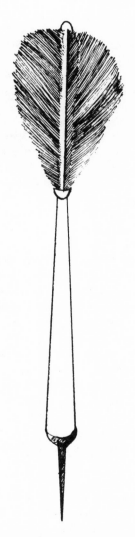

You Are In Control: You Will "Become" Your Decisions
Developing Your Career Shopping List

Have you ever had the frustrating experience of going to your guidance counselor for career advice only to be asked in turn: "But what would you like to do?" or "What type of work do you think you could do well?" Makes you wish you could reply: "Wait a minute, if I knew those answers I wouldn't be here. I came to you for those answers, not to have you ask me my own questions!" But before you give your guidance counselor an F for helpfulness, consider this fact: our government lists over 35,000 different job classifications. So where's your poor guidance counselor supposed to start without some hints from you?

It's the situation, the whole career guidance situation, that's frustrating. It's like circling over an unknown world looking for a place to alight without being able to recognize dry land from wet and not even knowing if you're meant to be a land or a water animal—all of which makes you feel mostly like a big, awkward turkey. Part I is designed to help you discover what type of terrain you'll thrive on so that you can land safely in the career world. It's designed to direct you to the landing strip that's right for you, make your landing less anxious, and take the "turkey" out of this whole affair.

The problem just outlined is essentially one of being asked to make a decision when you lack sufficient information. Circumstances have always forced young people to choose careers before they really know enough about career possibilities and themselves to make informed, intelligent, farsighted career decisions.

Part I is designed to help you resolve this dilemma. It begins by asking you to look inward in an attempt to discover who you are. It suggests some techniques you can use and experiences you can seek to help you discover, analyze, and "find" yourself. Next it pinpoints and carefully discusses the aspects of your life that will be most significantly affected by your career decision. That is, we identify what your career decision really involves. Finally, based on this knowledge of yourself and what your career decision involves, we ask you to define what you would consider the ideal circumstances under which you would prefer to live and work. In other words, Part I asks you to identify and define the ideal properties of the career you believe would maximize your happiness based on your personality, talents, needs, and desires. By way of preview, Part II then teaches you how to analyze actual career opportunities so that you can identify the career that best matches the ideal one you define for yourself in Part I.

You Are In Control: You Will "Become" Your Decisions

In understanding who you are lies the explanation for why you will become what your decisions allow you to become. As we shall see, you "are" what you have experienced. This is why it is so very very important that you make your decisions—especially your career decision—consciously so that you remain in control of what you experience and thus become. You can exercise great

Identification? Is this you too?

control over your destiny—but only if your actions are taken deliberately and you *consciously* choose the experiences you will have.

Have you ever tried to define exactly what you would identify as being you? It is true that you reside in your body, but you are not your body. If you lost your foot, your arm—even if you had a heart transplant—wouldn't you still have the same identity, still be you? Similarly, aren't all of the parts of your body including your brain merely "mechanisms" that serve your consciousness? Isn't your consciousness—the collection of thoughts, feelings, ideas, attitudes, and beliefs that you hold—the essence of you with which you identify? If this is the case, it follows that whatever shapes your consciousness also shapes you.

But isn't your consciousness limited to the environment that surrounds you? Hasn't your consciousness been shaped and molded by the environmental forces that you have been reacting to throughout your life? Now then, if we are our consciousness that is shaped by our environment, isn't it fair to maintain that we "become our environment"? It follows that by choosing to expose ourselves to the right set of environmental influences, we can deliberately condition ourselves along the lines we prefer. This conclusion is both hopeful and sobering. Hopeful because it means we can overcome the effects of the undesirable environmental contitioning we received in the past. Sobering because it makes us aware that we are in control of our own destiny. We are responsible for what we become because we generally choose the environmental circumstances that shape and mold our consciousness. We must always remember, however, that we can only continue to control what we become by consciously and deliberately choosing our environment.

The chapters in Part I discuss the various aspects of choosing the environment that will shape and mold you in the future. They deal with your people environment, your activity environment, and your location environment. They deal with becoming "who you are around, what you do, and where you do it." There is really very little that is new in all of this. Darwin pointed out that our bodies reflect what they had to be, how they had to develop, in order to survive in our physical environment. Generations of social scientists have documented the numerous ways we reflect our human environment. Just how these environmental forces have and will continue to shape and mold your consciousness will become much clearer as we move into Chapter Three, where, for example, we investigate the roots of our perceptions. The important lesson to be gained from this search for our identity is that we shape and mold ourselves, either consciously or unconsciously, by our choice of environments. You are in control of what you will become.

Developing Your Career Shopping List
Part I is designed to help you identify who you are and decide what you want most out of your life and your career. Discovering who you are and what kind of work is likely to satisfy and fulfill you will be a process rather than an event. Many ideas, feelings, and desires will enter your mind as you mull over the topics we shall discuss. To help you organize these thoughts, we have added several blank pages, referred to as Your Career Shopping List, at the end of this book. Each time you feel you may have tentatively identified one of your career preferences, jot it down on one of these pages.

Unless you know what you're shopping for, you are very likely to become overwhelmed and bewildered by all the considerations that will confront you when you enter the career market. It is important, therefore, that you develop your own detailed, well thought-out, shopping list in advance. You will need this list in order to coherently organize and integrate your many preferences when you complete your final career shopping list for the personal interviews in Chapter Eleven. But don't try to organize your list as you make it. Simply list each of your preferences as it occurs to you. Later, after you've completed your shopping list, you can begin to review it and start making trade-offs. Ultimately, you will have to trade-off all the advantages of the other careers that also interest you for the package of advantages offered by the career you choose to follow. You should tuck this reality into the back of your mind and allow it to temper your thinking as you go about constructing your shopping list.

One fundamental trade-off is central to all the chapters of Part I, especially Chapter Four. It involves your decision as to the importance you will attach to your career in relation to the rest of your life pursuits. This might be called *the* trade-off. It is analogous to deciding if you will major in your career, major in your non-career pursuits, or the degree to which you will major in both. This is the trade-off that should concern you most as you read Part I.

Finally, we should warn you that the author's preferences inevitably find their way into the text. At the Institute we prefer the more balanced approach of majoring to some degree in both career and non-career pursuits. One reader of an earlier draft pointed out that this preference was revealed not so much in what was said as in what was not said. She noted that we failed to discuss the alternative of working at something you don't care about purely to get the money you need to "live outside of your career."

You may choose to pursue this "working purely to live after work" alternative in which case you may be more interested in the monetary aspects of career decision-making that are discussed in Part II. Many people do pursue this alternative, but we have found that few people enjoy it or consciously choose it. Most people who work purely to live after work find they are stuck with this alternative as a result of inadequate career decision-making.

In order that people may be happy in their work, these three things are needed: They must be fit for it. They must not do too much of it. And they must have a sense of success in it.

John Ruskin

CHAPTER THREE

GETTING IT ALL TOGETHER: YOURSELF, THE JOB, THE PEOPLE

The difficulties that surround the career decision-making process are multiplied by the need to consider a large number of interrelated factors at the same time. It is much less confusing, however, to discuss each of these factors separately as shall be our practice. It is important, therefore, that the organization of this chapter into three separate discussions does not mislead you. Once you've reflected upon them separately, you will somehow have to weigh all three of these considerations as well as those we will discuss later and come up with an integrated "compromise" career decision.

FINDING YOURSELF

Sensible career planning must begin with the ancient Greek maxim "know thyself"—or what we refer to as "finding youself." Only after you know yourself and identify your real needs can you expect to choose a career that will satisfy you. By finding yourself we mean identifying your personality and talent traits. Finding yourself represents the first, or identifying, stage of what we shall refer to as the identity-match process. Once you have found yourself, the matching half of this process involves compatibly matching your personality and talent traits with broadly defined job functions for which these traits are desirable. Whereas we shall largely complete the identifying stage in this chapter, the matching stage of this process will occupy us throughout most of the rest of Parts I and II.

Are You Left-Minded or Right-Minded?

In her fascinating, award-winning book *The Brain Changers,*[1] Maya Pines reports on mind research that bears directly on career decision-making. Our minds are divided into two separate hemispheres, each of which controls the motor nerves on one side of our body, has its own personality, and governs some of the specialized functions like language that are the exclusive domain of one side of our mind. Each side can operate independently of the other side, but one side is always dominant and controls all the speaking. Thus we perpetuate the illusion that we have one mind. This illusion is destroyed, however, when the connecting tissue between these halves is severed, as in an operation to end the apparent war for dominance between the two sides in cases of severe epilepsy. Following this operation, the left and right minds literally do not know what each other has done and one of them may even be restraining the aggressive behavior of the other.

At birth, the connective tissues between these halves is only partially developed and duplicate, or parallel, learning occurs in both halves. By the age of two, both sides become fully connected and specialized learning begins. The right side is usually assigned tasks of synthesis, spacial perception, and music, while the left side gets all the sequential, verbal, analytical, computerlike activities. One side becomes dominant, and we develop into left-brained types who function most comfortably in a verbal world or right-brained types who rely more heavily on non-verbal forms of expression. This is what's important as far as career decision-making is concerned.

Because we tend to develop more of the talents that are the specialty of our dominant side, careers that utilize these skills are likely to come more easily and naturally to us. Knowing if you're right-minded or left-minded, therefore, can help you choose a career that's more likely to be a natural for you. Apparently, the direction your eyes turn when you think is a simple but very accurate test of which of your minds is dominant.[2] Your eyes will veer to the side opposite your dominant mind when you think. If you wish to learn which of your friends' minds are dominant, stare directly at them, ask them to count the number of letters in a long word, and observe the direction in which their eyes turn. If they veer to the right (that is, your friend's right), your friend is probably left-minded and more likely to be happy as a scientist, researcher, writer, or someone else who does analytical tasks. If they veer to the left, your friend is more likely to be happy following an artistic, musical, or a less verbal career.

Knowing of which mind your friends are may also help you improve the communication between you. When you know you're communicating with right-minded types, for example, you may choose to rely more heavily on hand gestures, graphics, and other non-verbal forms of communication. The primary benefits, however, can be expected from knowing which of your minds is dominant. For example, let's assume you're considering, or that your parents or someone else is pushing you into, an analytical type of career. If you learn that you are right-minded, you should reconsider your decision because you may be overlooking your strongest talents and interests. The degree of dominance varies a great deal, however, and this is not revealed by this simple eye test. Individuals whose two sides are most equally developed (with a slight amount of dominance) can be at home in both the analytical and the artistic world. This is an advantage in certain careers like architecture that require this type of balance. Because brain research is only now in its infancy, you'll be hearing a great deal more about it in the next few decades. At this point, many people view this subject as more interesting than useful.

Self-Image Psychology: Are You Limiting Yourself?

In his extremely popular book, *Psycho-Cybernetics,* Dr. Maxwell Maltz maintains that you may never realize your full potential unless you assume you have it. He bases his approach to greater self-realization on the solution-seeking procedures of the mind. This approach identifies the roles of the self-image, imagination, and positive thinking in expanding the possibilities available to the individual.[3]

Would you *try* to walk on water? Why not? Because you *assume* you cannot do it? Well, it certainly will be impossible for you to walk on water if your assumption that you cannot do it prevents you from ever trying to do it. These four sentences capture the essentials of the principle that explains how our self-image operates to set the limits of what it is "possible" for each of us to do in life.

There are two things that can make it impossible for us to do something: an assumption that we cannot that consequently stops us from trying or the reality that we cannot do it. If we expand our self-image—our idea of what we feel we can do—we will be able to do more because we'll attempt more and find we can accomplish more. Many times our incorrect assumptions alone can make it impossible for us to accomplish something because they block us from ever trying. Because it is largely the self-image that establishes the limits of individual accomplishment, if you expand it you also expand the "area of the possible." Dr. Maltz then goes on to explain how the mind seeks perfection.

The mind apparently seeks to achieve perfection through a process of trial and error in which, through feedback, it learns from and corrects its previous mistakes. It stores "programs" for tasks it does repeatedly and continually revises and perfects them each time they are used. This explains why practice makes perfect, even though we apply less effort and concentration. For example, after several weeks of trial and error, I found that unlocking my car in the dark became a simple, unthinking, automatic procedure. I also recall one of my earliest childhood memories that involved my first "Cheers, here's to you" with a glass of orange juice for me and wine for the big folks. Well, my glass went right up over my head without ever finding my mouth. "Not so far the next time" must have gone into my mind's corrected program for I never did that number again.

Finally, Dr. Maltz couples the self-image concept and the trial-and-error procedure with the fact that the mind cannot distinguish between an actual experience and one that is imagined vividly and in detail. He relays the following experiment that was reported in *Research Quarterly*. Sixty students were tested on their ability to shoot basketballs and were then divided into three groups of 20 each. For the next 20 days Group I practiced shooting baskets for 20 minutes each day, Group II did nothing, and Group III imagined they were shooting baskets for 20 minutes each day. "When they [Group III] missed they would imagine that they corrected their aim accordingly." [4] When they were tested again at the end of this period, the percentage improvement in these groups' scores was: Group I, 24; Group II, 0; Group III, 23! Psychologist R. A. Vandell achieved similar results in a controlled experiment that involved dart throwing.[5]

In its simplest formulation, therefore, Maltz's formula reduces to: (1) assume it's possible, (2) rehearse doing it in your imagination, and (3) do it. I was surprised to learn that one of my conservative boyhood friends has been successfully relying on this "technique of mental rehearsals" for years. He explained that although it works, it's not the kind of thing you talk about freely in the business world in which he has been immensely successful. "Most people are likely to question your competence if you raise the subject of mental rehearsals." Nevertheless, whenever he faces a difficult business meeting, he lies in bed early that morning and quietly goes over the upcoming meeting as vividly as possible in his imagination. He tries to anticipate every possible argument that may come up, prepares a response for it, and rehearses giving the response. When the meeting actually occurs, he is confidently prepared and has anticipated most of the moves that will come up. Under his management, his firm's sales have grown from $3 million to $12 million in just seven years; during this same period of time dozens of firms in his industry have folded. Call it by a different name if you like—it still works.

Dr. Maltz also maintains that the self-image concept explains why positive thinking works for some and not for others. It works only for those who expand their self-image to include the tasks under consideration within "the area of the possible." There can be no doubt that how we feel about ourselves affects our ability to perform. *Psycho-Cybernetics,* now in its twentieth-odd printing, is well worth reading. The suggested applications of the "technique of mental rehearsals" are especially interesting. Is your self-image limiting your career possiblities?

Inventory Approaches to Self-Discovery

The inventory approaches that are popular among many career specialists like Holland, Haldane, and Bolles are based on the assumption that one's past experiences can serve as a useful guide in making intelligent career choices for the future. These approaches begin by listing or taking an inventory of one's past achievements, activities, interests, memories, etc. These experiences, how they were chosen and how they are viewed, are assumed to reveal important aspects of an individual's personality and talents. Consequently, these inventories are then analyzed in order to identify common denominators that reveal the individual's personality and talent traits. Finally, studies of the personality and talent profiles of individuals who have been happy and successful in various occupations have made it possible to correlate the traits of these individuals with their career pursuits. The final assumption, therefore, is that if you have the same profile as those who have been happy and successful in an occupation, you too will probably be happy and successful in it. These are the steps and assumptions that are involved in linking up these inventories with occupational pursuits. We shall briefly outline the essentials of one of these inventory approaches.

Holland's Self-Directed Search Program

Dr. John L. Holland of Johns Hopkins University has long been a leader and careful researcher in the field of vocational guidance. His do-it-yourself Self-Directed Search Program has the advantages of being simple, and inexpensive and can be administered without professional assistance. If your school guidance counselor does not have a set of these materials, you may purchase a complete specimen set for $2.00 from Consulting Psychologists Press, 577 College Avenue, Palo Alto, California 94306.

Holland's program classifies work-related personality/skill traits into six categories: realistic, investigative, artistic, social, enterprising, and conventional. These terms have special connotations, however, in the context of his program. Students simply check "like" or "dislike" or "yes" or "no" to a series of questions under each of these six categories in separate activity, competency, occupational, and skill inventories. These results are then easily scored by the student to produce a three-letter summary code. Students then locate their summary code in a companion booklet that lists occupations that use these traits. This whole process takes less than an hour to complete. There is probably no easier or faster way to come up with a list of occupational possibilities, a few of which you might then choose to investigate in greater detail. I was impressed with these simple tests, the results of which seemed surprisingly valid in my case.

Other Techniques to Identify Your Talents and Interests

In his popular job-hunters' manual, *What Color Is Your Parachute?*, Richard Nelson Bolles suggests a series of practical exercises and aids to help you discover your interests and skills. Bernard Haldane, one of the original pioneers in career research, has written numerous books in which he suggests similar exercises to help you discover your talents and interests. His *Management Excellence Kit* is designed to help you discover your interests by analyzing what you consider to be your most important past achievements. You may find these and similar exercises and approaches helpful to you in identifying your interests.

Among the most widely used evaluative tools are the six types of psychological tests: personality, interest, aptitude, intelligence, achievement, and creativity. Your school guidance counselor can help guide you in selecting the type that is most appropriate to your needs. You should not view the results of these tests as infallible however. If they clash significantly with how you view yourself, you should carefully review your thinking before you reject them. But if, after careful consideration, you still believe the results are invalid, simply ignore them because they may indeed be invalid in your case.

IQ tests, for example, all of which attempt to measure an individual's capacity to reason and understand, have been fraught with unavoidable problems since their very inception. Although they're designed to measure intelligence, they invariably measure learned verbal or manual skills as well because these skills are used to complete these exams. The more you've used and thereby developed your verbal (manual) skills, the more points you'll score on a verbal (manual) IQ test. In addition, these tests are usually timed, which penalizes people who are cautious and prefer to check their answers carefully.

Likewise, these exams penalize those who are unusually nervous when tested. For all these reasons, the results of IQ tests should be interpreted cautiously. If you're able to do well in school, don't let your scores on IQ tests give you a complex. Consider them, but also consider your comparative ability to reason with your friends and classmates. IQ tests are always imperfect. There are many reasons why they may be wrong in your case.

Your parents, relatives, close friends, teachers—anyone who knows you rather well—can also be excellent sources of free career advice and information. Ask these people who know you well what career they could see you in and *why*. At the same time you ask them for career suggestions, also ask them for career information about their occupations. Just start asking questions— make a habit of it—about other people's careers and the careers of their friends. This experience will help you prepare for the in-depth interviewing you will be doing when you've completed this program. Much of the advice and information you collect during these early "warm-up interviews" may be of limited usefulness. That's not what's most important. At this stage your objective is simply to develop your interviewing techniques and start bouncing career ideas around in your head.

Make an Inside Job of It
There's just no substitute for first-hand knowledge. If you really want to know the story and whether you should be part of it, get inside where the action is and participate for awhile. This is one of the major themes of our approach.

Where are you in school? How many summers do you have left before you graduate to full-time employment? Why not get paid while you do your own on-the-spot career research next summer? Summer jobs and other part-time jobs provide good opportunities for you to organize your career plans. If they're well chosen, they can be very beneficial to you by helping you identify your personality, talents, and interests; probably prompting you to choose your school course work more wisely and apply yourself better because you'll know what you need to know and why; and giving you valuable work experience that will help you carry yourself better in job interviews because you'll be better able to explain why you want what you want. In short, well-chosen part-time work experiences will help you discover your work preferences, talents, and skills; give you a sense of direction; and help you focus your efforts to prepare yourself for your future career.

Your primary objective in choosing part-time work should be to accumulate the broadest type of experience you possibly can prior to starting your full-time career. You should view your part-time jobs as part of your preparation for a full-time career. Because they are primarily designed to help you find your career path, you should consider the amount of money these part-time jobs pay as a matter of secondary importance. In addition, you should not stick with any of these jobs very long—not more than one summer at the most—

because in the limited time you have, you want to find out as much as you can about the world of work and how you function in it.

Among the most important ways in which your future employers might vary are size (small, medium, large) type of organization (profit-oriented, non-profit institution, government) and subject treated (people, data, things). And much, much finer classifications can be made. You have a lot of sampling to do. Perhaps you feel you know enough about certain types of employers to rule them out without sampling them. OK, but be careful when you rule things out. It makes a big difference whether you're working with people, things, or data. Job pressures are quite different in non-profit as opposed to most profit-oriented organizations. You will have to reduce the list of career pursuits you consider strong possibilities and then simply do the best you can to experience as many of them as you can. But try not to base your decision on money. Finding your career niche is far more important than being less of an impoverished student by a few bucks. Since frequent job hopping is frowned upon after you start working on a full-time basis, hop around now and try to find yourself while you're still in school. The experience you gain from job hopping while you're still a student may spare you the initial years of floundering that so many students go through when they begin their careers

THE JOB AND YOUR LIFE-STYLE

Although we've stressed the point that your career decision will directly affect such things as your life-style and family relationships, these statements probably remain rather vague abstractions for many of you. The next few pages are designed, therefore, to provide specific examples that will give you a more tangible sense of and feeling for how the career positions you might choose would affect your life-style and family relationships. This list is not complete, however, and we will deal with many of these considerations in greater detail in the later chapters. These issues are being raised at this point merely to get your thoughts focused on the kinds of integrated considerations and compromises you need to begin making as you start "getting it all together."

We shall deal with three general types of life-style considerations: those that affect the amount of time you must devote to your job, the pressures associated with it, and the spillover effects your work will generate on the rest of your life, especially your family life. These are qualitative measures of your life that indicate whether you can spend it as you prefer.

Travel—Refreshing or Burdensome?
Most people enjoy and look forward to occasional business trips. These break up their work routine and introduce them to new people and places. On the other hand, most people find traveling burdensome when it becomes the routine. This is especially true of overnight and over-the-weekend trips. These

Well, Dad, do you think it's environment or heredity.

trips can keep you from your family and friends for long periods at a time.

Unscheduled travel creates even greater family problems. At the last minute you can't make it and your family is forced to change its plans. This can put great stress on family ties; after a while your family may just stop including you in its plans. Don't kid yourself; any significant amount of overnight travel will adversely affect normal family relationships. All personal relationships require spending time together if they are to be maintained and grow. Being away from home when your children need you will affect your relationships with them. Kids are very selfish—they just won't buy any of your excuses, period. They'll feel unloved and deserted if you're not there when they want and feel they need you. If you can't remember how you felt at that age, ask someone who has small children.

Two to five scheduled three-day business trips a year seem ideal for most people. These "working vacations from work" help keep you and your job fresh. And this amount of travel doesn't interfere greatly with family and personal ties. In fact, this much travel may keep you away from home just enough to make your family appreciate you a little more. But you should remember to bring them something to show you missed them too.

Because so much of business today is national in scope, all types of employees must travel more than they did a generation ago. However, certain careers such as management consulting, sales, and public accounting involve a great deal more traveling than most others. Travel requirements vary with the industry, the firm, and the career stage you're in. Depending on the nature of your work, the amount you must travel may increase or decrease as you advance in your career. Sales people tend to travel less later in their careers. General managers, on the other hand, usually travel more because they must supervise more operations.

Civic and Social Obligations

Employees are sometimes expected to represent their organizations after hours at civic events or to entertain clients socially. These activities can draw you away from your family and friends in much the same way, and with similar consequences, as too much travel. They, too, can become burdensome and prevent you from being the master of your own time and life. Always ask employers about their policy on these matters before you agree to work for them. Let them know where you stand in order to prevent any misunderstanding.

Vacation Time

You should consider three things about vacation time: how much you will get, when you can take it, and whether you can take more without pay if you wish to. It's also nice to be able to plan to take vacations when you want them. This is not possible in some fields. Skiing and accounting, for example, just aren't very compatible because the tax season happens to coincide with the ski season. Vacationing during this period is impossible for most accountants, and similar work/leisure conflicts exist in other fields as well.

Finally, it's important to be able to take several more weeks off without pay, especially if your vacation time is short. This flexibility will allow you to make an extended trip to Europe or Africa for example. It will mean you can take that vacation of a lifetime and really see something in detail. The option to extend your vacation time allows you to trade money for time, which means you can change the leisure/work balance in your life. You should also reach an understanding with your employer on this matter of extended vacations before you accept the job.

Flexible Hours and Dress

Being able to adjust your work schedule to accommodate your personal needs is a very big advantage. It goes a long way toward making you the master of your own time and life. The more your contribution at work is related to the contributions of others, the more difficult it is to keep flexible hours. It's also nice to be able to dress casually for work if you want to. It's a drag to have to run home to change before you go out at night.

Seasonal, Deadline, and Self-Imposed Work Pressures

Because each of us reacts differently to pressure, we shall simply note the incidence of pressures in certain fields. You alone must find out, for example, if you can deal with the Christmas schedule of a retailer. How will your family be affected by your absence at this time? Will you be civil or exhausted and hassled? You alone can determine if you can produce and thrive despite the deadline pressures associated with journalism and media work. If you're considering fields with seasonal or deadline pressures, try to test your reactions to these pressures as soon as you can. Then if you find them too unpleasant to cope with, you'll not have wasted as much time preparing yourself for work you won't want to continue doing.

The third kind of pressure is self-imposed. It comes from within us often because we're overly concerned about doing a good job. In the future, if you find that you're overly concerned about your work, you must realize that your overconcern is counterproductive. It probably won't help you to change jobs or fields because what will be needed is a change in your attitude. You will have to try to relax and not make your work more difficult than it need be. You've got to work on your own head to solve this problem.

Homework

Your work may tangibly infringe on the rest of your life in the form of work you do at home. Or it can intangibly infringe on the rest of your life in the sense that your mind and spirit are preoccupied with your work. Although you've gone home, you may have left your consciousness at work and you may not really be paying attention to what's going on. Many people, especially those who enjoy their work, have found they must fight this tendency to remain "at work."

If you start bringing tangible homework home on anything close to a regular basis, you should start asking yourself questions. Have I become a "work freak"? Maybe I should reorganize my work, change employers or fields? Homework indicates that you are having real problems balancing your needs. Since homework may affect your whole life, including your job, work on this problem immediately if it develops. Many professional people and self-employed people have a homework problem.

The Personalities You Meet at Work

Finally, it's important to consider who you'll be working with. Although there is a tremendous variety of people working in every field, each career field tends to have a "center." If I told you we were going to a cocktail party given by bankers, or doctors, or artists, wouldn't you expect each of these parties to be different? The people who work in a career field tend to share some common traits, interests, and motivations, etc. They tend to have a vaguely definable "center" and share a somewhat common mentality.

It's important that you feel comfortable with those in your career field because you will be spending a large portion of your life working with them. Furthermore, you are likely to draw a high percentage of your friends from among your associates at work. If you refuse to socialize with the people you work with, it can only hurt you. If you have a chance to mix socially with people who are working in the fields you're considering, take advantage of this opportunity to meet them. It may help you decide if you're about to make a career choice you can work with.

COMMUNICATING WITH OTHERS

Communication, in the sense we shall use it here, includes more than just getting the message across. It also includes dealing and working harmoniously with and through others to satisfy your mutual needs. In its broadest sense, the term *communicating* as we shall use it means navigating effectively in your people environment.

The skills you develop to help you communicate with others and sell yourself and your proposals to them may very well be the key ingredients in your future success and happiness. Time and again professionals in many career fields have told me, and I paraphrase: "A sizable cluster of practitioners of roughly equal expertise can be found in our field and most others as well. Only a few of them, however, also have the people skills that allow them to communicate their ideas and sell themselves as well as their expertise. They make others *want to believe* that they are the very best. And they frequently do become acknowledged as the leaders in their professions."

Our earlier discussion of the importance of communicative skills in fulfilling your future role as a problem-solver/decision-maker constituted only the beginning of the story about the importance of being able to communicate effectively with others. Indeed, nearly every aspect of your life—especially your career—will be affected by your ability to communicate and deal effectively with others. Others will decide to hire you, promote you, work with or against you, and to treat you fairly or unfairly, kindly or unkindly, warmly or coldly. They may trust, help, respect, and love you or do just the opposite. This is why communication is so important. You must learn to communicate effectively with others in order to gain their cooperation in working toward your mutually beneficial ends. You want people to work with you, not against you.

Three Types of Communication Gaps

Communication gaps can be graphically represented in the space between individuals A and B in Figure 3–1, which is an extension of Figure 2–1. Let's imagine that individual A on the left has a message to communicate to individual B in the center. The roman numerals that appear between A and B's mental wheels mark the various steps through which the message must be transmitted. Blockage at any of these junctures will cause a communication gap.

Type I gaps are the result of the message sender's inarticulateness in formulating the message. The message is garbled at location I as it leaves A's

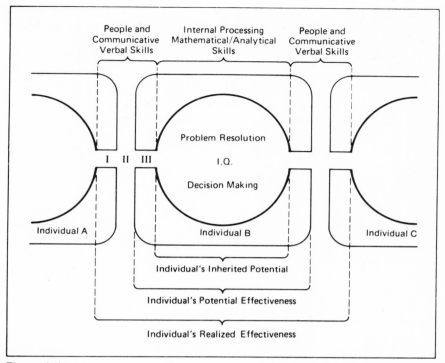

People and Communicative Verbal Skills

Internal Processing Mathematical/Analytical Skills

People and Communicative Verbal Skills

Problem Resolution

I.Q.

Decision Making

I   II   III

Individual A

Individual B

Individual C

Individual's Inherited Potential

Individual's Potential Effectiveness

Individual's Realized Effectiveness

Figure 3-1

off-loading tube. For example, A's message may be incompletely, incorrectly, or incoherently expressed.

Type II gaps are much more interesting and common. They result essentially from the sender's insensitivity to the receiver's feelings and differences from the sender. This second type of communication gap involves the rejection of a proposal to cooperate that both parties view as fair and mutually advantageous. In this case, the proposal is not rejected because it is unattractive per se, but because of some form of rejection, disapproval, or lack of trust, etc. in the one making the proposal. The person making the proposal may be rejected personally or his or her real intention may be questioned. Type II gaps can be caused by any one of a large family of often subtle "language problems" that make the communication ineffective because of the form in which it is presented. In short, the communication is blocked because it is "packaged" improperly.

The vocabulary we use, the analogies we draw, the timing of our delivery, our manner and the mannerisms we use, the role we assume (for example, that of a peer, friend, advisor, etc.) with the receiver—all these nuances constitute the packaging of the communication. Body language is a communicative nuance that has received a good deal of attention recently. Our voice is another; and it alone can vary in terms of tone, inflection, cadence, accent, what we emphasize, and we could go on and on. We can use these nuances of expression to say something sarcastically and completely change its meaning. Communicating is clearly a very involved and complicated process. This is why artful communicators personalize all communications whenever possible, why they present or package the same message differently for each of us in accordance with our background and circumstances. They know that the improper choice of any of these subtle nuances can cause a type II communication gap. They realize that these gaps are not so much the result of what we say as how we choose to say it.

The receiver is responsible for type III communication gaps. They are caused primarily by inattentiveness and reading incorrect motivations and intentions into the sender's communication. The sender can avoid many potential type III gaps by anticipating them and taking effective steps to hold the receiver's attention and reassure the receiver that the message is straightforward.

How Communication Gaps Originate
Communication gaps originate, for the most part, from the same sets of conditions that cause each of us to be individuals who are slightly different from everyone else. This point can be illustrated by examining how the human mind and a modern computer function. Both the mind and the computer are created blank and must be given background information before they can provide any answers. In addition, the accuracy of both the mind and the computer is wholly dependent upon their being given accurate information in the first place in a format that they can understand. This very limited and imperfect "analogy" can help reveal a great deal about why we frequently fail to communicate what we wish to communicate to others.

Our minds receive their initial "programing" from our parents and the other members of our immediate family. Confusion and communication difficulties are inevitably guaranteed by this arrangement whereby each of us receives his or her programming from a different set of individuals, all of whom perceive the world and its "realities" somewhat differently. The information or programming we receive simply cannot be completely accurate because each of our family programmers is guilty of the same types of inaccuracies, biases, prejudices, and misperceptions shared in varying degrees by all human beings. Thus, inevitably, from day one we begin to acquire a perception of reality that is, objectively speaking, as inaccurate and unrealistic as our family's circumstances and experiences are unique.

To make communication still more difficult, the combination of "languages" used by each family is also unique. For example, some families teach and condition their members through a system of rewards whereas others rely on punishment. Each family also has its own special mannerisms, symbols, verbal and non-verbal forms of expressing itself—all of which constitute part of its unique "language." And then there are the "languages" of all the other environmental and cultural influences that touch us and shape our consciousness. Look at yourself. Can't you see how your ethnic, religious, economic, regional, and national affiliations have affected your thinking and the "languages" you understand and attempt to communicate with?

Our communication difficulties begin, therefore, at home, where each of us is programmed with partially inaccurate information and taught "languages" that are never fully understood by those outside our home. Consequently, we communicate poorly—just what we should expect of a group of maverick computers, each programmed with different information and its own unique language. Overcoming these inevitable communication difficulties requires that we consciously seek to avoid language problems and that we deliberately seek to expand and modify our limited perception of reality.

The broader the environment in which one hopes to be active, the greater the need for modification of one's original perceptions. If you grew up in a small town and plan to spend your life there, you need never learn to communicate with people outside it. But if you plan to leave a small town for the city, you'll need to learn to understand city people in order to communicate and deal effectively with them. It is also wise to learn how to cope with people you find unpleasant and disagreeable because circumstances at work, in your neighborhood, and elsewhere will force you to deal with a few such people.

Some Secrets of Communicating Effectively

By now you can realize why type II communication gaps are so common. Being sensitive to individual differences and anticipating that these individual differences in programming, background, experiences, and "language" will cause communication problems are *the* secrets to communicating effectively. This sensitivity and understanding will enable you to formulate communication approaches that will help you avoid type II gaps. The next few sections offer some specific examples of approaches that rely on these principles of effective communication.

Draw on the Other Person's "Library"

This principle of effective communication is designed to help you conceptualize the ways in which people are different. It represents an extension of the arguments we have just made. In terms of our earlier discussion, this principle might also be called "Speak the Other Person's Language."

Try to imagine what it would really be like to get inside someone's head—to stand and peer outward from the center of the mental wheel in the illustrations we have been using. What we would see might be considered analogous to a vast circular library with books, bulletins, clippings, sounds, smells, tastes, and all manner of images, etc.—all these arranged under such major subject headings as "art," "food," "music," "sex," and "sociology." Under these there would be subheadings like "fiddles," "peanut butter," and "Elton John." The volumes and entries under each subject might be classified as vicarious information, first-hand information, and imagined or synthesized experiences to reflect how these acquisitions were made and the sources from which they came. One spin around in their heads and we'd have a good idea how people had spent their time, what interested them, and what we could talk to them about. And, of very special importance to fulfilling our objective of more effective communication, one glance at the subheading "languages" would reveal how we could best communicate with them.

The nearly blank mind of a child does eventually evolve into something that functionally resembles such a vast library. When people relate to each other about their common interests, concerns, and experiences, they can be thought of as exchanging or Xeroxing the volumes they find interesting in each other's libraries. Type II communication gaps are analogous to attempts to exchange books that don't interest or cannot be understood by the other person. These books may be written in the wrong language, on the wrong subject, about subjects that are considered too private, or they may be presented or "packaged" so as to make them unacceptable to the other person. All of these are examples of the common mistake of being insensitive to the other person's differentness from yourself.

When you first encounter people with whom you want to communicate, therefore, you should look for clues as to the "languages" they will understand. You should also look for a subject of common interest that can serve as a satisfactory opener to establish a dialogue with them. These techniques will help you gain acceptance as a person, after which you can begin to push your proposals or communicate whatever else you wish.

You can get many clues about the "languages" and interests of people by being a good listener and sharpening your powers of observation. Listen to the vocabulary, analogies, and symbols they use. Observe their manner of speaking, dress, and temperament. Becoming skillful in relating to people is something you can really learn only through experience. "Drawing on the other person's library" is merely the first important step that gets you past the very common blunder of being oblivious to individual differences and consequently attempting to relate to everyone the same way. Be sure to relate to people as individuals, and then just experiment until you've developed your own successful style. Since you'll be handicapped without these skills, keep practicing—do whatever you must—until you become a skillful people handler.

Being Competent Is Not Enough

Earlier we noted that the leaders in most fields become acknowledged as such because, in addition to the necessary expertise, they also have the people skills needed to promote themselves and their work. In some instances, the acknowledged leaders may not even be the best technicians. But they have made the public *want to believe* that they are, and this is their secret.

Each of us has needs that force us to deal with other people. In most cases, however, we have some choice as to whom we will deal with. And we typically choose to deal with the people who, in addition to appearing able to satisfy our specific needs, provide us with supplemental reasons for wanting to deal with them. In fact, we often base our choice primarily on these other reasons because we are unable to adaquately evaluate their expertise.

It is unwise, therefore, to rely purely on your competence to promote your career interests. If you are also able to meet their human needs for understanding and friendship, people will want to believe you are competent because they will want to deal with you rather than with others. In addition to being sensitive to their differentness, therefore, also be sensitive to the human needs of those with whom you are relating. Work on developing a genuine interest and concern for others and mix warmly with them. That is, work on developing a healthy and mutually rewarding other-person orientation. This is simple, perhaps obvious, advice. But it can make all the difference in singling you out from the others who are being interviewed for a job or considered for a promotion and it can greatly enrich your non-career life as well.

Use Good Timing

Communicating effectively also requires being sensitive to the immediate moods and preoccupations of others. Try to approach them when they are not tired, irritated, upset, or preoccupied with something else. Trying to put yourself in their position will help you become sensitive to their differentness, their human needs, and their immediate moods as well.

You would be wise to begin now to continually develop and perfect your people skills. People are at least half the battle in life. You need their cooperation.

Seek Social Experiences in College

You should not wait until after graduation to begin improving your people skills. College life provides a multitude of opportunities for you to practice developing them in a relatively unpressured context. Becoming active in any of your on- or off-campus organizations will help you to learn how to deal with people. Living in a fraternity, sorority, or any other autonomous group setting can also teach you valuable lessons. These group experiences will teach you how to make proposals, negotiate, and reach compromises with others. As we shall see later, in today's world we function as team players and many decisions are reached collectively through committees. The more group experience you gain in college, the better prepared you'll be.

CHAPTER FOUR

WHAT WILL YOUR MAJOR BE IN LIFE?

God asks no man whether he will accept life. That is not the choice. You must take it. The only choice is how.

Henry Ward Beecher

This chapter deals with what we referred to earlier as *the* career/life trade-off. This trade-off involves the decision as to how you will divide your time between your career and your other life interests. It is equivalent to deciding whether you will major in your career, major in your non-career pursuits, or the degree to which you will major in both.

Having to work is a reality very few of us can successfully dodge for very long. We typically find that those who have dropped out to try a subsistence routine are eventually back at work on terms they find less attractive than those they were offered earlier. Although our material needs force us to spend time providing for them, we also have less obvious spiritual and other non-material needs, such as the need to form and maintain close relationships with others. We should spend time providing for these needs too because we reap from these relationships in direct proportion to the time and energy we put into them. The answer lies, therefore, in discovering how to strike a happy balance between our various competing life needs. Finding and maintaining such a balance is the topic of this chapter.

No one but you can decide what the central focus of your life ought to be. Consequently, rather than answering this question for you, this chapter's discussions are designed to make you explicitly aware of the implications of the choices you might make. We shall discuss the uses of time, their rewards, and how Americans use their time. These more general discussions are followed by an examination of some of the specific trade-offs you will face in making your career decision. The final section illustrates the impact of commuting and overtime on your "time money" and develops a simple index to help you monitor the leisure/work balance in your life.

OUR "TIME MONEY" AND MATERIALISM

If you sit down and quietly ponder the nature of your existence, you'll realize, if you don't already, that time is the essence of life, that time is really all we human beings have. Everything we acquire—money, knowledge, possessions, skills—simply represents a transformation of our time and energy. When we use our time to work, study, or practice, we convert or transform our time into money, things, knowledge, or skills. We "pay" for all these things with the one thing we can't buy: our time, a piece of our lives. It follows that time is *the* scarce resource, or the ultimate "money" each of us has to spend.

Most people agree that to be as happy as possible in life is a worthwhile goal. Even if they can't always define it or say what they want, they seek happiness and wonder how to get it. The following discussions are designed to help you decide how you can spend your time money to gain the greatest amount of happiness during your lifetime.

Happiness can be defined as your state of mind when you react favorably to the circumstances that you face. These circumstances, in turn, depend on how, where, and with whom you spend your time. It follows that the outlook for your overall happiness will be favorable if you enjoy your career, on which you will probably spend more of your time money than on any other single activity. The time that you convert through working into money and into the material things money can buy will also be a source of happiness. But money cannot buy friends, love, or an understanding of one's family. These can only be "bought" directly with time. Since these are rich sources of human happiness, your time is also well spent on them. Essentially, therefore, you must decide what combination of material and non-material "time purchases" will maximize your happiness.

Three key considerations or requirements should concern you most when you're choosing a career. Your career should satisfy your financial needs, your individual needs, and leave you with enough time and energy to meet your family's needs—if you have a family. What you must look for, therefore, is a viable three-way compromise.

You might begin by analyzing what appear to be interesting career opportunities to see if you feel they would fulfill you personally. If they pass this test and you also feel you possess the required personality and talent traits to do them well, you can proceed to analyze their financial potential. Finally, you can analyze the careers that meet both these criteria in terms of your family's needs for you in the future. If you plan to eventually have a family, will the career you're considering allow you to spend as much time with them as you want to? When it comes to spending your time money, you really do get the kind of personal and family relationships you pay for. Will you have the time and energy to cultivate happiness at home as well as at work?

Finally, it must be noted that the viability of your career decision will depend on the viability of all three of these parts. That is, if any one of these needs is not met, the others will probably not be met satisfactorily either. All three parts are mutually interdependent and affect each other favorably or unfavorably. Individuals who are unhappy with their work will probably bring that unhappiness home to infect their family relationships. Likewise financial problems can torpedo a marriage and a bad marriage can ruin a career. Your happiness rests, so to speak, in a critical three-way balance.

Are Americans Too Materialistic?

America and Americans in general have sometimes been criticized for being too materialistic. Before we attempt to evaluate these criticisms, however, several points must be made. First of all, materialism should not be confused with material goods. It cannot logically be concluded that Americans are materialistic simply because they happen to have a relative abundance of material goods. Materialism and material circumstances are not the same. In this book, we use the word materalism to refer to a preoccupation with material things—a tendency to seek them, to stress their worth. Materialism is not an index of how many material goods are enjoyed; rather, it is an index of how interested people are in increasing the amount of their material goods.

Furthermore, when we attempt to evaluate these allegations that America and Americans are *too* materialistic, we must bear in mind that *all* judgments made in regard to material circumstances must be based on *relative* comparisons. Wealth and poverty are relative concepts that cannot be defined in absolute terms, but only in terms of a particular time and place. In 1976, all Americans are well off by eighteenth-century American standards or by present-day Indonesian standards. Yet future generations or unknown beings in outer space may view us as poor. Wealth is a concept that depends on our perspective—where and when we live and, most important, what we know others have. There will always be rich and poor lands, people with more and people with less.

Thus all questions that pertain to materialism inherently involve making value judgments. Such judgments should, therefore, be left to the individual. These value judgments should be made consciously; they should not be "fudged" or decided in a biased way, as most people usually do. The discussions that follow are designed to correct this situation and to help you consciously make your own decisions on how much of your time money you would be wise to spend on material goods.

Our values are taught to us by our environment: they are part of the programming our minds receive from our families, our institutions, our society and the world at large. American values, therefore, are not really our "personal" values but those our American environment has taught us: we did not choose them any more than we chose to be born in America. In reality, the values we hold are just another example of how we have "become our environment." If we wish to be objective, we should be willing to try to determine how well these values conform with our present circumstances and our individual needs.

Values are slow to change and usualy do so only after they have been proven inappropriate in the face of changed circumstances. Since our material circumstances are dramatically different from those of our parents from whom we acquired our material values, shouldn't we double-check the consistency of our inherited material values with today's material realities? Even though this is difficult, we must attempt it. The following paragraphs that ask you to rethink these values should not be construed as an attack on American values, your values, or the importance of work and the material things work produces. Rather than degrade the importance of work and material things, these discussions are designed to develop an objectively balanced perspective of their importance.

What Do the Figures Tell Us?

Income and employment statistics support the claims that ours is a materialistic society. From 1941 to 1972, the average American's real income (after adjustment for inflation) increased by 109 percent.[1] Even though we became more than twice as wealthy, however, Americans continued to spend exactly as much time working. The average industrial work week was 40.6 hours both in 1941 and 1972.[2]

Working women, especially since 1950, have been largely responsible for our increased wealth. It is even more interesting, however, to learn which women have entered the work force. Whereas the percentage of working women with no children under the age of eighteen increased by 36.6 percent, those working women with children under the age of six increased by 134.6 percent during the period 1950 to 1972.[3]

Although these figures also reflect other considerations such as the increased incidence of divorce, they nevertheless smack decidedly of materialism. Despite the fact that our material wealth has more than doubled, we have shown no interest in spending more of our time on non-material pursuits. In fact, much of our added material wealth has been purchased with the time money of women, especially those with infant children, who have been added to the paid work force. If we consider the family to be the basic social unit, we must conclude that our society has impoverished itself in terms of time. And this has been done to add to our material wealth, which was already greater than any other nation's in 1950. Why have we made these choices?

Is Economic Theory Wrong or Have We Been Conned?

That people should become more wealthy, and then work harder, is hardly what economic theory predicts. It maintains that people will work until the value of the things they acquire through working equals the value they place on their time. As a nation becomes wealthier, economic theory predicts that part of its additional income will be used to "buy" additional leisure time. That is, as people get richer, they will work fewer hours—just the opposite of what has in fact happened in America.

An example will clarify this point. Economists working in less-developed countries have found that higher wages result in fewer hours worked. After receiving their pay checks, workers feel so wealthy that they simply refuse to return to work until they again need money. For the time being, they have enough money to satisfy their needs, and they prefer additional leisure time to more money. In such areas, cigarettes, Coca Cola, bicycles, and transistor radios have sometimes been introduced in order to counteract these workers' preference for leisure time. That is, deliberate attempts have sometimes been made to hook these workers on consumption goods in order to keep them working.

In effect, this is precisely what Professor John Kenneth Galbraith claims has happened to the American worker/consumer. In *The Affluent Society* he argues that many of our products are unneeded. Advertising, nevertheless, convinces us that we must have them. He claims that advertising, through contrived want creation, produces the need for additional work to produce and pay for these unneeded products. Do you think Professor Galbraith is correct? Has advertising added to your family's work week and diminished its leisure time? Although we are wealthier, have we been conned into working more?

Do We Lack Adequate Leisure/Work Options?

To some extent, certain individuals are purchasing more leisure time. This is especially true at the extreme ends of the working-age group. Older people are retiring a few years earlier, and a lot of young people are dropping out of the work force for long periods at a time. Some of them take off several months, or even years, between jobs or careers. More of this might occur if it were encouraged by our institutions.

It seems that institutional rigidity now stands in the way of shorter working hours. Most employers offer a 40-hour work week or no work at all. If workers were given the option of working 30 hours a week, many of them might accept less money for the additional leisure time. Shorter work weeks are being tried, as are work schedules with extended weekends (for example, ten-hour days with three-day weekends, or ten-hour days with one seven-day week on and one week off). Some individuals have been able to arrange shorter work weeks because their firms don't want to lose them.

But so far, few employers have been forced to consider shorter work weeks and longer vacations. However, if present experiments with shorter work weeks and longer vacations are successful and become popular with employees, employers will be forced to reconsider. If large numbers of employees want more leisure time, a few smart employers will begin offering it. These few employers will have many more job applicants than jobs. Consequently, they will be able to choose the cream of the available work force. As this happens, more and more employers will be forced to follow suit or suffer from a relative lack of first-rate personnel, their most valuable resource. If people really want more leisure time, competitive market pressures will eventually force employers to offer more of it. This has already begun to happen on a small scale.

The Habit Hypothesis

Much, if not most of, human behavior can be explained in terms of habits. Habits save us valuable decision-making time and energy, and we develop them to handle virtually all of life's repetitive routines. The problem with habits, however, is that we often fail to modify them to fit the changing circumstances we face. Unthinkingly, we continue to practice them after they are no longer practical and efficient. There is no reason to believe that our habitual attitudes toward work are an exception.

The Protestant work ethic must clearly be counted among the environmental influences that have shaped our values. So must the harsh economic realities of the Great Depression of the 1930s that helped mold the attitudes of our parents' generation. Indeed, we should expect that these older Americans have handed down habitual attitudes toward work, money, and materialism that may no longer be appropriate for today's economic conditions.

As a Depression child, my mother was often hungry; she dreamed of owning a grocery store so she wouldn't be hungry again. Many who experienced real want in that time fear the return of another depression, and for some people no surplus seems to be adequate. Their materialism was born of need. Wouldn't we be wise to review our attitudes toward material things lest we perpetuate materialism out of habit? In fact, wouldn't you be wise to periodically review all your habits and revise them in accordance with the new realities you face?

To be sure, all of us are greatly indebted to the self-sacrifices of the generations of hard-working Americans who preceded us. Their sweat and toil, not ours, is primarily responsible for the high standard of comfort, security, and freedom we enjoy today. Nevertheless, when we work we pay with our time money—pay with a piece of our lives—and we must carefully evaluate the sensibleness of that trade-off. I cannot scrutinize that balance for you nor would I welcome your deciding for me in these matters. Likewise our forebears have not chosen for us but rather improved our options. We alone must judge for ourselves and for our families. There is no more important, or difficult, task than deciding what will be our major in life.

How Can You Cope with Materialism

Despite everything that has just been mentioned, there are no absolute answers as to how much of their time and energy nations and individuals should spend working to meet their material needs. This involves making value judgments that only you can make. But let's assume that after careful reflection, some of you find American values too materialistic for you. How can you cope with these values? How will you be able to choose more leisure time without becoming envious and spiteful as you watch others collect material possessions? Will you have to break from the mainstream, adopt another life-style, and assume a new identity as many young Americans have done? Perhaps you admire their courage but find their course too radical for you. Do you have more moderate options? We will offer some answers to these questions in the next two sections.

Impose Your Own Perspective

If you choose to spend more of your time money on non-material pursuits, you will have to learn to accept less in the way of material things. There's no way to escape the realities of this trade-off. There are ways, however, to avoid becoming excessively envious of your fellow citizens who opt instead for more material things. Most of these ways depend upon the perspective with which you choose to view your circumstances, as the following example will illustrate.

Shortly before his death, my grandfather, who had grown up with tired horses and bumpy buggies, took me for a spin in his new Cadillac. At that time he was not aware of superior automobiles and was therefore totally content with his new car. Nero probably felt the same way about his last chariot. But wave a magic wand and bring them both back today in their vehicles, and both would feel disadvantaged. They would both be unhappy now simply because they would be aware of better alternatives.

Likewise, imagine how envious an ancient ruler might be of today's television, air conditioning, jet travel, movies, and penicillin. If she had had the choice, would Cleopatra willingly have switched placed with Carly Simon? Or play the forward version of this game, and imagine how miserable we could make ourselves by looking into the future. Imagine it. No more acne! Instantaneous travel! Six-month vacations! Could we make ourselves envious and miserable! Or go out tonight, lie down, and ponder the uncountable stars that constitute our universe. Imagine how sick with envy we could make ourselves if we only knew the delights we were missing out there in the universe.

Yes, it's quite easy to make yourself miserable by comparing what you have with what others around you have now or will have in the future. On the other hand, if you compare your circumstances with those of your ancestors, you are more likely to find your lot satisfactory. If you decide, therefore, that you prefer to spend more of your time money on non-material pursuits, why not try to compare your material circumstances with those of your parents or grandparents when they were your age? This comparison will reveal that you can enjoy many more material advantages than they did, without sacrificing nearly as much of your time money. Your parents, and even Nero, didn't enjoy the variety of entertainment you get at little cost from television. They couldn't jet off to Europe, Mexico, and the Caribbean. Many things that were considered a luxury by your parents' generation are now considered necessities, and you will be able to afford them with a modest income—an income you can buy with a more modest expenditure of your time money.

Or approach your decision with the perspective that there cannot be any absolute winners in envy's materialistic game. Even if you had chosen to spend all your time money on material pursuits, you nevertheless would have been poor by the standards of the future or, perhaps, those of outer space, if not by those of today's superrich. Since you could not choose the age into which you were born, why allow its material standards to make you unhappy? Set your own standards and enjoy spending your time money as you see fit. You must develop the perspective and *courage* that you have consciously chosen what you have decided is best for you and that you are willing to accept the consequences of your decision.

How About Working to Meet Your Needs?

As we have seen, our real income has more than doubled since 1941, yet we are working just as hard as people did in 1941. When will America start "buying" leisure time with its increased productivity? Why do we continue to work as long and as hard as people did in 1941? Unnecessary want creation through advertising, the institutionalized forty-hour work week, envy, and a lingering depression mentality have been cited as possible explanations, to which finally the force of habit has been added.

People often get so tied up in their daily routines that circumstances are allowed to perpetuate themselves. Today's problems carry them into tomorrow, and tomorrow's problems into the next day, etc. The future is never planned; the past remains unevaluated; unthinkingly life proceeds. Income is earned and spent. This could happen to you.

Before you start to work, therefore, it might be wise to ask yourself what your material needs really are. Why not determine your needs, and then let your needs determine how much you will work? Work to satisfy your needs, and then enjoy life and the things you have worked for. Do you really need foot deodorant and blue toilet bowl water, or would you be happier if you spent more time fishing, reading, or relaxing with those you love?

TIME AND CAREER: SOME SPECIFIC TRADE-OFFS

Thus far we have been talking in general terms about *the* trade-off, or the decision as to what your major in life will be. You will also have to make a whole series of less important trade-offs. Focusing, as we shall now, on a few of these that are specifically related to time will help sharpen your decision-making skills. Each of us should learn how to make difficult choices wisely, because we cannot avoid making difficult decisions. The following choices are examples of such decisions.

Time or Money?

Here is one of the most difficult trade-offs. Which do you want most: money or time? Which do you want more of? Usually you cannot get more of both.

No matter what career you choose, you will have competitors—others who will have chosen the same career you have selected. Together, you and your competitors will constitute the supply of labor to your chosen career field. Since many, if not most, people prefer short work hours and long vacations, career fields that offer large amounts of leisure time attract large numbers of potential employees. Because many people are looking for work in such fields, employers in these fields can afford to be choosy. And they need not pay high wages.

Enough people will be so interested in the additional leisure time that they will accept lower pay in order to get hired and be able to enjoy more leisure

Life's a balancing act.

time than they would have in higher-paying fields. Those unwilling to accept such low wages will be unable to find employment in these fields. In effect, they will have priced themselves out of the labor market in these fields.

The situation above is an example of the market laws of supply and demand in action. The greater the supply of labor, the lower the wage. If you have difficulty understanding these supply and demand relationships (as many people do), they will become more understandable when we reach Chapters Six and Seven, where they are spelled out in detail with examples.

Time or "Success"?

A work freak is a type of person you will soon encounter if you don't already know several. They are everywhere, in every career field. Student work freaks are known as bookworms. Work freaks, or WF's, appear unbalanced because they are compulsive about work. As a general rule, if you are awake, the WF is working.

WF's are not simply born, they develop. Somewhere along their career path they become too interested in getting a promotion or good grades, an unhappy personal relationship embitters them and they channel almost all their drive into their work, or they convince themselves that their entire self-worth depends upon their achieving a certain career goal they have set for themselves—for example, straight A's. Whatever the reason, the extent of their leisure time drifts lower and lower on its way toward zero. Once the balance is lost in the developing WF's life, his or her ultimate personal tragedy becomes increasingly more difficult to avoid.

Because the work freaks' work occupies a larger part of their lives, they have less time to relate to others and less time to pursue outside interests. Their friends and non-career interests become neglected. On the few occasions the WF's join their friends, their friends find them increasingly more boring to talk to and more difficult to relate to because of the lengthening time intervals between the occasions on which they see each other. Neglect has spawned rejection. Their friends no longer wish their visits. Finally the WF's stand alone with their work. The vicious circle is closed, the tragedy complete.

WF's have been very well represented among our most accomplished and famous personalities. Nevertheless, the sacrifices WF's make in terms of the balance in their personal lives do not seem worthwhile to most of us. Most of you would probably like to avoid becoming a WF. How? Just being aware of the WF trap should help you avoid it. Also, later in this chapter you will learn how to construct your own leisure/work index, which measures the balance in your life. Here's a suggestion. Why don't you compute your leisure/work index at least once each year, on your birthday or on New Year's Day? Call it your career insurance against the onset of the WF syndrome.

Would you like to have an interesting job? Of course you would, but would you still want an interesting job if it brought you dangerously close to becoming a WF? Think about it. Having an interesting job and becoming a WF are related. Extreme examples can best illustrate this point. Would you have to become a WF in order to become President of the United States? Would you have to become a WF in order to be recognized as *the* leader in your chosen field?

We are uncovering another one of those difficult trade-offs. Many intelligent, hard-working, ambitious individuals are active in every career field. They will be among your competitors in your chosen profession. And guess what? Some of them will be the biggest WF's you could find anywhere. The most interesting jobs at the very, very top of your chosen field will probably be occupied by various degrees of WF's. That's not what they are called, of course. "Dedicated," or a similar euphemism, will be used to describe them.

Since they are compulsive about work, WF's will trade almost anything to reach the top. They have allowed their work to become almost their whole life. Unless you are extremely bright and can outperform everyone in your field, including the WF's, with relative ease, you might be wiser and far happier not to aim for the very top.

After all, what makes a job interesting? Should a job be considered interesting if it consumes almost all your time and interferes with or destroys your personal and family relationships? Maybe you should consider the job that will stimulate you without destroying the balance in your life as the most "interesting" job you could have. Perhaps such a measure of career success would serve your overall interests better. Wouldn't we all be wise to settle for a stimulating, rather than an engulfing, career position?

Time and Flexibility

"Fairy Godmother, where were you when I needed you?" is a line that I recall, but can not place, from a children's story. When the little children in your life need you, will you be available? When a glorious day finally comes along, will you be able to drop your work and complete it in the evening? When your favorite aunt or an old college friend visits you, will you be able to reminisce together until the wee hours without facing the alarm clock at 7 A.M.?

In addition to the amount of time your career will demand of you, don't you owe it to yourself to consider the flexibility of your work schedule? Will you be able to tailor your work schedule to allow for your other life needs? A flexible time schedule is a very attractive fringe benefit. It can go a long way toward making you the master of your own time and life. If you are a student, you probably enjoy the benefits of a flexible time schedule—perhaps without fully appreciating them. Do you have friends who are employed? Ask them about this fringe benefit the next time you meet. And when you do arrange to meet, notice which one of you sets the time and why that hour is chosen. This experience should increase your appreciation of the benefits of a flexible work schedule.

How about seasonal deadlines and pressures? They can destroy your life for weeks and months at a time and make you an irritable, tired, absentee parent and spouse. Are you willing to face the seasonal pressures of a tax accountant or retail merchant? Can you make these sacrifices? Should you? You have many factors to consider in choosing your major in life.

THE IMPACT OF COMMUTING AND OVERTIME ON YOUR TIME MONEY

This section focuses on the balance between the time you spend working at your career and the time you have left to spend on your non-career pursuits. These discussions and the statistics used to illustrate them are drawn directly from the Appendix to Chapter Four. The seven tables that appear near the end of this book in that Appendix demonstrate precisely how commuting time, overtime, and vacation time affect the balance between your leisure time and your work time on a workday, weekly, and annual basis.

The Impoverished Commuter

Commuting is a problem that has grown larger along with our cities. You will face it when you choose a job and a location in which to live. If you are a student, school is your work and the time you spend getting to and from school and walking between classes is your commuting time. You may logically consider your commuting time as additional working time, because if you weren't working, you wouldn't have to spend time getting to and from work.

Five hours per workday is the maximum amount of leisure time you are assumed to have if you are well-organized, sleep eight hours, and commute only fifteen minutes one way to work. Based on these assumptions, Table 4–2 reveals that each additional five minutes you commute represent a loss of 3.3 percent of your potential workday leisure time. Every half hour added to your one-way commute represents an additional 20 percent reduction of your potential workday leisure time. Commuting impoverishes you in two ways. It nibbles at your pocketbook and it gobbles up your leisure time. When you've chosen a job and are looking for a place to live, you may wish to consult these tables to see how much of your potential leisure time your alternative choices will cost you.

Is Working Overtime Worth It?

The extra hours one spends working outside normal working hours are called overtime working hours. Working overtime forces us to pass up other activities. For example, the extra time you spend cramming for next Monday's history midterm may mean that you can't go away this weekend or that you must miss a football game. Or because you must spend so much time preparing for your psych midterm, you can't polish up your English paper as well as you would like to. You may regret having to cut your favorite anthropology class which meets the period before psych. These are examples of the kinds of sacrifices that working overtime requires us to make. These sacrifices will become even more difficult when there are others in your life who depend on you.

Later, when you are employed and if you have children, overtime work may force you to miss your child's music recital, performance in the school play, or tennis match. Do you remember how disappointed and unloved you felt when one or both of your parents were a "no show"? Children usually don't accept these things. Overtime, as well as unpleasant work and long commutes, can be expected to have adverse effects on your family and personal relationships.

Certain careers can be expected to involve a great deal of overtime work during a peak season. Accountants, for example, should anticipate working long hours during the winter months prior to tax time. Those who work in retailing positions in department stores probably won't be at home much around Christmas time. Other careers provide opportunities for free-lance work which must be completed after normal working hours. And some firms expect personnel to work longer than eight hours. Before accepting a position that will require overtime, you may find it helpful to consult Table 4–3.

Most salaried professionals are not paid directly for overtime. Even if they were compensated for working overtime, would they be wise to trade additional leisure time for additional dollars? In your mind, does it make sense to add to your workday, which is already eight hours long, by subtracting from your daily leisure potential of only five hours? Table 4–3 shows that people who spend just one extra hour each day at work sacrifice 20 percent of their potential leisure time.

Finally, if you are offered compensation for working overtime, don't forget to base your decision on the dollars you can keep after taxes. If you live in New York State and already have a taxable income of $20,000, roughly half of every additional dollar you earn working overtime will be lost in state (12 percent) and federal (38 percent) income taxes.

The Leisure/Work Index: A Monitor
of the Balance in Your Life
The balances we have been discussing throughout this chapter can be easily lost in the pull and tug of life's competing demands. The leisure/work index is designed to prevent this. It measures the balance between the hours you are devoting to your work and the leisure hours you are free to spend as you like. Computing your own leisure/work index requires only one simple division which is completed as follows by expressing your annual leisure hours as a percentage of the time you spend working each year:

$$\text{Leisure/Work Index} = \frac{\text{Annual Hours of Leisure Time}}{\text{Annual Hours of Work}}$$

In order to use this index, you must first decide how you want to divide your time income between leisure and work hours. Next you must compute the leisure/work index which that division represents. This will give you your standard, or preferred, leisure/work index. Then all you must do is periodically record your actual leisure and work hours, compute your actual leisure/work index, compare it with your preferred index, and make the adjustments needed to reestablish the balance you desire in your life. This index is a handy little device. It can help you realize your goals and become the master of your own time and life.

CHAPTER FIVE

Home, in one form or another, is the Great object of life.

                                    Josiah G. Holland

THE RELATIONSHIP BETWEEN GEOGRAPHIC
MOBILITY AND CAREER CHOICE
    The "People Professions" Offer Greater Geographic Mobility
    Industry Location Affects Geographic Mobility

WHAT YOU GET WHEN YOU CHOOSE A CAMPSITE
    Climatic Considerations
    Cultural Considerations
    Economic Considerations
    State and Local Governmental Services

SPECIALIZATION: MIDWIFE OF THE NOMADIC
SOCIETY AND OTHER CHANGES
    Specialization: The Price of Progress
    Job Insecurity: An Unpleasant Consequence
    The Bright Side of Specialization
    Work: The Individual's Identification and Satisfaction

CHAPTER FIVE

HOW TO CHOOSE BETWEEN "CAMPSITES"

Welcome to the Nomadic Society. Based on a recent survey, the U.S. Bureau of the Census predicts that twenty-five-year olds with some college training will move between seven and nine more times during their lifetime.[1] This unprecedented degree of geographic mobility indicates, in effect, that we've become a nation of modern-day nomads—especially those of us who are better educated. It follows that most of you could probably benefit from some advice on how to choose between campsites.

Some of you may consider choosing where you'll live one of the most important decisions you'll grapple with while you're reaching your career decision. You may feel a special attachment to a particular city, region of the country, the sea, the mountains, family or friends, and wish to remain close to them. Or you may not care so much where you live as long as you can avoid the often traumatic uprooting associated with moving every five years or so. And a few of you may actually prefer a nomadic existence and want to know what types of careers will facilitate it. This chapter has been organized to accommodate readers whose interests span the full range of these extremes.

The first section examines the dependent relationship between geographic mobility and career choice. The subsequent section classifies interlocational differences by origin as climatic, cultural, economic, or governmental. Organizing your thoughts and preferences along these lines will help you weigh the many considerations that enter into your locational decisions more systematically. The final section identifies increased occupational specialization as the major cause of our progressively more nomadic way of life and explains how increased specialization has changed the rewards we can expect from our work.

THE RELATIONSHIP BETWEEN GEOGRAPHIC MOBILITY AND CAREER CHOICE

The "People Professions" Offer Greater Geographic Mobility

Those who work in professions such as teaching, law, nursing, and medicine—those who serve the needs of the general public—enjoy the largest degree of geographic mobility. Wherever people live, they will need to learn, be healed, and receive legal council, which means that people in these professions can choose to live anywhere. On the other hand, many of these same professionals have very little geographic mobility once they begin their careers. Doctors, lawyers, veterinarians, and morticians, for example, spend a long time building a reputation and a practice among their clients. They become tied to their practices and avoid moving elsewhere because this would require their rebuilding a new practice from scratch.

Those who work in these people professions and others who enjoy this type of geographic mobility appear to be blessed for at least two reasons. First of all, it's an obvious advantage to have more control over your life and have the freedom to choose where you want to live. Most of us apparently live in large cities not by choice but out of necessity. A recent Gallup poll shows that only 13 percent of the Americans living in large cities would remain there if they had a choice.[2] Second, an even bigger blessing in terms of family and personal relationships is that these people can stay put—they can live in houses rather than tents. Many view the "Dallas this year–Los Angeles next–Boston in three years syndrome" as a very dangerous and unfortunate aspect of corporate/executive life. The following quote from the *Wall Street Journal* explains why the nomadic life-styles of these executives often produce alcoholic wives and/or husbands and lonely problem children. "Moving is a severe trauma probably as great as divorce," says Robert Seidenberg, a Syracuse, N.Y., psychiatrist, many of whose patients are victims of multi-moves. "It's like uprooting a tree or a bush—you simply can't flourish transplanted five or six times."[3] Incidentally, executives who wish to avoid this nomadic life can do so by working for smaller firms that are located in fewer locations or perhaps only one location.

Although those who are employed in the "people professions" can live and work anywhere there are people, where they choose to live can affect the nature of their work. As a general rule, the more specialized one becomes, the larger the city one must live in. For example, a general practice lawyer could survive in a town of 10,000 whereas a criminal lawyer couldn't. Likewise, a psychologist couldn't survive in a small town that could, however, support a general practice physician.

Industry Location Affects Geographic Mobility

A few industries are rather highly concentrated within one region or city. Consequently, by choosing to work in these fields, you are simultaneously limiting where you can live. For example, New York City is the center of America's publishing, fashion, advertising, performing arts, and financial industries. Because most of the activity in these industries is located in Manhattan, it would be unrealistic for you to think you could pursue a career in these fields without spending some time there. You'd probably at least have to go there for training, and success in these fields would probably lead you back again to Manhattan. The auto industry is in Detroit; the steel, coal, and other natural resource industries are regionally based, and so on. Consequently, if you have a strong regional or city-size preference, you should take these into consideration when you choose an occupation. Sounds simple enough, but I myself never realized while I was getting a Ph.D. that as an economist I would most probably be living in New York City if I wanted a business career. The large corporations that hire Ph.D. economists usually assign them to their international headquarters, many of which are located in New York City.

WHAT YOU GET WHEN YOU CHOOSE A CAMPSITE

When you select a community in which to live, you will be accepting a package deal with climatic, cultural, economic, and governmental dimensions. The following sections identify the most important factors in each of these categories. These factors represent the considerations you should carefully weigh when you are choosing between alternative locations.

Climatic Considerations

The climate of the location you choose affects your welfare by determining the kind and extent of outdoor activities you can participate in. Access to outdoor forms of recreation and exercise is especially important and necessary to the health of college graduates, most of whom have sedentary jobs. Outdoor recreational opportunities depend on the nature of weather conditions and the type and proximity of surrounding natural formations like mountains, rivers, lakes, and the sea. The availability, quality, cost, and accessibility of camping, fishing, swimming, hiking, biking, skiing, boating, and hunting opportunities are among the outdoor activities you should consider. The length of the season for each of these and the dependability of weather conditions should also be considered. Denver, for example, enjoys 300 days of sunshine annually. In Seattle, you've got the sea in your front yard and the mountains in your back yard. It costs $20 an hour for tennis courts in Manhattan. Temperature, humidity, and winds also play a role. Have you ever been blown down Chicago's Clark Street?

Health is also directly affected by smog and other pollution factors. The importance of health is often grossly underestimated by young people, who tend to take it for granted. Ask someone who's been seriously ill if it's silly to stress the importance of outdoor health-related activities. We need exercise to keep fit both mentally and physically.

Cultural Considerations

When you choose a location in which to live, you invite the culture and values of that region to invade your consciousness and shape your children's consciousness. As imperfect as regional labels like "liberal North East," "conservative Midwest," and "traditional South" are, there are distinct regional differences in values, the way people perceive the world, and the way they act towards one another. Cultural differences are felt, not measured. You must experience these differences and decide if you're able to cope with them, willing to accept them, or if you simply can't be comfortable living with them.

The nature of cultural differences also makes a big difference. Many people find it difficult to accept different racial, religious, and ethnic attitudes. Compromises are less difficult to make on matters that involve the

community's commitment to cultural activities like the theatre, concerts, and museums, or differences in life-styles. However, a colleague of mine left New Mexico after only one year because he couldn't stand the walls that separated people's yards. For him, it was too cold and unneighborly to live behind high masonry walls in what he felt was a "stockade atmosphere."

Before you move to a different region of the country, you should try to discuss the region in detail with a friend who has lived there. Then visit the region for as long as possible before you decide to move there. One comforting consequence of our nomadic life is that wherever you go you'll find others who have also been transplanted there from your region of the country.

Economic Considerations

Among the most important economic dimensions of the region you choose to live in are: its adjusted cost of living, the industrial balance in the local economy, its growth rate, and how much you'll have to spend to travel back "home" to visit family and friends. The cost of state and local taxes, which is also a very important economic consideration, is discussed in the next section on governmental services.

The adjusted cost of living, which makes allowances for local wage and price level differences, is most significantly affected by factors like city size, which affects housing costs and life-styles. Housing costs vary by as much as 100 percent because of local differences in the cost of construction labor, materials, and the type of materials used, which depends on climatic factors; city size, which affects the cost of land and the type of dwelling units, apartments or single-family homes, that are built; and local real estate taxes. These differences can quickly whittle down what looks like a sizable salary increase for transferring to a big city. When coupled with the extra tax bite taken out of the salary increase, a 30 or 40 percent salary increase may really represent a salary cut in terms of real purchasing power. In addition, moving from town to city or city to town may involve a significant change in life-styles; for example, the change from a private home to apartment living. Incidently, the 50 percent increase in housing costs that occurred between 1970 and 1974 appears to have lifted the cost of single-family homes above the reach of most American households. Single-family housing starts, which represented 78 percent of all housing starts in the early 1960s, slipped below 50 percent in 1973 and are expected to drop to one-third of all starts by 1990.[4]

The extent of industrial diversification or balance in the local economy affects all residents, especially local business and professional people. If a city or state is largely dependent on a single industry, as Detroit and Michigan are on the automobile industry, the local economy has all its eggs in one basket, so to speak.[5] Its fortunes will move up and down Yo-Yo style with those of that one industry. Even if you're not employed in that industry, your life will be affected by what happens to it. Housing values, for example, are likely to rise and fall with the fortunes of this key industry.

The rate of growth of the local economy is one of the better indicators of what is likely to happen to local employment opportunities, property values, and the adjusted cost of living. Depending on your viewpoint, you may welcome growth or dislike the change and congestion that it may bring. Finally, before you move, you may wish to consider how much you'll have to spend to keep in touch with and periodically visit your family and the friends you don't want to let slip out of your life.

State and Local Governmental Services

When you select a location in which to live, you agree to accept the costs and benefits of its state and local governmental services. Most important among these costs are property, sales, and state and local income taxes. The most important benefits include public school and state university educational programs, highway and mass transit systems, police and fire protection. All of these are rather easily identified and evaluated. Property taxes can vary tremendously—by as much as 10 times—for comparable housing in different locations. Poor public schools and high crime rates are the governmental service deficiencies most people try hardest to avoid.

This concludes our discussion of locational decision-making. We have seen that there are a great number of factors to consider when you choose your campsite. NICP has developed a special Geographic Preference Index that enables the decision-maker to deal effectively and objectively with these many considerations. With the aid of this analytical tool, it becomes a mathematically simple, albeit tedious, task to simultaneously consider the many factors involved in deciding among locations. Individuals who are willing to spend at least 20 hours evaluating their geographic preferences may find this index helpful.[6]

SPECIALIZATION: MIDWIFE OF THE NOMADIC SOCIETY AND OTHER CHANGES

Our nomadic way of life is one—but only one—of the important effects of the increased occupational specialization that has become the hallmark of work today. Thus it is both necessary and desirable that this discussion take us well beyond the subject of choosing a campsite. This is necessary because the effects of increased specialization are interrelated and must, therefore, be treated collectively in a single unit. The inclusion of these other considerations is desirable because they also bear directly upon your career decision-making in many significant ways. In addition to noting how and why specialization has produced the Nomadic Society, we shall also reveal how specialization has changed and affected job security, the nature of our work, the rewards we can expect from it, and how we can partially compensate for these changes.

The sections that follow continue the investigation we began in Chapter Two into the nature of the work about which you are deciding. Now our focus has shifted, however, and we will become much more reflective. Whereas until

now we have concentrated on the functions you will perform and how to prepare for them, we turn now to an analysis of the work itself. How varied will
your work be? How much independence will it allow you? How closely will you
be able to identify with it, etc.? Among other things, an improved understanding of these realities of the world of work will enable you to formulate
plans to largely avoid those realities that you find most disagreeable.

Specialization: The Price of Progress

Even though UFO pilots may find our twentieth-century civilization primitive,
human beings have never enjoyed anything approaching America's present
standard of living. Nevertheless, we're working less now than in previous centuries. Have we become smarter, discovered a miracle? What has made this
progress possible? What price have we paid for it?

Although we may wish to believe otherwise, we are not any smarter, just
better organized than before and the beneficiaries of the continued development of technology. We've assigned ordinary people to ever-more narrowly
defined, specialized tasks in which each of them can become a superworker—
superfast, superefficient, and, unfortunately, sometimes superbored as well.
Through better organization we've become, effectively, a supernation. Being a
jack-of-all-trades may provide more varied and interesting work, but one
wastes too much time changing tools and learning how to use all of them
efficiently.

When you enter the work force, therefore, you should expect to "pay" for
our high standard of living in terms of more routine, less varied work. That's
part of the hidden price we pay for antibiotics, stereos, jet travel, and air
conditioning. Moreover, the disagreeable side effects of specialization are no
longer limited to blue-collar work. We now have one-organ doctors, divorce
lawyers, and labor economists. Of course, you can avoid the most disagreeable aspects of specialization, but only at a price. Everthing is a trade-off for
something else.

The organizational efficiencies of specialization have also forced companies and their divisions to become narrowly specialized. This has in turn
forced these employers to move into larger and larger national and international markets in order to find outlets for their highly specialized products. Just
like heart specialists, specialized firms must draw their clients from larger markets. This explains why many of you will be transferred as often as eight times
during your career as the nationwide companies you work for move you
around from office to office, plant to plant.

As a result of specialization, we have also become critically interdependent upon one another. We function much more as team players and less as
individuals. We depend on others for our supply of such necessities as food,
clothing, and shelter. Food production has become specialized, and we have
crowded together in cities. Government has become more necessary to main-

tain order in these close corners. And our economic dependence on each other has spawned a larger federal government that tries to guarantee uninterrupted production.

Increasingly, as we have grown more interdependent, power has been transferred from the individual to larger and larger collectives. This centralization of decision-making has inevitably had an homogenizing effect. Individuals have also lost a great deal of their independence as a result of increased specialization and the larger markets it has spawned. Specialists are part of a team, and they must follow the playmaker's commands. Because they have very little productive value off the team, specialists have relinquished much of their independence to the organizations that employ them. This explains, for example, why it is so difficult for them to refuse transfers to another location. As specialists we've become important cogs in the organizational wheel. Our importance, however, depends on our remaining a part of that wheel. This is another of the unpleasant realities—we've become partial prisoners of our organizations. They shape and mold our lives.

Job Insecurity: An Unpleasant Consequence

Increasing specialization and the accelerated technological change it has fostered have also contributed to job insecurity and made labor markets generally more perilous. Although intelligent governmental policies could largely offset this adverse effect of specialization, they have typically been shortsighted—politically rather than economically inspired. Consequently, governmental policies have frequently been and are likely to continue to be a major cause of economic instability. Job insecurity, therefore, is very much a part of the economic reality with which you will have to deal throughout your career.

Although technological change is the very engine of progress that pulls our standard of living even higher, its immediate human consequences can indeed be cruel. Overnight, whole industries may disappear or be subjected to painful pruning, dislocation, and transformation. The fact that the automobile ultimately created millions more jobs than it destroyed—new jobs for steel workers, oil drillers, road builders, motel personnel, pollution equipment makers, etc.—provided little solace for the carriage makers and buggy whip salespeople who immediately lost their jobs when the automobile revolutionized the transportation industry. You may very well choose a career that will slate you for a fate similar to that of yesterday's carriage makers.

Specialists are particularly vulnerable to unemployment that results from technological change. They are trained to do specific jobs. If and when technological change eliminates the need for these jobs, their skills are no longer in demand. They are left bereft of both jobs and useful skills, must seek retraining, enter the unskilled work force, or remain unemployed—all painful alternatives.

Enough of this gloomy side; we would not have you become pessimists.

You will make very few decisions during your life, however, that will be as important as your career decision. Specialization, technological change, boredom, inept political decision-making that results in job insecurity—these are some of the unpleasant realities that will affect you when you enter the world of work. We feel obligated to discuss them and point out their likely impact on your life. Enough said. Now let's take a walk on the bright side.

The Bright Side of Specialization

The medical advances wrought by our specialized technology represent the most dramatic improvement in our standard of living. Whereas in previous centuries only the lucky survived to a ripe old age, today only unlucky Americans fail to. Although specialization has fostered urbanization and the resultant loss of more of the individual's freedom to the political authority, urbanization has also augmented the individual's freedom by affording a broader set of choices. The concentration of large numbers of people in urban centers has made specialty markets economically viable. A large city, for example, can support restaurants of virtually every nationality and specialty. Of far greater significance, individuals who live in large cities also have a much wider choice of friends and potential spouses. It wasn't long ago that the stamina of your horse determined how far you could search for a compatible spouse and friends that shared your interests. Our specialized technology has provided us with a mixed bag of costs and benefits. It has altered the options we face—destroyed some of our old freedoms even as it has created more new ones.

Modern travel and communication possibilities are dramatic examples of the costs and benefits of our specialized technology. Without these possibilities, markets would be regional rather than national and international in scope. Consequently, our lives would be less subject to the often traumatic experience of being transplanted that most executives must endure as they are moved from city to city throughout their careers. Many more children would grow up knowing their grandparents, and more parents would grow old with their children. On the other hand, jet travel brings the most remote reaches of the world within one day's travel of home. Space travel may enable our descendants to find a new home in the universe before our sun ultimately burns out.

Our communications gadgetry, like television and the movies, bring the world into our living room and provide us with far better entertainment than that enjoyed by the richest rulers in all antiquity. Our communications technology is probably also responsible for a more humane world. Each of us is made a personal witness to the horrors of war and the problems of minorities and women. We become aware of and sensitive to these and other human needs and our world is changed for the better. Technology has also revolutionized the nature of our work, making it increasingly less toilsome and less time consuming. These are a few of the advantages we must balance against the negative aspects of specialization.

Work: The Individual's Identification And Satisfaction

We can summarize what we have learned about the nature of today's work by saying that it serves our collective needs more adequately than it serves our needs as individuals. Specialization is a rational way to organize our collective efforts. Collectively through specialization we are able to make a much bigger "pie" than the sum of all the separate pies we could make as unspecialized individuals.

Specialization benefits each of us by ultimately providing us with much more pie for less effort. But we pay for these benefits in the form of less varied, often more boring work with which each of us can identify less as individuals. Each of us adds a single ingredient to or performs a single operation in the production of the collective pie. Unlike the carriage maker, most of us cannot adequately express ourselves as individuals through our work. We merely assemble the machine-made pieces that collectively make up the supercarriages that none of us can identify as our individual handiwork.

Thus, while collectively more productive, today's work is typically less satisfying for the individual. The moral of all this: now, more than ever, the individual must seek sources of personal identification and satisfaction that lie outside his or her career pursuits. Because our work has become increasingly more specialized, depersonalized, and collectivized, it is much more difficult for most of us to gain a satisfactory measure of our individual worth through our work. On balance, ours is a great time to be alive. In this age, however, we should expect to express ourselves as individuals largely outside our work.

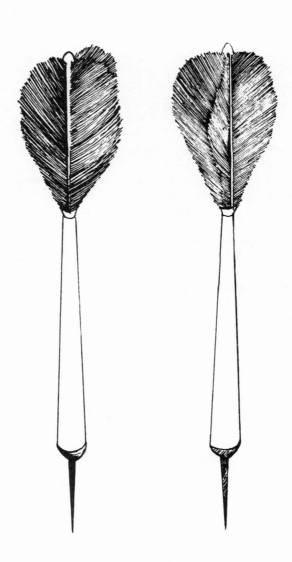

PART II

ANALYZING YOUR CAREER ALTERNATIVES

*If a man neglects education, he walks lame
to the end of life.*

                              Plato

Career Economics
The "Laws" of the World of Work
Increasing Your Employability

By now you should have some pretty firm ideas about what you want most from a career. If career opportunities had detailed labels that accurately described and explained the possibilities they offered, you'd be in a good position to make your career decision. You could simply check off the items on your Career Shopping List against these labels and choose the career that offered the best match. We are in effect going to put you in a similar position, because the chapters in Part II will show you how to write up accurate labels for the career opportunities you investigate.

Unlike Part I, the chapters in Part II ask you to deal with what is, with the analysis and evaluation of circumstances as they are, as opposed to what you would like them to be. You will learn how to critically analyze, identify, and evaluate career opportunities and how to get current career information that is specifically tailored to your needs and interests. Upon completing Chapter Eleven, you will be prepared to discover and recognize the career opportunities that most closely resemble the ideal career circumstances you defined for yourself in Part I. In other words, the tools and analysis of Part II are designed to lead you back from the realm of dreams into the realm of reality along the paths that will bring you most closely to the realization of the objectives you formulated in Part I.

Career Economics

Have you ever played one of your friend's favorite games when you knew none of the strategies and barely even understood the rules? Unfair! Yes, but that was only a game between friends. If you're like most Americans, you probably understand just about as little about the strategies and rules of the market game in which you earn and spend your money.

As long as you continue to work and live in the Western world, you will be selling your labor services in the labor market. Then you'll use the proceeds of that sale to make all your purchases in the many, many markets for consumer goods and services. Don't you wish you had a better understanding of how our market system works? Doesn't it seem rather foolish and ostrich-like to continue to live and work in a market economy and not seek to educate yourself regarding how market mechanisms function simply because you find this subject difficult to understand or boring? Doesn't this lack of understanding make you feel somewhat vulnerable? If you do feel this way, you'll feel much better after reading Part II, because you will then be able to greatly improve your odds of winning in our market economy. Knowing how markets function, you will be able to conduct your affairs more intelligently in the job market.

In attempting to give you enough economic reasoning to participate as an informed worker/consumer in our market economy, it was sometimes difficult to decide where to draw the line on what should and should not be included. Obviously, you need to understand the fundamentals of supply and demand, particularly as these apply to the labor market. The industrial characteristics

"What, me worry.!"

that generate job insecurity and cause periods of unemployment also had to be identified and explained. But beyond these subjects, it became increasingly a matter of judgment as to what would and would not be included.

A few additional economic concepts, like the concept of opportunity costs, have been introduced to help explain and illustrate points that are directly relevant to the discussion of wage level determination. More than one-third of our income is spent today by politicians who frequently and sometimes deliberately mislead us on important economic issues. Therefore, we discuss the role of politicians in making economic decisions and how these decisions affect you. While the economic decisions of our political leaders may not seem directly relevant to the labor market, they are, in fact, central to its performance. General economic conditions such as unemployment and inflation are almost always the direct result of bad national economic policies. You need to realize this as a citizen and voter as well as in your capacity as a job seeker. But only part of what you'll learn in Part II bears directly on economic considerations. The very interesting topic of career Position Analysis will take us beyond the realm of economic laws into a realm that involved the formulation of a completely new set of "laws."

The "Laws" of the World of Work

Gradually, as we continued to analyze the results of several hundred comprehensive career information interviews, it became clear that the world of work could be characterized as being governed by a body of "laws." In fact, this is how *The Career Game* was first conceived. In effect, the world of work, into which you are about to graduate, is shaped and conditioned by a set of constraints that are analogous to those that operate in nature.

In nature, features like mountains, plains, and swamps and forces like wind, temperature, and pressure determine the life forms that can survive and proliferate in nature's varied microenvironments. Life forms must be surefooted to thrive in the crest of the mountains and they must be strong swimmers to make of the open river a home. Some of the "laws" that govern the world of work also have their origin in nature in the sense that nature shapes the character of much of the work we must do. More often, however, the laws that govern the world of work reflect the nature of people. This is not surprising since people decide what work is desirable, what will be done, and who will do it.

The generalizations and principles that are presented in Part II explain the operating dynamics of the employment scene by revealing the whys of the labor market. The underlying assumption of this approach is that if you understand the whys and hows of our system, you will be better able to formulate strategies that will enable you to work in and through it. Understanding the likely consequences of the career decisions you might make will enable you to make decisions and follow strategies that are much more likely to produce the results you prefer. Upon completing Part II, you should be a much more self-sufficient career decision-maker, capable of independently formulating your own intelligent course of action. This is the overall objective of these chapters in which the format is analytical, the focus is on decision-making, and the emphasis is on finding happiness in your career and life.

Specifically, Chapter Six deals with job security, or what makes an industry a likely candidate for layoffs during recessionary times. Chapter Seven introduces an analysis of how supply and demand affects wage and salary levels. Chapter Eight expands this discussion to include the Big Money Game and certain other "special situations." In Chapter Nine, we enter the next phase of career decision-making and begin to evaluate positions or jobs as opposed to career fields. This discussion of Position Analysis is based on the knowledge we gleaned from interviewing several hundred people about their career positions and rates of advancement. Chapter Ten explains what you can do to hedge your career decision when you remain undecided about it. Finally, Chapter Eleven summarizes everything you learned in both Parts I and II by taking a young man named Lee Wade step by step through the entire career decision-making process. We begin with his self-identification and continue through the interviewing process to the selection of a career and his first job.

Increasing Your Employability

Hopefully you haven't forgotten our opening comments and warning. If you haven't heeded our advice and reread that section, please reread it now.

An essential purpose of Part II is to prompt you to start thinking of ways to make yourself more attractive to employers. When you are ill and need a doctor, you hire a doctor based solely on his or her ability to cure you—the arrangement is strictly one of business. Likewise, when employers consider hiring you, their decisions will be primarily, if not exclusively, based upon your ability and training to handle the job. This is the basic reality regarding the way in which potential employers will view you.

As you read these chapters, therefore, you should consciously be searching for ideas as to how you can make yourself more employable in the eyes of your prospective employers. In view of the competitive pressures fostered by the baby boom, you should also keep asking yourself, "What can I do now and in the future to improve my competitive position so as to enhance my chances of career advancement?" Discuss your ideas with your friends, call on your economics department if you get stuck, but in any case, start making your initial career information interviews as soon as possible. Nothing will serve to clear up your understanding of these matters faster than the insights you will gain from these interviews. They are an absolute must.

In view of their special employment difficulties, it is doubly important for liberal arts students to begin conducting exploratory career information interviews early. The majority of the employers who responded to The College Placement Council's 1974 survey reported that they would consider hiring more liberal arts majors if they had taken certain business-related courses or if they had done co-op or other experiential work. Thus, if liberal arts majors find out what employers in their career fields want early enough, they can arrange to satisfy these requirements and greatly improve their odds of getting hired upon graduation.

CHAPTER SIX

WHAT MAKES A JOB SECURE FROM UNEMPLOYMENT?

What's the difference between a recession and a depression?

We're in a recession when someone else loses their job; we're in a depression when I lose my job.

                                    Anonymous

Economics is a subject that generally either frightens or bores most people. If you want strangers to leave you alone, tell them you're an economist. If you've got my luck, you'll get a disappointed, half-frightened "ooh" and one of those "you-must-be-weird-even-if-you-don't-look-it" looks. If they hang around after that, they're either after stock market tips, or they're very, very lonely. I've learned to refer to myself as a writer.

The field of economics frightens most people because they don't understand the mathematical, graphic, and statistical tools and lingo used by economists. Moreover, much of the economics taught today is irrelevant to students' daily lives, which helps to explain why so many of them find it boring. Mathematics, graphs, and statistics have not been used in the exposition that follows. Words alone have been used to convey the whole story. The economic relationships that we shall begin to investigate in this chapter are of immediate relevance to your daily life and material well-being. Consequently, acquiring an understanding of these particular economic relationships should frighten you much less than the alternative of remaining ignorant of how they will affect the likelihood of your becoming unemployed in the occupation of your choice.

The earlier sections of this chapter identify the forces and circumstances that determine job security. These influences are organized and set forth in the form of general principles that apply to every career field. This exposition is self-contained and assumes no prior understanding of economic reasoning. Everything you need to know in order to understand and later apply these principles is presented and illustrated with tangible everyday examples. The postwar data presented in the final section reveal the operation of these principles during recent recessionary periods.

A Note on Language Usage

Language is often a problem. It can be confusing, and it can be tiresome. The financial and economic press uses many different words to refer to the things that money can buy. Most of these words mean the same thing although they sometimes have slightly different connotations. The words *good, product,* and *commodity* all mean the same thing within the context of this book. They all refer to something that is produced and sold by a firm or an individual.

The word *service* is very similar in meaning to the words *good, product,* and *commodity,* but it has a slightly different usage. When people pay to have something done for them, to themselves, or to something they have, we call this a service. Lawyers, dentists and most other professional types who deal directly with people provide services. Services such as psychological help or entertainment at a rock concert are often intangible. House painting, automobile repairing, and hair styling are examples of tangible services. When we are employed, we always provide services. We do something for our employers or to the materials that become their products.

The term *employer* applies to the individual, institution, organization, or, more typically, the business firm that grants the job. The terms employer and *firm* (by itself) are used as synonyms to refer to all types of employers. Some readers may be confused by the term industry. All those employers that produce similar products or services make up an *industry*. It is helpful to discuss the topic of job security within the context of an industry because all the employers in an industry will be similarly affected by any given set of general economic conditions. For example, if consumers stop buying cars, the employees at GM, Ford, Chrysler, and AMC will probably all face lay-offs at the same time. These four employers are the separate pieces that make up the automobile industry in America.

Finally, many different words, all of which have the same meaning and connotation in this book, are used to refer to the payments employees receive for their services. *Wages* (which is the term we shall use most often), *salaries, compensation, pay,* and *fees* all refer to the same thing. We also use the words *workers, employees,* and *personnel* interchangeably.

THE DETERMINATES OF JOB SECURITY

It may already be obvious to you that when you begin working in an industry, your fate as an employee becomes directly linked to the fate of the industry in which you are working. *The demand for labor in an industry is derived directly and solely from the demand for the products and services produced by that industry.* When people stopped wearing hats, hatmakers lost their jobs. Your labor services will be needed by your firm only as long as the fickle consumers who buy its products continue to do so. If consumers stop buying your firm's products, you will be out of a job because your firm will no longer be willing or able to pay you wages. Consequently, in order to evaluate the likelihood that you will become unemployed because consumers stop buying the commodities you labor to produce, we must investigate the nature of consumers' needs for the products of the industry in which you work.

Classifications of Economic Goods

Since we live and work in a free-enterprise economic system, we must learn to cope with occasional periods of economic insecurity. Ours is an economy of ups and downs. When the public mood becomes pessimistic regarding the future, when bad economic times threaten or actually do occur, individuals look for ways to reduce their spending. If you are employed in one of the industries whose products consumers do not need or can postpone buying during recessionary times, it is much more probable that you will experience periods of unemployment sometime during your career.

Economic goods can be classified into categories that reflect the extent to which they are needed, the uses to which they are put, and the extent to which the demand for these goods is sensitive to general economic conditions. It is important that you understand these classifications when you select an industry in which to work, because the likelihood of your becoming unemployed during a recession will depend largely upon which category of goods your employer produces.

Necessity Goods and Luxury Goods

The distinction between necessity goods and luxury goods is based on the ability of the consumer to do without the product. Among the goods classified as necessities are food, clothing, shelter. and medical care. These goods and services satisfy the most basic biological needs for the continuation of life itself. Obviously, however, not all foods can be considered necessities. Filet mignon, caviar, and fresh strawberries in February are food luxuries. Similarly, fur coats, vacation homes, and Pucci dresses are not necessities either. We can get along quite well without luxury goods.

Whereas expenditures on luxury items can and will be drastically reduced during difficult and uncertain economic times, expenditures for commodities that are truly necessities will remain stable. In fact, expenditures for some low-priced necessities may even increase somewhat during recessionary times, because consumers may substitute inexpensive necessities for the more expensive necessities they bought during good times. For example, sales of blue jeans and uncut cloth may actually increase while those of dress slacks and ready-made women's dresses may actually decrease during a recession.

Most typically, however, necessities hold their own, whereas expenditures for luxury items such as furs, jewelry, expensive entertainment, vacations, air travel, and pleasure boats are greatly reduced during a recession. Because an industry's demand for labor is derived from the demand for its products, the more its products resemble necessity goods, the more job security it can provide its employees. If your firm produces luxury items, it will have to lay off a large percentage of its employees during a recession—and you may be among them.

If you accept work in a luxury goods industry, you would be wise to insist on a salary that is high enough to compensate you for the additional risks of unemployment you will incur. You should also anticipate being periodically unemployed and structure your personal savings program accordingly. During good times, luxury goods industries usually earn handsome profits. If your employer has a profit-sharing or employee bonus program, or if you are a salesperson working on a commission formula, these compensation packages may compensate you for the additional hazards of unemployment associated with working in a luxury goods industry.

We have seen that classifying goods as necessities or luxuries is helpful because it tells us how much job security we can expect in the industries that produce these goods. We can learn even more about this subject by making finer distinctions. This requires additional classifications that often overlap. Just as a person can be classified as tall, thin, and ambitious, an economic good can also have several classifications. Each of these classifications helps to reveal a little more about the job security of those who work to produce this economic good.

Necessity and luxury goods are two subclassifications of a much broader classification of economic goods called *consumption goods*. This classification identifies who buys these goods. Since individual consumers buy consumption goods, anything that affects the level of their incomes will also affect job security in consumer goods industries.

Consumer Goods: Nondurable and Durable

Consumption goods, which include literally everything from tooth paste to sail boats, are subclassified into nondurable and durable goods. These subclassifications are based on the expected useful lifetime of the goods, which indicates whether consumers need to continually purchase them or whether they can postpone buying them when they feel economically insecure and want to reduce their spending. Consequently, these subclassifications serve exactly the same function as those of necessity and luxury goods.

Products that consumers fully use within roughly one year of the date of purchase are called consumer nondurable goods because their useful lifetime is rather short. This definition is not very precise, however. All clothing items, for example, are considered nondurables even though some clothing items are used for many years. Food items, cigarettes, cosmetics, inexpensive accessory items, etc. are examples of nondurable goods. The key characteristics of nondurables are that they are relatively inexpensive, used quickly, and must be rather frequently replaced.

Because they are relatively inexpensive, consumer nondurables are not the first things that consumers stop buying when hard times threaten or actually do set in. The demand for them is rather insensitive to economic fluctuations. Consequently, the demand for employees in nondurable goods industries is also largely unaffected by general economic conditions. Employment in these industries is stable and secure in much the same way, and for similar reasons, as in necessity goods industries. In fact, these classifications overlap each other to a considerable extent.

Consumer durable goods, on the other hand, have an expected useful lifetime of more than one year. Most of these items, such as major household appliances, cars, cameras, stereos, are rather costly. When consumers are unemployed or apprehensive about the future, these are some of the first items they do not buy or postpone buying. When you are unemployed or fear you may become unemployed, you do not seriously consider buying a new refrigerator. If your present refrigerator breaks down during times like these, you have it repaired rather than replaced. Because the demand for consumer durable goods is sensitive to general economic conditions, jobs in consumer durable good industries are less secure than jobs in consumer nondurable good industries.

Capital Goods

The final goods classification we shall study is called *capital goods.* This classification is based on who buys the goods. Capital goods are bought by business firms. They make up the second major classification of all goods as either consumption goods or capital goods. The term *capital* confuses everyone, including economists at times, because it has several different usages, all of which are closely related.

Business people, especially those who work in finance, refer to the funds a firm has invested in its operations as its capital. Therefore, the words *capital* and *money* are frequently used interchangeably on Wall Street. Firms seek money in order to grow and expand their businesses. In order to expand, business needs machines, equipment, and buildings in which to place them— these are called capital goods. The word *capital,* as used by us in the sense of capital goods, refers to these goods themselves rather than to the money firms buy them with.

Analytically, capital goods are distinguished by the fact that they are bought by firms and are used to produce other goods. Computers, drill presses, trucks, the tools and equipment used on assembly lines, the structures and buildings in which these are located—any machine or building that firms use to process materials into products or to package and distribute their products—all these are examples of capital goods. Since firms use capital goods to produce their products, the demand for capital goods is directly related to the demand for their products. As we shall see, however, the demand for capital goods is much more unstable than the demand for consumption goods. This is true largely because the useful lifetime of most capital goods is many years. In this sense they are similar to consumer durable goods, but the demand for capital goods is even more unstable.

Ultimately, all capital goods are used to produce consumption goods. They are the tools used to make the products and to provide the services that consumers want. Firms require capital goods either to replace their production tools that have worn out or to expand their production to meet growing consumer demands for their products. The demand for new capital goods to expand the present level of consumption goods production will exist only when the economy is growing or when new technology is developed that mandates a wholesale scrapping of obsolete production techniques—for example, when transistor technology replaced tube technology in the electronics industry. This fact alone contributes greatly to the instability of the demand for capital goods, but this problem is made much worse by the nature of our modern production techniques.

The highly mechanized production technology used in America is very capital-intensive, or capital-using. As our economy has developed, an increasingly larger percentage of our labor force has been assigned to machine making, tending, and monitoring. Today, our machines do most of the work that our great grandparents toiled to complete. The average American firm employs three-dollars' worth of capital goods to produce one-dollar's worth of consumption goods. Because the same capital goods are used over and over again for many years, however, the total value of the consumption goods they ultimately produce far exceeds the initial cost of these capital goods. Nevertheless, the fact that three-dollars' worth of capital goods are used to produce one-dollar's worth of consumption goods does significantly affect the stability of employment in the capital goods industries. It means that when the demand for consumption goods expands, the demand for capital goods and, consequently, the demand for labor in the capital goods industries, expands up to three times as much.

Conversely, and also because of the fact that capital goods are used for many, many years, when consumption demand contracts, the demand for capital goods contracts by an even larger multiple. When the demand for consumption goods declines, business people cannot fully utilize the capital goods they already have on hand, and they certainly are not interested in buying more.

For all these reasons, employment in the capital goods industries is less secure than in any other industries. The construction and industrial machinery and equipment industries that produce capital goods are the most unstable industries in our economy. When the rest of the economy catches a cold, these industries come down with pneumonia. Conversely, when the rest of the economy experiences growth, capital goods industries experience supergrowth, backlogs of orders, and handsome profits. To be associated with these industries is like being on a perpetual roller coaster ride. Employment in them is most perilous and the number of job positions is continually expanding and contracting.

Scientific Fields May Be Insecure

Many of the more scientifically oriented professions experience a kind of job insecurity similar to that in the capital goods industries. Take those employees in research and development for example. Research and development departments are concerned with their firms' long-run or future competitive positions. Employees in these departments discover and develop the ideas and products that will make their firms successful in the future.

When a firm experiences difficult times, it focuses its concern on the more immediate problem of survival. Since the profits that were being used to fi-

nance research and development expenditures have declined, these activities are cut back. Engineers of all categories, basic research personnel, and those individuals who support these scientists can expect their employment opportunities to rise and fall somewhat with the state of general economic conditions.

However, because firms are very concerned about their future and because they invest large amounts in research and development activities, they do not want to curtail these activities and fire workers unless the threat to their financial survival is immediate and very real. Workers in these fields will suffer in two ways during difficult economic times. Those who are already unemployed or have just entered these fields will find it very difficult or impossible to locate jobs because no one is hiring new employees. Those who are already employed will find it very hard to change jobs, get wage increases, and get their firms to spend money for their projects. They will be temporarily locked into their jobs, which may become less interesting because they are less free to pursue their work aggressively. Some of those already employed may also lose their jobs during such times.

Individuals who seek careers in capital goods industries and, to a lesser extent, those who work in a research and development capacity or in consumer durable goods industries would be wise to follow the advice given those who work in industries that produce luxury goods. Insist on receiving additional compensation for the added risks of unemployment you will incur by working in these positions. Furthermore, be sure to set some funds aside for the rainy days that you should anticipate.

Obviously, there are other industries and occupations in which job security is limited. When you are choosing a career, evaluate this aspect of your potential employer's business and plan accordingly. Studying a firm's sales patterns during recent recessionary periods will give you some indication of how risky it may be to work for it. You should also ask others who have worked in your field about the job security you can expect in it.

Mixed Industries

Many industries do not fit very nicely into any of these classifications. Instead they fall somewhere between one or more of them. In some cases, it is analytically more correct to treat the individual firms that make up an industry differently. This is true of many service industries. For example, if a law firm were to specialize in servicing Wall Street investment firms, its legal practice would fluctuate with economic conditions on Wall Street. Employment security with such a law firm would be quite different from that with another law firm which specialized, for example, in physician malpractice cases or patent law cases. Likewise, job security in advertising firms will depend on the nature of their clients' products.

The principles we have learned still apply in these cases. However, you must identify the nature of these service firms' businesses. Job security in these firms is directly linked to the nature of their clients' products. In effect, you may treat such service firms in an analytical sense as "employees of their client firms." For example, whatever determines the demand for oil will directly affect the demand for the services of consulting firms that specialize in giving advice to firms that drill for oil. Because of the increased price of oil, such firms became flooded with new business after the oil embargo of October 1973.

Although it is more difficult, it is still possible to determine the amount of job security you can expect in mixed industries. In many instances, as for example in the service industries, firms are not overly specialized. They often have clients whose various products fall into many classifications. If this is the case, these firms offer a good deal of job security. Their business can be expected to fluctuate moderately with general economic conditions.

The Firm Matters Too

Although your fate as an employee is linked primarily to the fate of the industry you work in, it is also linked to the fate of the particular firm you work for. When an industry experiences good times, almost all of the firms in it grow and prosper together. Greater personal opportunity almost inevitably comes with growth. As your firm prospers, it will need your services and valuable experience more than ever. If it doesn't promote you and increase your salary, one of its competitors will be likely to hire you and your firm will lose your talents and experience.

On the other hand, all of the firms in an industry usually suffer together during difficult times, and some of the weakest are frequently forced out of business. Whereas in bad times you may lose your job if you work for one of the weakest firms in your industry, you may only find it difficult to get raises and promotions if you work for one of the stronger firms in your industry. Consequently, it is also important that you consider the relative industry positions of potential employers when you are job hunting. You should compare your potential employers' sizes, growth rates, profit rates, investments in research and development activities, and the modernness of their technologies in order to evaluate their ability to withstand difficult times. In Chapter Eleven we will discuss how you can get this information.

WHERE UNEMPLOYMENT HIT, 1957 TO 1974

Table 6–1 provides tangible proof of the connection between the nature of your employer's products and the likelihood that you may become unemployed during recessionary times. The general principles we just developed are clearly born out in these data that span the recessions of 1957, 1960, and 1969.

Table 6–1 shows how unemployment rates varied in six key industrial classifications during the period 1957 to 1974. Although these figures conform very well to our expectations, these data contain important limitations that require special comment. The industry classifications used in Table 6–1 were developed by the U.S. Department of Labor to serve a multiplicity of uses. They are much too broad and overlapping to ideally suit our special purposes, but they are all we have to work with. Durable and non-durable goods, for example, should be further subclassified into luxury and necessity goods for our purposes. If this type of subclassified data were available, the product/ unemployment relationship could be seen in much sharper focus. Nor is the National Bureau of Economic Research's official definition of a recessionary

TABLE 6-1
UNEMPLOYMENT RATES BY INDUSTRY, 1957-1974

INDUSTRY (Wage and Salary Workers)	1957*	1958*	1959	1960*	1961*	1962	1963	1964	1965	1966	1967	1968	1969*	1970*	1971	1972	1973	1974*
Construction	10.9	15.3	15.3	13.5	15.7	13.5	13.3	11.2	10.1	8.0	7.4	6.9	6.0	9.7	10.4	10.3	8.8	10.6
Durable Goods	4.9	10.6	10.6	6.4	8.5	5.7	5.5	4.7	3.5	2.8	3.4	3.0	3.0	5.7	7.0	5.4	3.9	5.4
Non Durable Goods	5.3	7.7	7.7	6.1	6.8	6.0	6.0	5.4	4.7	3.8	4.1	3.7	3.7	5.4	6.5	5.7	4.9	6.2
All Industries	4.5	7.3	7.3	5.7	6.8	5.6	5.6	5.0	4.3	3.5	3.6	3.4	3.3	4.8	5.7	5.3	4.5	5.3
Transportation and Public Utilities	3.3	6.1	6.1	4.6	5.3	4.1	4.2	3.5	2.9	2.1	2.4	2.0	2.2	3.2	3.8	3.5	3.0	3.2
Government	1.9	2.5	2.5	2.4	2.5	2.1	2.2	2.1	1.9	1.8	1.8	1.8	1.9	2.2	2.9	2.9	2.7	3.0

Source: U.S. Department of Labor, Bureau of Labor Statistics, unpublished data.
*Officially a recessionary year

year ideal for our purposes. It measures recessions in terms of sales rather than the unemployment rate. Since most employers are hesitant to lay off their workers when sales first fall off and also hesitant to rehire them when sales first pick up again, unemployment rate changes lag behind the official recession benchmarks. The unemployment rate typically peaks in the second year of a recession and continues at a high level into the first year of the official recovery.

The product/unemployment relationship is most clearly revealed during a recession and in the year immediately following it. The data shown in Table 6–1 completely span three such periods that officially began and ended as follows: August 1957 to April 1958; April 1960 to February 1961; and December 1969 to November 1970.[1] The six industries shown have been arranged from most to least susceptible to unemployment.

The construction industry, which produces the buildings and highways needed by an expanding economy, heads the list as the most unstable employer. The other capital goods industries, such as the industrial machinery manufacturers and the steel industry, would also head our list if we had data on these industries. The likelihood of unemployment in these industries would be similar to that in construction, which, during recessions, is 2 to 2 ½ times as high as the average for all industries and more than 6 times as high as in government, the most stable classification. These data also reveal that unemployment in the construction industry is high even during good times. This is due in part to the fact that economic growth does not occur uniformly throughout the country. Even during boom times, some areas of the country are not growing and their local construction industry remains largely unemployed. This is not typical, however, of capital goods industries in general.

The steel industry, for example, serves the entire nation from several regional centers. No matter where the economy is growing, jobs for steel workers are created in these centers of steel production. Because it is more locally based, the construction industry, on the other hand, faces especially troublesome problems of matching job opportunities with the availability of local construction workers. Whereas steel can be shipped to where the growth is presently occurring, it's much more difficult to relocate construction workers to these areas. Consequently, rapidly growing areas experience shortages of local construction personnel at the same time that pockets of persistently high construction unemployment exist in areas that are growing less rapidly. This results in an exceptionally high average level of unemployment in the construction industry, even during good times.

If we had data on its classifications, the luxury goods industry would probably be second in the rate of unemployment. While the durable and non-durable classifications generally conform to our expectations during the recessionary years, these data would conform much better if more refined subclassifications (for example, luxuries, necessities, capital goods, etc.) were available. Most of the services that are classified under transportation and public utilities, for example, are necessities, and the unemployment rate in this category is considerably below the average during all the recessionary years. Trains, buses, and the electric company continue to operate during recessions and you will still be able to turn on the gas after your sweetheart phones to tell you it's all over. Necessities like these are recessionproof.

Unemployment is least likely if you work for the government. But, again, finer subclassifications would have been desirable. Of the various levels of government, unemployment is least likely during a recession if you work for the federal government. Washington has the responsibility of fighting recessions, and it alone can finance its deficits by simply printing more money. Cities must borrow to finance their deficits. When they run out of credit, they too must lay off employees—as New York City did in 1975. States and counties are in the same position as cities; while employment with them is secure, it is less secure than with the federal government.

As you have undoubtedly noticed, we have carefully avoided commenting on the most recent recession of 1974-1975. We've done this because the unusual nature of this particular recession mandates a separate, quite special analysis. In fact, the inflation/recession of 1974-1975 constitutes a classic example of circumstances in which an economic novice should preferably seek the advice of an economic authority. This period in our economic history was unusual in almost every respect. If you prefer to, you may simply record 1974-1975 as an exception to the general rules and not trouble yourself with trying to understand what happened during this atypical period. The next four paragraphs, which attempt to explain the rudiments of what happened in the simplest and briefest terms, are strictly optional. You will lose nothing in terms of the continuity of our general discussion if you fail to fully understand these paragraphs or if you elect to skip them altogether.

The Recession of 1974-1975: A Special Case

As is virtually always the case, the seeds that matured into the bitter economic harvests of 1974-1975 were sown much, much earlier. The first of these seeds were planted during the war years beginning in 1965 by Congresses that lacked the discipline to fully finance the war and their other expensive programs with higher taxes. Instead they relied partially on "borrowing from the Federal Reserve" to close the gap between their runaway expenditures and the insufficient taxes they levied. If we took the time to explain what "borrowing from the Federal Reserve" really involved, you would quite simply and correctly realize that this is a cover-up term for printing more money, which is precisely what was done. This extra money was the first seed—we'll call it the "money seed."

If we took the time to explain another economic riddle, you'd realize that when an extra dollar is printed it has a fully expected way of "multiplying" until it ultimately grows to become eight dollars. This process takes some time, however, and it was not until the late 1960s that Congress's money seed matured. The inevitable result was inflation, which was forecasted way back when Congress first planted its money seed. Inflation, which is simply an imbalance between money and the things it is exchanged for, occurs whenever the money supply expands faster than the supply of things. Things become scarce relative to money, and their prices shoot up until the surplus money is dissipated in the form of higher prices and a new, higher money/things balance is established. To stop an inflationary price spiral, therefore, the money/things balance must be restored in favor of things. This can be accomplished either by producing more things or eliminating the extra money by, for example, raising taxes and destroying the money that is collected. Congress did neither. Instead it blamed business and labor for the inflation and enacted four phases of wage and price controls.

Wage and price controls have never worked well. And these particular controls, which for purposes of administrative simplicity were applied only to large firms, were especially counterproductive. Because large firms get supplies from thousands of small firms whose prices were not controlled, they were soon caught in a vicious and irrational environment of increasing costs and fixed prices for their products. Many firms stopped expanding and some stopped producing altogether. Bottlenecks and shortages developed throughout the economy, and the money/things balance became even worse. When controls were finally lifted, we inevitably got the pent-up inflation anyway. But businesses finally started to expand again and carry out the modernization programs they had postponed in the irrational atmosphere of controls. This represented the first step toward the long-run curtailment of the inflationary price spiral because it increased the supply of things.

Then, on the heels of controls came poor harvests and the Arab oil embargo which sent food and energy prices rocketing upward. Inflation raged across the board as the prices of almost all items were marked up to reflect the higher energy costs of producing and transporting them to market. Since food and energy are necessity goods, consumers could not reduce their consumption of these items. Consequently, the demand for virtually all nonnecessity items fell off as consumers were forced to economize on these items in order to continue buying food, heating their homes, and driving to work. And yet, as we entered this recession, many of the capital goods industries were experiencing boom times. Why? Because these industries were still working overtime to fill the backlog of orders they received immediately after decontrol when business suddenly tried to implement the expansion and modernization programs they had postponed during the period of wage and price controls. This was indeed a very strange set of unique economic circumstances. These conditions also constitute an alarming testimony to the unnecessary suffering that can be wrought by a body of powerful, self-serving politicians.

The Job Function Matters Too

Table 6–2 provides tangible proof that the likelihood of your becoming unemployed depends not only on the nature of the demand for your employer's products but also on the "divisibility" of your job function. Social work and medical care are examples of job functions that we shall define as divisible. If the quality of service is to be maintained, additional social workers and medical personnel must be added as the number of cases and patients increases. Machine tending is an example of a perfectly divisible job function: machines and machine tenders are added and dropped in fixed proportions as the volume of the firm's work expands and contracts. The job function of the plant manager, to cite the opposite extreme, is completely indivisible. The plant manager cannot be laid off unless the entire plant closes. Likewise, the need for an organization's professional staff remains largely unaffected by changes in the volume of its business. Adding or dropping zeros from the figures that appear on a firm's contracts or on its balance sheet does not affect the firm's need for a lawyer and an accountant.

As long as an organization continues to operate, it will continue to need its various departments. It's the divisibility of your department's job function and how its work load varies with changes in your firm's total work load, therefore, that affects your job security. Job security is inversely related to a department's size and the divisibility of its job function. Job security is maximized, therefore, in a one-person department. These truths are substantiated by the data presented in Table 6–2. These unemployment rates by occupational classification were also compiled by the U.S. Department of Labor. They are arranged in order from the least to the most likely occupation to experience unemployment during a recession.

TABLE 6-2
UNEMPLOYMENT RATES BY OCCUPATION, 1958-1974

OCCUPATION	1958*	1959	1960*	1961*	1962	1963	1964	1965	1966	1967	1968	1969*	1970*	1971*	1972	1973	1974*
Managers and Administrators	1.7	1.3	1.4	1.8	1.5	1.5	1.4	1.1	1.0	.9	1.0	.9	1.3	1.6	1.8	1.4	1.8
Professional and Managerial Workers	1.8	1.5	1.6	1.9	1.6	1.7	1.6	1.3	1.2	1.2	1.1	1.2	1.7	2.4	2.1	1.8	2.1
White-Collar Workers	3.1	2.6	2.7	3.3	2.8	2.9	2.6	2.3	2.0	2.2	2.0	2.1	2.8	3.5	3.4	2.9	3.3
Clerical and Kindred Workers	4.4	3.7	3.8	4.6	4.0	4.0	3.7	3.3	2.9	3.1	3.0	3.0	4.1	4.8	4.7	4.2	4.6
Blue-Collar Workers	10.2	7.6	7.8	9.2	7.4	7.3	6.3	5.3	4.2	4.4	4.1	3.9	6.2	7.4	6.5	5.3	6.7
Operatives and Kindred Workers	11.0	7.6	8.0	9.6	7.5	7.5	6.6	5.5	4.4	5.0	4.5	4.4	7.1	8.3	6.9	5.7	7.5
Non-Farm Laborers	15.1	12.6	12.6	14.7	12.5	12.4	10.8	8.6	7.4	7.6	7.2	6.7	9.5	10.8	10.3	8.4	10.1

Source: U.S. Department of Labor, Bureau of Labor Statistics, unpublished data.
*Officially a recessionary year

CHAPTER SEVEN

Every short statement about economics is misleading (with the possible exception of my present one).

Alfred Marshall

CHAPTER SEVEN

WHY JOBS PAY WHAT THEY DO

You don't have to be money crazy to want to be able to predict how much you'll be able to earn in the occupations you're considering. All of us would be better able to plan our futures and achieve greater mastery over our affairs if we were better able to judge how much we could earn in our prospective careers both now and in the future. Paying the rent and buying food are among our most basic and inescapable responsibilities. It just doesn't make sense, therefore, to work and live in a market system that is regulated by forces you don't understand. Why set yourself up to be disappointed or "plucked" by the bad guys?

This chapter presents the rules of the game in the market economy in which you will work and spend your income. You'll learn the rudiments of supply and demand, and how these forces interact to determine prices. The analysis will be directed specifically toward the determination of your occupational wage, the single price that will concern you most during your working years. You'll learn the key economic signs to look for in forecasting your financial future in whatever career field you're considering. And by the time we're finished, you'll be much more confident about your ability to distinguish a good deal from a bad one and to prevent yourself from losing your feathers to those bad guys.

How Our Market Economy Functions

Our market economy is made up of many, many smaller pieces called *markets*. There is a separate market for every product and service and every classification and grade of labor that exists. Each of these markets has two sides: a providing or supply side and a taking or demand side. The individuals who make up each side of a market can be thought of as playing a serious competitive game against the players on the other side of the same market. During the course of this game, the product or service is exchanged from the suppliers to the demanders and the "score" is recorded in terms of the price at which the product is exchanged. The suppliers, those individuals or firms that provide something for sale, are motivated to seek the highest possible price. The demanders, those individuals or firms that come to the market to buy, are motivated to seek the lowest possible price. The higher the price, the more the suppliers have won; and, conversely, the lower the price, the more the demanders have won.

Throughout this chapter we try to ascertain what will determine the level of your wages in the occupations you might choose. Here is red flag number one. Your future wage is a price, and like all other prices it will be set by the competitive, tug-of-warlike forces of *both* supply and demand acting together. Supply conditions directly affect price, but they do not set it. Demand conditions also directly affect price, but they also do not set it. Price is set by both supply and demand conditions acting together. For example, if hail were to destroy half of this year's peach crop, this supply condition by itself would tend to raise the price of peaches. But suppose someone on a television talk show presented preliminary evidence that linked the pesticides used by peach growers to cancer. If enough peach buyers were convinced by this evidence and stopped buying peaches, this reduced demand condition might fully offset the lower supply of peaches. As a result, this year's price of peaches might be even lower than last year's, when the peach harvest was twice as large.

Competition also exists between the players on the same side of each market. This competition, which gives free markets their self-regulating quality, will also be very important in the determination of your future wages. While the individuals who make up either side of a market share a common price objective, they are in direct competition with each other and this competition directly thwarts their common price objective. Department stores would all like to get the highest possible prices for their goods—this is the common price objective shared by these suppliers. However, in competing among themselves for customers, they tend to offer deals that force all of them to sell at lower prices. The amount of competition and the extent to which the common price objective is thwarted are directly related to and increase with the number of participants on either side of the market. The more department stores there are, the lower their prices are likely to become.

Likewise, the more buyers there are in a market, the more difficult it is for any of them to buy at a low price because in competing among themselves for the limited supply of a commodity, together they bid up its price. Ticket scalping, the illegal practice of reselling tickets for popular, sold-out, entertainment events at exorbitant prices, is an example of how buyer competition drives up prices. The willingness of many motorists to bribe gasoline station attendants with tips in order to get more gasoline during the 1974 energy crisis is another example of how buyer competition drives up prices. Examples of the effects of supplier competition can be seen in the market for very costly items such as homes, cars, and major appliances whose prices can often be negotiated by the buyer. When you appear serious about buying a new car, car dealers usually ask about the specifics of the offers other car dealers have made you. Their desire to know their competitors' offers, and their frequent willingness to meet or better them, are examples of how supplier competition lowers prices.

We can draw the following conclusions about the determination of wage levels. Like any other price, the wage level of any particular type of labor is determined simultaneously by the interaction of the participants on both the supply and demand sides of that particular labor market. The smaller the number of workers and the larger the number of employers there are in that market, the higher the wage level will be. Conversely, the smaller the number of employers and the larger the number of workers there are in that market, the lower the wage level will be. In other words, wage levels are a direct reflection of the extent of supplier and buyer competition in a field, and anything that affects the extent of this competition will also affect a field's wage levels.

The Economist's Implied, Ever-Present Qualifier

One of the most common economic stumbling blocks occurs because wage levels are set not by supply or demand forces but by the simultaneous interaction of both these forces. In fact, it is simultaneous relationships like this that are responsible for most of the conditional qualifying statements used by economists. These simultaneous relationships make it literally impossible to tell the story straight (that is, without these qualifying clauses), which explains all the "economic doubletalk" you're accustomed to hearing. Any statement about the effects of supply forces on wages can be contradicted by the opposing forces on the demand side of these simultaneous relationships. And, vice versa, what is said about the demand forces can be contradicted by the supply forces. It is possible to explain the operation of the forces on either side of the market, therefore, only in a context in which you assume the forces on the other side of the market to be inoperative. This is typically accomplished with the phrase "all other things remaining the same." This technique gives you a piecemeal understanding of these simultaneous relationships. Once you have grasped both halves of this story, you can patch them together and you'll finally have the story "straight."

We shall turn first to an investigation of the forces that affect wage levels from the supply side of the market. As we proceed with this and the subsequent discussions, some of you will say: "Yes, but I know that can't be true because this or that force can override what they're saying." You may be right, but only because you may have forgotten our qualifier that all other things are assumed to remain the same. Try to remember this qualifier and why it is being used. This will make understanding the operation of these market forces much easier.

The standard qualifier that all other things are assumed to remain the same must be added to virtually all the economic generalizations we shall make in this book. Because constantly repeating this same qualifier is tiring, we shall adopt an alternative technique. We shall include this qualifier in the initial generalizations we formulate and subsequently omit it from most of the rest. *The qualifier that all other things are assumed to remain the same is to be implied, however, in any and all of the economic generalizations we shall make throughout this book.* We're leaving it up to you to read this qualifier into them.

SUPPLY FORCES THAT AFFECT WAGE LEVELS

The effect of supply-side market forces on your future wage level will be directly related to the number of other workers who enter your career field. This is what we earlier termed the extent of supplier competition. The extent of supplier competition in your career field will depend on two things: (1) how many other people are also willing to enter your career field and (2) how many of these people who are willing to enter are also able to actually gain entry into your chosen field. We shall first discuss the most important factors that affect the willingness of most individuals to seek work in an occupation. Although many of these are rather obvious, it is nevertheless helpful to organize them systematically.

Factors That Affect the Willingness of Individuals to Seek Work in an Occupation

The more attractive an occupation appears to be, the more people there will be who are willing to seek work in that occupation. Provided there are no significant entry barriers (discussed in the next section) that prevent people from seeking jobs in fields they find attractive, employers in these fields will be well supplied, perhaps even swamped, with job applicants. Consequently, there will be a great deal of supplier competition for the relatively few job openings that exist, and this competition will serve to suppress wage levels.

Those qualified applicants who really want jobs in a field they consider attractive will be prepared to accept lower wages if necessary as "the price they must pay" in order to get the kind of work they really want. Employers in every occupational classification of labor are interested in paying the lowest possible price for the quality of labor they need. Those individuals who are unwilling to accept the relatively low wages paid in "attractive" occupations will have effectively priced themselves out of these labor markets.

Obviously, not all of us have similar preferences. Whereas most individuals dislike pressure, a few thrive on it. Similarly, most individuals prefer to avoid insecure jobs, working in isolated locations, and physically dangerous work. Nevertheless, a few people deliberately seek jobs that have these characteristics because they prefer these circumstances, not because these jobs, which most people dislike, are relatively highly paid. Individuals who have work preferences that are unlike those of the great majority of the work force do not significantly affect wage levels, however. Wage levels are overwhelmingly determined by the preferences of the majority of the working-age population.

The list below gives the most important characteristics that make occupations attractive to most people. All other things remaining the same, the more of these characteristics an occupation has, the lower its wages will be. Conversely, occupations that have fewer of these characteristics and/or directly opposite characteristics will tend to have higher wages, all other things remaining the same. Employers in these relatively unpopular fields will have to offer more money in order to compensate their employees for the additional unpleasantness that the majority of them associate with their work. Supplier competition will be relatively weak in these unpopular fields; and without the added attraction of higher wages, too few employees would choose to work in these fields.

Preferred Occupational Characteristics

Job Security (discussed earlier in Chapter Six). Examples: Most types of government work, necessity goods industries, and consumer non-durable goods industries.

Short Hours and Generous Vacations. Examples: Teaching, in-the-air airline personnel, and seasonal occupations like skiing and swimming instruction.

Low Levels of Pressure and Stress. Examples: Most types of government work, working for most non-profit institutions, and college and university teaching.

Reduced Responsibility and Accountability. Examples: Positions further down the managerial ladder, and staff positions as opposed to line positions. The terms *staff* and *line* are borrowed from military terminology. Staff people do not generally have direct profit or management responsibility. They act in a capacity of supporting, advising, and giving technical assistance to a firm's line personnel, who are directly responsible for profitability, determine and administer policy, and have the ultimate decision-making authority. Whereas the line directs and decides, the staff follows, investigates, proposes, and occasionally carries out the line's decisions. Staff people are usually more specifically trained technician types whereas line people are more likely to be generalists. Individuals in line positions bear a larger amount of responsibility, and more pressure, and receive more compensation. Technical aides and administrative aides of all types occupy staff positions.

Attractive Non-monetary Fringe Benefits. Examples: Airline and travel agency work because of the travel benefits; certain aspects of the publishing business because it offers variety, intellectual stimulation, and immediate involvement with the world of fresh and ever-changing ideas; work in the media business because of the constant change, contact with personalities, and the travel which may or may not be viewed as a plus; college and university teaching because of the intellectual stimulation and freedom to pursue ideas.

Social Prestige and Respectability. Examples: The clergy. Much of the prestige that was once associated with the professions of medicine, law, and teaching has vanished. However, highly educated people still command somewhat more respect than others.

Work Located in Preferred Climates and Locations. Examples: California and Colorado are two very popular regions. The City of San Francisco is another one. Most San Franciscans could earn more money in other large cities but prefer not to leave the Bay Area. However, those who work in preferred locations are not always paid less.

An Absence of Physical Danger. In this instance it is easier to present coun-
terexamples. Police and detective work, mining and iron workers (those individuals who assemble the superstructures of tall buildings).

While each of the job characteristics listed above tends to lower the level
of wages in a field, the effects of any and indeed all of these characteristics
can be neutralized by circumstances that prevent individuals from being able
to enter the field. The amount of supplier competition and, therefore, the extent to which it affects the wage level are determined by the ability as well as
the willingness of individuals to enter a field. We shall now focus on the determinates of the ability of individuals to enter an occupation.

Factors That Affect the Ability
of Individuals to Enter an Occupation

Anything that prevents individuals who are willing to seek work in a field from
being able to qualify for employment in that field shall be called an *entry
barrier.* Without exception and regardless of their specific nature or how and
why they originated, all entry barriers have a common effect on an
occupation's wages—they increase them. By reducing the number of workers
who enter a field, entry barriers reduce the amount of supplier competition
which in turn reduces the extent to which workers themselves collectively bid
down and restrain the wage level. Consequently, it is in the selfish interests of
those already employed in a field to erect as many entry barriers as they can.
By keeping many potential workers out of a field, entry barriers limit supplier
competition and thereby maintain wages at a higher level than they would be
without the barriers.

We shall discuss three types of entry barriers: educational, financial, and
legal. These are the most common, and, therefore, the most important barriers
that prevent people from entering fields they might otherwise choose to work
in.

Educational Entry Barriers

Employers often refuse to consider workers for jobs the workers feel they
could do. The employers tell them that they are not qualified, that they lack the
necessary educational credentials. Let's try to understand why this happens.

Hiring is a serious business because employers incur large risks when
they hire new people. They must spend time and money training new workers,
and many things can go wrong. An employee's mistakes can result in lost
production, damaged products, and customer dissatisfaction and can disrupt
the work of the firm's other employees. Even if none of these disasters occur,
the employee may simply not like the job and quit. Then the firm must repeat
the whole selection and training process and incur still more expenses.

Consequently, firms want to minimize the risk of hiring those who will do a
job poorly or leave because they don't like the work. Those individuals who

have the responsibility of hiring new employees are especially interested in hiring people who will work out well and remain with the firm—too many "bad hires" and they themselves will be fired. They're people too, and it's no fun for them to have to fire employees who don't work out. For all these reasons, the firm and its hiring officers always want to hire the best person for the job. But how can they identify that person?

When most of us seek jobs, we are completely unknown to our potential employers. Consequently, we are asked many questions. Regardless of how many questions they ask, employers really want to know the answer to just one question: How soon will we be able to do the job well? What do employers have to rely on when they guess about our ability to do a job well?

If we have worked before, employers can assess our previous work record. Experienced workers got their training and made their initial mistakes at the expense of other employers. Firms incur lower training costs and fewer risks by hiring them. Therefore, firms are willing to pay experienced workers more than inexperienced workers. If experienced persons with demonstrated ability to handle the work can be hired for reasonable wages, they will be hired first.

When firms must hire inexperienced people, they look for other indications of an applicant's ability to do the job. Educational backgrounds and scholastic records are heavily relied upon in these cases. Why? Because, while the firm knows almost nothing about you, they do know how people with your educational background have tended to work out in the job you want. "Math major" is a more useful label than "Margie Kipp." "Top fifth of his class at Utah State" is a more reliable label than "Bill Woods."

Over the years, employers have been forced to hire many unknowns. Their experience has shown that unknowns with certain educational backgrounds cost less to train and make fewer mistakes in certain job categories. As a result, firms feel that they incur fewer risks by hiring persons with these educational backgrounds. Some employers may simply show a preference for applicants with certain educational backgrounds. For example, many banks prefer to hire business and economics majors because they require somewhat less training and have already shown an interest in the matters bankers deal with.

Employers in some fields require, rather than simply prefer, specific educational backgrounds. This is the case in scientific and technical fields. In these occupations, the knowledge acquired in school is directly applied on the job. Without having studied engineering, you cannot get a job as an engineer. Only chem majors will be considered qualified for positions as chemists. Employers in some fields are permitted to hire only those individuals who have completed a specified course of study. Most schools are prohibited from hiring teachers who do not have a four-year college degree. Publicly owned corporations are required to hire certified public accountants to audit their financial statements.

Many employers impose educational requirements for less obvious reasons. They may feel their educational requirements act as a filter that improves the quality of their work force. Their experience may indicate that such requirements reduce the time and expenses they incur training new employees. Or they may find that these requirements add to their firm's prestige.

Regardless of how or why educational requirements become prerequisites for employment in a field, they have the same effect on the field's wages: they raise them. Acquiring an education is difficult, time consuming, and expensive. Consequently, educational requirements discourage and prevent many individuals from entering a field. Because fewer people qualify for jobs in the field, those who do qualify face less competition and are therefore able to earn higher wages. The smaller the number of workers there are in a field, the less tendency there will be for them to bid down their own wages when they attempt to find jobs. Incidentally, educational requirements result in higher wages for a second reason. Unless people can expect to recover the costs of educating themselves, most of them would be unwilling to pay for their education. For example, if college students did not feel they could earn more after college, most of them would not spend their time and money getting a college education.

Finally, in discussing the relationship between educational barriers and wage levels, stress must again be placed on the qualifier "all other things remaining the same." Advanced research degrees like the Ph.D. usually place their holders in a staff as opposed to a line position. As noted earlier in this chapter, top staff people usually earn less than top line people, few of whom hold Ph.D.'s. However, the other differences in the nature of staff and line work account for the higher pay received by top line personnel. In order to accurately see the relationship between education and wage levels in this case, the wage rates of less well educated staff people must be compared with those of better educated staff people. When staff personnel are compared with other staff personnel and likewise line personnel are compared with other line personnel, the requirement that most other things be held constant is met and these comparisons do reveal that better educated personnel earn higher wages.

Financial Entry Barriers

Anyone who is willing to qualify for employment in a career field but is unable to do so for financial reasons, has been blocked by a financial entry barrier. In a broad sense, therefore, college and graduate school tuition and living expenses are financial barriers for some students. These financial barriers can and have been overcome, however, by millions of students with the aid of scholarships, grants, loans, and part-time wages. We shall focus on the more difficult financial barriers encountered by those who plan to become self-employed.

Those wishing to become self-employed face serious financial barriers and should carefully evaluate their financial needs. One of the primary reasons most new businesses fail is because they lack the financial resources necessary to carry them through the difficult start-up years in which losses are more common than profits. Most people who start new businesses tend to be overly optimistic, and they almost invariably underestimate their financial needs.

Becoming self-employed is *relatively* easy for most professional people. In fact, many of them experience greater financial difficulties while getting their training than in opening their practices or businesses. Doctors and dentists are able to borrow with relative ease. Lawyers only need an office, some books, and some secretarial assistance. Psychologists can operate out of their homes. Most professional people can work for or in association with others in their profession until they have developed the reputation and practice they need to operate independently. And of even greater significance, the payroll expenses of most professional self-employed people are minimal in comparison with most self-employed business people.

The financial resources needed to enter most business fields constitute insurmountable financial barriers for most people. Increased urbanization has resulted in larger markets that have in turn spawned larger businesses. Consequently, opportunities for self-employed business people with limited financial resources are disappearing. This has continued to be the case since World War II. Many capable individuals have remained as managers of other people's firms simply because they lack the funds needed to start their own businesses.

Farming is another example of how the scale of business has grown. Land, equipment, and fertilizer costs are large multiples of what they were a generation ago. Today, most types of farmers need hundreds of thousands of dollars to operate on a profitable scale. The real estate development business and the construction business have also become bigger businesses. Whereas these firms used to be locally based, now they are often regionally based. Retail businesses such as grocery stores, clothing stores, automotive supply stores, department stores, hardware stores, and drugstores have all entered the chain store age. Chains buy in large volume at lower prices and are usually more efficiently managed. Therefore they can charge lower prices that drive their smaller competitors out of business. Although consumers have benefited from chains because they get what they want at lower prices, chains have greatly reduced the opportunities for self-employed business people.

The small business opportunities that still exist are largely confined to fields that are service-oriented. Many real estate brokerage firms and insurance agencies of all types remain small in size. Small business opportunities still exist in the local restaurant and entertainment businesses. Repair and maintenance firms are other examples.

Many nationally known businesses such as McDonald's and Dairy Queen offer local franchises to business people. However, franchises like these can still cost hundreds of thousands of dollars, and you will have to demonstrate that you have business experience and know-how. *This experience you should require of yourself in any case if you plan to open your own firm.* With such experience, you could possibly overcome the financial hurdles by finding someone with money to back you in a joint venture. Finally, you should note that most of the business fields that are still open to people with modest amounts of money are very competitive, risky, and often overcrowded. These are not easy fields in which to make a living, and struggling to do so may become your whole life.

Legal Entry Barriers

Whereas educational barriers are understandable and often necessary, and financial barriers may be accepted as an unavoidable consequence of greater urbanization, the vast majority of legal entry barriers cannot be condoned. They harm all of us as consumers because their consequences are higher prices and a reduced supply of some of the products and services most vital to our welfare. They also effectively deny many the freedom of occupational choice. Let's try to understand why they exist and examine their effects.

The practitioners in an occupation have a lot in common. Not only do they share a common wage objective, they also face similar problems and they can benefit from each other's mistakes and successes. It is only natural that they should organize. Once they've organized, it's also only natural that they should attempt to use the political influence of their organization to raise their occupation's wages. Through their organization they typically cite the need to protect consumers from incompetent practitioners as the reason the state or local government should establish a regulatory body to pass judgment on the qualifications of would-be practitioners in their trade or profession. Of course, only another plumber can judge the competency of other plumbers and, likewise, only a dentist can evaluate the work of other dentists. Therefore, the watchdog body must itself be composed of practitioners of the occupation it regulates. This unwise arrangement, which places the members of the occupation in a position to regulate the degree of supplier competition in their own occupation, is like having the wolf guard the hen house.

The regulatory body's effective control over its occupation's wages increases as regulation progresses through the three stages of registration, certification, and finally licensure. The legal entry barriers, which become progressively more difficult to overcome through each of these stages, include fees, schooling and educational requirements, apprenticeships and other experience requirements, and increasingly more difficult examinations. All of these requirements, many of which are of questionable relevance to the competent provision of the occupation's services, have three common results. They increase the amount of time would-be practitioners must spend preparing to enter the occupation, they increase the costs of this preparation, and they reduce the likelihood that candidates will ultimately be accepted into the occupation. Consequently, these barriers produce their intended result: they discourage and prevent many would-be practitioners from entering the occupation. Thus by reducing supplier competition these barriers raise the wage level from what it would otherwise be. Occupational regulation is successful for those in the occupation, not for the consumers of its services.

Professor Milton Friedman addresses the problems of occupational regulation at greater length in his book *Capitalism and Freedom*. This stimulating little book, which investigates the relationship between political and economic freedom, is written for a lay audience. You may find it quite interesting. Friedman illustrates the arguments against occupational licensure by examining its consequences in the field of medicine, for which the strongest case in favor of licensure can be made. He shows that even in this field licensure has produced undesirable consequences. The association he is citing in this quote is the American Medical Association.

A dramatic piece of evidence on the power and potency of the Association as well as on the lack of relation to quality is proved by one figure that I have always found striking. After 1933, when Hitler came to power in Germany, there was a tremendous outflow of professional people from Germany, Austria and so on, including of course, physicians who wanted to practice in the United States. The number of physicians trained abroad who were admitted to practice in the United States in the five years after 1933 was the same as in the five years before. This was clearly not the result of the natural course of events. The threat of these additional physicians led to a stringent tightening of requirements for foreign physicians that imposed extreme costs upon them.[1]

Today, we still have a severe shortage of doctors in the United States. American doctors are paid more than doctors anywhere else in the world—more both in dollar amount and in comparison with the members of other professions. Despite this fact which has been true for several generations we have fewer doctors per capita than most other developed nations. We continue to pay more for our doctors and receive relatively fewer of them. Despite these high wages, we still have a doctor shortage; this, too, is clearly not the result of the natural course of events.

When you choose a career, you are likely to encounter legal entry barriers. Dentists, lawyers, morticians, auctioneers, real estate brokers, plumbers, barbers, stock brokers, pharmacists and the practitioners in scores of other occupations are licensed by various municipal and state governments. If you choose any of these fields, you will have to spend time and money preparing yourself for entry; and you will find much of this preparation difficult to justify but nevertheless legally necessary.

DEMAND FORCES THAT AFFECT WAGE LEVELS

In Chapter Six we explained that the demand for labor is derived from the demand for the products that labor is used to produce. We learned that whatever determines the demand for a firm's products also determines its demand for labor. And we reasoned from this that if a firm can no longer profitably sell its products, it will be both unwilling and unable to continue to hire and pay its labor force. The principles and analysis that were discussed during that investigation into the determinates of job security apply directly to this section as well. But now our focus is much broader. Our present study will include investigations into the roles that profitability, growth, technological change, interindustry, and international competition play in the determination of occupational wage levels.

Because the demand for labor is ultimately derived from consumers' demands for products, we shall begin by first investigating the determinates of consumers' demands for products. You can also relate to the demand for consumption goods more readily. Understanding these consumption relationships, therefore, will serve to introduce and facilitate an understanding of the derived demand for labor. Because the total demand for any product equals the sum of all individuals' demands for that product, we can use one individual's demand to illustrate the determinates of consumption demand. You will be that individual. This will make things more personal and more fun.

The Demand Game

I'm going to trick you. My students and I have had a little fun and learned a great deal from this game. Imagine you were hungry, liked apples, and wanted to buy some to eat now and to store in your refrigerator. Now I'm going to ask you several questions. *Each time you see a question mark immediately stop reading and answer the question. Don't ruin the game by peeking ahead!* Each question illustrates a different determinate of the demand for consumption goods.

You're off to the market to buy apples. How many apples are you going to buy? You're kidding! We haven't told you how much money you have to spend. Since you're broke, you can't buy any apples at all. *Income* is obviously one of the determinates of demand. That was what Chapter Six was all about. When consumers' incomes are reduced because of unemployment, the demand for consumption goods is directly affected. Okay, now we will give you two dollars which will be the income you have to spend each time you go to the market for apples from now on in this game.

You're off to the market to buy apples. How many apples are you going to buy? What was that you said? Apples are very, very scarce because of a late frost that destroyed the apple blossoms, and the only ones available are selling for one dollar each. Maybe that price will change your mind? We have identified another determinate of demand: *the price of the product*. From now on it should be easier to answer the questions because the price of apples for the rest of the game will be 25 cents each.

You're off to the market to buy apples. You have two dollars, and you know that apples are selling for 25 cents each. How many apples are you going to buy? Do you really want any apples at all? At the market you find your favorite fruit on sale for 10 cents a pound. Maybe that will change your mind. We have identified another determinate of demand: *the prices of substitute goods.* Substitute goods are goods that can be used in place of other goods. Oranges are substitutes for apples and for any other kind of fruit. Chicken is a substitute for beef and vice versa. Television and the movies are substitutes for each other. Aluminum, steel, and plastic beer cans and glass beer bottles are substitutes for each other. The demand for any good is affected by the price of goods that can be used as substitutes for it. For example, when you go food shopping you may intend to buy some steak. If you find that chicken is on sale for 39 cents a pound, however, you may buy it instead of steak. In this case you might substitute chicken for beef, not because of the price of beef, but because of the price of one of beef's substitutes. Substitution is very important and occurs frequently. In fact, in a very strict and pure sense, the prices of all other goods affect the demand for every good in some small way. But this fine point is unimportant for our purposes. For the rest of this game, you may fix the prices of all substitutes for apples at any reasonable levels you wish to choose.

You're off to the market to buy apples. You have two dollars, the price of apples is 25 cents each, and you know the price of all substitutes. Now finally, can you tell us how many apples you are going to buy? Have you changed your mind again! On the way to the market you learn that the U.S. Department of Agriculture recommends that apple growers spray this crop 12 times a year with various pesticides.[2] Your taste for apples has suddenly vanished, and you don't want them any more. The final major determinate of demand has been identified. It is consumers' *tastes.* Consumers are often fickle. Changes in their tastes dramatically affect the fashion industry and have even brought Chrysler, Ford, and General Motors to their knees. During the gasoline shortage of 1973-1974, consumers abruptly stopped buying big cars and these giant auto makers were suddenly stuck with tens of thousands of big new cars they couldn't sell.

Our game is over. We have identified the four major determinates of consumption demand. They are income, the price of the good, the price of substitutes, and consumers' tastes. If any one or all four of these determinates change, it will affect the demand for labor in the industry that produces the product—the apple industry in our example. To be sure that you understand these relationships, we shall work through an actual example. In this case we will extend the example to reveal the effects of consumer demand changes on the derived demand for labor.

The standard-sized American car market will serve as our example. In the mid-1950s Volkswagons were introduced into the American automobile market at much lower prices than larger American cars. These *substitutes* became popular, and other inexpensive foreign cars also began to be sold in America.

Detroit manufacturers lost more and more sales and jobs to European carmakers. Finally American carmakers began to produce small cars too. This in turn helped save employment opportunities for those who built cars in America. In 1965 the unemployment rate dipped below 4 percent, and consumers' *incomes* rose sharply to new record levels. Consumer spending on all durable goods including large automobiles also set new records for the next several years in a row. The demand for labor in the large automobile industry rose sharply.

In 1974 two things happened simultaneously. The cost of gasoline nearly doubled, and automobile prices rose sharply because of inflation. Consequently, the cost or *price of operating large cars* increased sharply and suddenly. Consumers also could not buy enough gas and changed their *tastes* in favor of small cars. Large cars sat around in dealers' lots while small car buyers had to wait months for their new cars. As a result, tens of thousands of auto workers who made large cars lost their jobs. These examples demonstrate how changes in consumers' demands directly affect the demand for labor to produce consumption goods. With this understanding we can begin to investigate the other determinates of the demand for labor more directly.

The Importance of Understanding Why
The discussions that follow will reveal two facts: (1) that your future wages are likely to be higher if you work for a profitable firm in a profitable industry, and (2) that the prospects of your receiving higher wages in the future are even better if you work for a firm in an industry that is not only profitable but also growing. You are being told these facts in advance in order to drive home the benefits of the "why approach" that we tried to justify earlier in Chapter Two. As you will realize during the course of the following discussions, the simple knowledge that profitable and growing employers are good employers is by itself of limited benefit to you in formulating sound career plans. Hopefully you will later recall this example that helps demonstrate how you can know the facts about many things and nevertheless understand the meaning of nothing.

Understanding why a potential employer is profitable and/or growing completely eclipses the importance of simply knowing that such an employer is profitable and/or growing. Understanding why your potential employer exhibits these characteristics now will enable you to evaluate their permanentness. Only this deeper understanding can enable you to forecast whether this employer is likely to be a good one in the future as well as today.

The factors we are about to discuss—technological change, growth, and profitability—are all interrelated and associated with each other through a variety of cause-and-effect relationships. This produces a number of difficulties in trying to explain them—difficulties that make it impossible to tell the story "straight," because several simultaneous relationships are involved. Technological change usually results in growth. Growth, in turn, is usually sustained by profits, and the search for profits sometimes results in technological change. Thus, it is also impossible to explain any part of this story separately but even more hopeless to attempt to relate everything at once. Our decision to begin by explaining the role of profitability is, therefore, arbitrary.

Profitability's Effect on Wage Levels

It's good to be employed in a profitable industry because employers in profitable industries can afford to pay high wages. Firms in these industries are producing products that consumers want and are willing to buy at profitable prices. Because these firms want to continue to make profits, they will not allow other firms to outbid them in the labor market. Unions in profitable industries also find it easier to obtain wage increases because management can afford them. If union workers are well paid, the firm's other personnel are also likely to be well paid.

High profits also facilitate and usually induce expansion. Most firms would like to expand in order to make more money but only profitable firms are earning the cash they need to implement their expansionary desires. Because they are successful, profitable firms also enjoy good credit ratings. This enables them to borrow additional money if they want to grow even faster than the inflow of their profits alone will allow. This brings us to growth, but we will be returning to profitability again later.

Growth's Effect on Wage Levels

Firms in growing industries are even better places to work than merely profitable firms. Industries simply cannot grow unless they are profitable. But in addition to being profitable, growing industries have a growing need for labor. If you work in a growing industry, you are almost certain to be promoted to a position of greater responsibility and higher pay much earlier in your career.

As we noted earlier, employers prefer to limit their risks by hiring experienced personnel. Growing profitable firms are no exception, but their very success makes it impossible for them to hire enough experienced people. Firms like IBM, which grew by more than 20 percent a year for many years, more than quintupled in size in less than ten years. If you were to enter such a firm, in less than five years time the firm would have doubled in size and you would be more experienced than most of its employees. After ten years with such a firm, you would be more experienced than 80 percent of its employees. This explains why firms in rapidly growing industries simply must place relatively inexperienced people in responsible positions. They have no alternative.

Firms in rapidly growing industries must continually attract new personnel. They accomplish this by bidding them away from other employers both inside and outside their own industry. For example, imagine that you had been working for IBM for several years during the 1960s. If IBM didn't promote you, Control Data, Burroughs, or one of the other computer companies might have hired you away from IBM. Meanwhile, all of these firms were also stealing talent from other industries. Growing firms have many problems. Their continued growth and profitability depends on their finding good problem-solvers, and they will pay them well. Any way you look at it, employees in rapidly growing industries work in areas of great opportunity. They enjoy all the advantages of working for a profitable firm, plus they are likely to be promoted rapidly.

Technological Change: The Prime Mover Behind the Scene

Technological change—the discovery and development of new and/or more efficient production techniques—is the basic source of many changes in the ways people spend their money. Technological change results in the development of new products and changes in the costs of established products. As a result, consumers spend their money on new and different goods. This in turn directly affects the demand for labor. New jobs and new industries are created, and some old jobs are lost in other industries. Some firms blossom, while others wither and die.

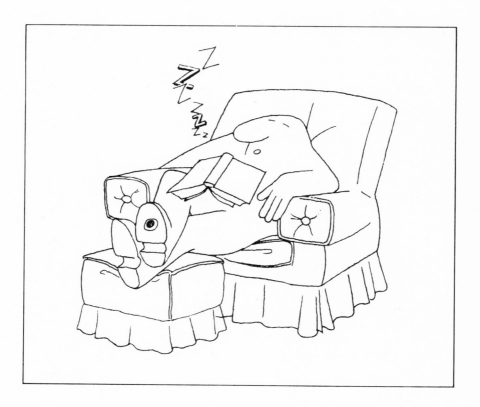

Industries such as the computer industry that develop suddenly and grow extremely rapidly usually do not satisfy new human needs. Human needs are unlikely to change very rapidly. In most instances, rapidly growing industries satisfy already established human needs in better ways and/or at lower cost. Behind most rapidly growing industries lies a revolutionary technology that replaces an existing technology. The more dramatic the improvement, the greater the rush to convert to the new technology.

Many of the functions performed today by computers were formerly done by armies of clerks, bookkeepers and statisticians. Computer technology performs these functions more rapidly and at less expense. During its childhood, the computer industry had to grow rapidly simply to catch up with the established demand for its products.

Along with a new technology come new possibilities. By making it possible to work on new problems, computers created far more work than they replaced. Without them, for example, space exploration would have been impossible. During its adolescence, the computer industry continues to grow in order to exploit the opportunities made possible by its revolutionary technology.

Technological change is a double-edged sword, however, and the birth of a new industry usually results in the death of an existing industry. When Robert Fulton sailed up the Hudson in the first steamship, he acted both as the midwife of the steamship industry and the harbinger of death to the then proud and flourishing clipper ship industry. The derived demand for labor effects that were unleashed by Fulton's voyage were indeed far-reaching. They never could have been foreseen fully by anyone. Lumberjacks, builders of wooden ships, sailmakers, and ropemakers would ultimately lose their jobs. New jobs would be created for boiler makers, steel workers, and many more sailors. Mark Twain would steam up the Mississippi River valley, which could now be developed, and the peoples and products of the world's continents would be brought closer together by months of traveling time. Steamship technology revolutionized the transportation industry. In doing so, it destroyed many jobs but created many, many more. Technological change cannot be fought successfully. If the industry you happen to select is revolutionized in this manner, switch industries, don't fight.

Technological change provides examples of *substitution* in a different context. A cost-saving new technology is substituted for an existing technology. The wholesale conversion to the new technology results in a new, rapidly growing, profitable industry. Causality flows from technological change to growth and profitability. We shall now return to profitability, to which technological change is linked in an important second way.

Profits are defined as the differences between the sales price and the production costs. Consequently, profits can increase for two reasons. If demand increases, buyer competition will bid up the sales price, which will result in higher profits. This is what happened in the computer industry. The demand for computer technology was very strong, thus enabling firms like IBM to sell their products at very high, profitable prices. Profits can also increase as the result of reduced production costs. This is what computer users experienced and why firms were eager to buy computers. Firms that used computers had reduced production costs and therefore earned greater profits.

Consumers also share in the benefits of technological change. The first firms to use computers earned greater profits than their competitors who did not have them. These more profitable firms wanted to expand in order to earn even larger profits. In order to increase their sales, however. they had to lower their prices to induce their competitors' customers to start buying from them instead. Thus, consumers also saved money.

Firms that had not yet adopted computer technology were threatened with the loss of their customers and were also less profitable. Nor could they bid as competitively for labor. Because the firms that used computers had lower costs, they could sell their products at lower prices, still make high profits, and attract other firms' customers. Firms without computers were forced to get them in order to lower their prices and keep their customers. The benefits of technological change are shared by many groups.

Competition and Profitability

There is yet another cause of profitability. Profitability can result from a lack of supplier competition. If a firm does not have competitors, consumers cannot find substitutes for the firm's products. Firms that do not have competitors are called *monopolists*. Since a monopolist is the sole supplier of a product, it controls the market and can set the market price at a very profitable level. The third reason an industry or a firm may be very profitable, therefore, is because it has relatively few or no other competitors.

Consumers have no bargaining power with a monopolist because they have no alternatives. They cannot substitute another supplier's product because there are no other suppliers. If they need or want the product, they must buy it from the monopolist at the price asked for. If apples were the only kind of fruit available, you would have to buy them at the price that was asked or not eat any fruit at all. In this example, if only one firm produced apples, it would be a monopolist.

There are very few examples of pure monopolies. Public utilities are monopolies, but their prices are regulated by the government. *Monopolistic* is an adjective used to describe industries that have few suppliers and therefore tend to resemble monopolies. There are a large number of monopolistic industries. The automobile, aluminum, and computer industries are industries that have few suppliers and are therefore termed monopolistic.

Because there are relatively few suppliers in monopolistic industries, supplier competition is limited and the tendency of suppliers to bid down prices is greatly reduced. Since they are so few in number, firms in monopolistic industries have relatively little trouble keeping themselves informed of one another's activities. These firms sometimes even develop an informal tradition of following the pricing lead of one of the larger firms in their industry. When it changes its price, the others change their prices, often by almost exactly the same amount. In effect, their collective actions tend to resemble those of a single monopolist. Consumers really don't have much bargaining power under these circumstances. They can substitute one supplier's product for another, but they still pay roughly the same price.

As the number of suppliers in an industry increases, it becomes increasingly more difficult to hold prices at profitable levels. The larger the number of suppliers, the more likely it is that one of them will not follow the pricing practices of the rest of the suppliers. If one firm sells its products at a lower price, it begins to attract more and more of its competitors' customers. Eventually the rest of its competitors also have to lower their prices or go out of business.

One of the most effective ways to increase supplier competition is to encourage imports. In America we have only four automobile manufacturers. Foreign cars provide American consumers with dozens of additional alternatives that make substitution possible. In the 1950s many Americans began to substitute smaller, less expensive foreign cars for American cars that were becoming larger and more expensive each year. As a result, American car makers were forced to start making smaller, less expensive cars too. Foreign suppliers have made, and continue to make, the automobile industry much less monopolistic. As a result of the competition they provide, American car buyers enjoy lower prices and cars that are smaller and better suited to their needs.

Domestic suppliers do not welcome foreign competition because it results in less profitable prices for them. Just as professional people try to erect legal entry barriers, industries try to erect tariffs and quotas to block the entry of foreign goods. In almost all cases, their arguments in favor of tariffs and quotas are invalid. One of these commonly voiced fallacious arguments is that without these trade restrictions America will lose jobs to other nations. The next two paragraphs, which explain why these seemingly plausible arguments are false, constitute somewhat of a bonus. It's to your advantage to understand these matters because they directly affect your welfare both as a citizen and as a consumer. The discussion of these matters has been included here because they are important and because many of you might otherwise fail to become aware of them. But since this topic is not directly related to career decision-making, these two paragraphs are optional and you may skip over them if you prefer.

If you want to grasp what's really going on when nations trade with one another, it helps to think of them as single individuals and to focus on their possible motivations for trading with one another. In order to buy something, an individual must be able to sell something else to get the money to pay for the purchase. It's no different with nations. America simply cannot buy goods from other nations unless it also sells some of its goods to them. When America buys, it pays with dollars, the only kind of money it has. America's paper dollars are utterly worthless to other nations, however, unless they ultimately plan to spend them to buy American goods. This explains why the argument that other nations, because of their cheaper wages, will undersell all American products is clearly ridiculous. If this silly argument were indeed true, we would be living not in America but in Heaven. A few Americans could then print paper dollars. In exchange for these dollars America could then buy everything it needed from the rest of the world. Then all of us, except the few work freaks who wanted to print the dollars, could retire permanently.

The underlying reason why it makes sense for individuals and nations to trade with each other is called *comparative advantage.* Let's assume that you can catch two fish or one rabbit each day and that I can catch one fish or two rabbits a day. Under these assumed circumstances you have a comparative advantage in fishing and I in hunting. If we each specialize in the catch we do best and then trade our catches with each other, both of us will enjoy a more plentiful, better balanced diet. It is just as intelligent for nations to specialize in the work they do best. Trade restrictions, on the other hand, prevent nations from specializing in the work they do most efficiently. As a result, people throughout the world must labor harder to produce less, and the wealth of all nations is diminished. When trade restrictions are used to block the importation of foreign-made goods, we are spared the temporary costs of relocating workers into more efficient industries. For this we sacrifice the permanent benefits of specialization and incur higher prices forever. International trade barriers tend to make nations jacks, rather than masters, of trades.

Regardless of their specific nature, all trade barriers limit supplier competition and therefore increase the profitability of the protected industry. Industries can also be sheltered from foreign competition in other ways. It may simply cost too much to transport foreign goods to the domestic market—for example, glass bottles. Or it may be physically impossible to import the product—for example, buildings.

Industries like the construction industry are sheltered not only from international competition, but also from domestic competitors outside their region. It is impossible to profitably construct buildings in Chicago with workers and materials that come from very far away. It costs too much to ship the materials and relocate the workers. Consequently, the profitability of such industries is largely determined by the extent of local or regional supplier competition. Profitability can vary greatly from region to region in such regionally based industries. If you intend to work in such an industry, therefore, you should assess your particular firm's competitive position and profitability.

Competition can also come from outside an industry. This frequently happens as a result of technological change that allows one industry to make substitutes for the products of other industries. The container industry provides lucid examples of interindustry competition. Soft drinks and beer used to be packaged exclusively in glass bottles. Now steel, aluminum, and plastic cans are also used. Suppliers from four industries now compete for the business that was once controlled exclusively by glass suppliers. Technological change is a very effective antimonopolizing agent. New technology provides consumers with additional substitute goods. Substitutes increase supplier competition and make prices less profitable.

Summary: Profitability, Growth, Technological Change, and Supplier Competition

The benefits of career decision-making are harvested not only today and tomorrow but over a lifetime. Ultimately, therefore, the benefits of understanding the relationships between profitability, growth, technological change, and supplier competition, and an employer's circumstances lie in being able to predict the likely course of that employer's future wage level. This requires that you understand the flow of causality within these relationships, which, in turn, necessitates our "why approach." We have seen that profitable industries and firms are good places in which to work because they can afford to pay good wages. The more profitable a firm currently is, the better able and more willing it will be to outbid other employers in today's labor market. But we must understand why an employer is profitable in order to predict the probable future course of that employer's wage levels.

High profitability may simply be the result of little supplier competition. In this case it is important to know why there is little supplier competition and whether these circumstances are likely to change. Supplier competition may increase if foreign imports are introduced, other industries begin producing substitute products, or more domestic suppliers enter the market. If supplier competition increases, prices will become less profitable and wage levels will suffer in the long run. Consequently, if you intend to work for a profitable firm, you should know why it is profitable in order to evaluate the likelihood of its remaining profitable.

Technological change may also be the basic source of profitability. Firms that are profitable because they are using technological advancements (the early computer users in our example) tend to be innovative and progressive. The managements of such firms have demonstrated that they are effective competitors, and they can be considered more likely to remain progressive and profitable. Such firms are therefore more likely to continue to be able to pay good wages.

Firms in industries that are producing technological change (computer makers in our example) are even better employers. Their products are very much needed, and they must grow rapidly just to catch up with the established demand for their products. Growth produces opportunities for employees to gain more responsibility and higher pay much earlier in their careers. Rapidly growing firms, therefore, offer all the advantages of profitable firms plus early career advancement.

F. Scott Fitzgerald You know, Ernest, the
rich are different from us.
Ernest Hemingway: Yes, I know. They have
more money than we do.

THE ROLE OF OPPORTUNITY COSTS IN WAGE-LEVEL DETERMINATION
   What Economic Theory Says You'll Be Paid

EXAMPLES OF THE ROLE OF OPPORTUNITY COSTS
   Medicine
   Law
   Managers and Other Key Personnel
   The Bread Breakers
   Tickets to the Big Money Game

WHAT DETERMINES WHO MOVES UP WHEN PRODUCTIVITY
IS HARD TO MEASURE?

CHAPTER EIGHT

THE BIG MONEY GAME
OR
HOW CAN ANYONE BE WORTH A
SIX-FIGURE INCOME?

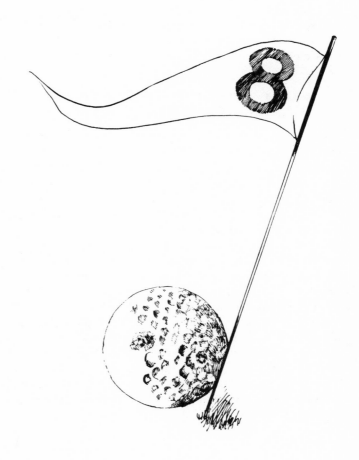

We've seen how wage levels are set by the interaction of the forces that determine the extent of buyer and supplier competition. Although these principles can explain most cases, there are a few very interesting special situations that are much more easily understood if you have a little "inside information" on how markets function and how bargaining is done. At this point, we're going to open the economists' bag of tricks and very selectively pull out what is perhaps their best trick. This one is very useful. You'll be able to apply it not just in the Career Game but every time you go out to buy anything from strawberries to a new car.

Imagine we paid your salary and expenses and sent you out into the world to discover why people are paid what they are paid. After awhile you'd most likely return with answers similar to the following ones. "Sometimes it seems to depend on their employer's ability to pay. Other times it seems to depend on how many people want the job. And, well, sometimes it's really hard to tell, but it seems to depend on how much their employers fear they might lose if their workers didn't work for them." All these answers would be right, but you probably wouldn't realize that all three of them could be explained by the single concept of *opportunity costs*. This concept is the "trick" that explains how someone can truly be worth tens of thousands of dollars a year more than most other employees.

THE ROLE OF OPPORTUNITY COSTS
IN WAGE-LEVEL DETERMINATION

Opportunity costs are invariably encountered in decision-making and all other circumstances that require us to choose between alternatives. The very nature of these circumstances reveals that "we can not have our cake and eat it too." Choosing one alternative "costs" us the other alternatives, and these are what we call our "opportunity costs." That is, opportunity costs are what we choose to forego when we opt for something else. For example, let's imagine that on Sunday afternoon you could either go ice skating or watch a football game. If you decide to go skating, you will have to miss the football game. Not watching the football game would be the opportunity cost of going ice skating. Very simply, *opportunity costs are the opportunities you forego to do something else.*

Everything we choose to do involves opportunity costs, only a small percentage of which are easily measured in terms of money. Our most important opportunity costs arise out of decisions that affect our physical, emotional, and spiritual health, and these cannot be valued in dollars and cents. The concept of opportunity costs, therefore, is not used exclusively by economists. Economists just happen to use this concept more because the trade-offs that concern them professionally can be conveniently measured and compared in standard monetary units. Now that you understand what opportunity costs are, we're prepared to evaluate what economic theory has to say about how much you'll be paid for your labors.

What Economic Theory Says You'll Be Paid

According to economic theory, you'll be paid what you're worth. You're shocked? You thought economists were more clever than that—a little strange, yes, but at least clever. Moreover, this isn't even an answer. It simply raises another question: what are you worth? The truth is you're worth what your employer would lose if your job went undone. This is called your employer's opportunity cost of not hiring you. You'll be paid whatever you agree to work for, however, and this should lie between two extreme limits. You should be paid no more than what you're worth to your employer (that is, no more than your employer's opportunity cost of not hiring you). You should accept no less than another employer is willing to pay you for work you find equally as attractive. You're confused? Let's work this out step by step.

What people are worth depends in part on what they're doing. Their labor services can't possibly be worth more than the value of the things they produce. Let's assume that you are a geologist and that your labor services could add an average of $100,000 a year to the revenues of the prospecting firm that wanted to hire you. If you were a very shrewd bargainer and held out for $100,000, this firm would be no worse off with you than without you. You could conceivably get the firm to pay you $100,000, and we'll see later how this might actually happen. This would be the extreme upper limit in this example. If you worked catching fish rather than as a geologist, on the other hand, your labor services couldn't possibly be worth more than the value of the fish you caught. We now have at least part of the answer. What you're worth depends in part on what you're doing.

Now suppose there were several other geologists besides yourself who also wanted to work for the prospecting firm. Let's assume that all of you have similar knowledge, training, and experience and that each of you could add $100,000 to this firm's revenues if it hired you. And, finally, let's assume that you and the other geologists have only two employment alternatives. Each of you can either fish or work as a geologist for this particular firm. You guessed it: supplier competition among you and the other geologists would cause you to bid down your wages to about the value of the fish one of you could catch. That is, the firm would have to pay you only what your labor services were worth in your best alternative job. This amount, which is called the employee's *opportunity wage* rather than opportunity cost, in our example would equal the value of the fish one of you could catch. This gives us another part of the answer. You'll at least be paid your opportunity wage, or what you could earn in your best alternative job.

Does the example of geologists fishing for a living upset you? This doesn't normally happen. However, when Congress drastically cut spending on the space program in the late 1960s, thousands of scientists were forced to take whatever jobs they could find. Some of them became cab drivers, and some of them probably did work as fishers for a while.

Normally, the number of geologists and the number of firms needing their services are about in balance. We've seen that when there are a lot of geologists and just one firm that can hire them, the firm has them over the barrel. It can hire one of them for peanuts. But we might have turned our example around. If there were several firms that wanted a geologist and you were the only geologist, you'd have the firms over the barrel. Then buyer competition between the firms would force them to pay you almost the full amount that your labor services could add to their revenues. If your services could add $100,000 to any one of the firm's revenues, then any one of them could increase its profits by hiring you for a wage of $99,999.99 or less. As the only available geologist, you could rely on buyer competition to bid your wage up to nearly the limit of your potential employers' opportunity costs of not hiring you. That's how you could actually reach the extreme upper limit of your potential wage.

As we said, under normal conditions the supply and demand for geologists are pretty well balanced. Furthermore, once a few of the firms that could use geologists have hired them, geologists are no longer worth as much to any of them. Why? Because when there were no geologists at all, these firms were making some rather simple geological mistakes that could have been relatively easily corrected. When the first geologist to be hired corrected these simple mistakes, the other firms imitated the firm that had employed a geologist. Consequently, the firms that didn't hire geologists nevertheless received some of the benefits they might have gotten by hiring one. As a result, these firms could no longer add $100,000 to their revenues by hiring a geologist. The second geologist will be worth less than the first because the first gave away some of the geological secrets. As more and more geologists are hired, more and more of their practices become widely known and imitated. Therefore, the amount a firm can gain from having its own geologist continues to decline. Our example is somewhat unrealistic only because geology is a well-established science. The first scientists and other specialists to offer needed services in a new field do actually encounter circumstances similar to those we have depicted in this hypothetical example.

In the long run, when the market for the services of geologists is in balance, the wages geologists receive should be about equal to the amount their services contribute to their employers' revenues. Geologists should be getting paid just about what they're worth, and this amount should be just high enough to encourage about as many young people to become geologists as are needed to replace those who are retiring and to fill the new positions that are opening in this field. When this happens, the market for geologists is said to be in long-run "equilibrium," or balance. We can see that under normal conditions, therefore, what you're worth and what you're paid should be one and the same figure.

Finally, sometimes it's very hard to determine what someone's worth. The third part of our answer, therefore, is that sometimes people are paid what their employer thinks they're worth. Under certain circumstances it may be relatively easy for employees to fool or trick their employers into believing they're worth more than they are. It's unreasonable to assume that people will always be paid what they're worth. Sometimes they are underpaid. Sometimes they're overpaid. It depends on what their employer thinks they're worth, and employers make mistakes too.

We can summarize what economic theory has to say about how much you'll be paid as follows:

1. Under normal conditions, when the labor market is in long-run equilibrium, or balance, you should be paid an amount that is about equal to the value of the services you contribute to your employer. This amount is called your employer's opportunity cost of not hiring you.
2. Under no circumstances, even when the labor market is out of balance, should you accept less than your opportunity wage, which is the amount you could earn in your best alternative job.
3. However, because under certain circumstances it is particularly difficult to measure how much someone's labor services are worth, and also because people sometimes make mistakes, there are times when people are paid strictly what their employer thinks they're worth. Their employer may underpay or overpay them.

In other words, wage offers are made and accepted on the basis of the employers' and employees' calculations of their alternatives. Employees will accept the highest paying alternative they're offered; and employers will accept the lowest costing alternative they can find, providing it costs them no more than they feel the labor services are worth. Economists refer to these alternatives as opportunity costs and opportunity wages.

Of course, since we are reasoning here as economists, the implicit qualifier of economists that *all other things must remain the same* must be read into what we've been saying. We shall make this qualification explicit and amend what we have been saying by adding that employees must consider alternative jobs as equal in all other respects before the decision and the opportunity wages involved can be compared in monetary terms. This fine point that often confuses students can be illustrated as follows. Suppose you were offered two jobs as a campaign worker. One for $150 a week by a politician whose policies you agreed with. Another for $175 a week by a politician whose policies you did not agree with as much. These alternatives cannot be compared solely on the basis of the wages you are offered. Job offers almost always vary in more ways than just the amount of money you would be paid. It is only when the job offers are identical in their non-monetary aspects that the decision boils down to strictly a matter of pay. When the jobs you're offered are otherwise identical or nearly identical, then and only then can your decision be based on a simple comparison of your opportunity wages.

In the example used, you may accept the job for $150 and still be acting rationally on economic grounds. In effect, economists would say that you chose to "pay" $25 a week to work for the politician whose practices you agreed with more completely. This is a relatively minor point that may confuse you more in reading about it than if you were faced with such a choice in the real world. If you were offered a safe job with the Mafia, would you take it even if it were the best paying job you could get? Perhaps this example clarifies the point that money does make a difference, but other things do too—and they can be more important than money.

EXAMPLES OF THE ROLE OF OPPORTUNITY COSTS

In our earlier discussions of wage levels, we emphasized the roles played by the forces that determine the extent of supplier and buyer competition. On the demand side we focused on the employer's ability to pay as determined by profitability. Profitability was found to depend on such things as product demand, competition, and technological change. Our focus in this chapter will be on how opportunity costs determine how much an employee will be paid. We'e looking at the situation from a different angle or, more precisely, we're telling the rest of the story rather than another story. The ability to pay and opportunity costs both weigh heavily upon the determination of wage levels.

It is sometimes easier to understand wage, salary, and fee levels if you put yourself in the shoes of those who are paying them and try to evaluate their opportunity costs as they might view them. It is especially enlightening to do this if you are pondering the charges levied for the performance of a vital task. Viewed from this perspective, how much they pay seems directly related to their ability to pay and what they fear might happen if the job were not done by a particular employee. The fees for many professional services vary substantially and offer a good case in point. It is also often very difficult to evaluate the quality and value of these services. Under these circumstances the employee's reputation and ability to negotiate fees and the employer's assessment of what's at stake all play an important role in the determination of what the employee is paid. Let's see how some of the participants in the Big Money Game do their thing.

Medicine
Let's imagine you are very wealthy and become seriously ill. If you feel that only one particular doctor has the skills needed to heal you, how much would you be "willing" to pay that doctor to heal you? The answer can be found by

analyzing the alternatives you face, by analyzing your opportunity costs.

Let's assume that you fear you will die if this particular doctor does not attend to you. In this case you imagine the opportunity cost of going without the doctor's services would be your life, which would also mean the loss of your fortune. Another possible alternative would be to pay any fee the doctor asked, up to the full amount of your fortune. If you accept this alternative, you'll still have your life plus the part of your fortune that remains after you've paid the doctor's fee. In this case you feel the opportunity cost of not getting the doctor's services is life itself. Faced with these alternatives, you'd be acting rationally if you paid any fee up to the full amount of your fortune.

Rich people who need or want medical services usually don't quibble about fees since their health or vanity is at stake. Doctors reputed to be the best cancer specialists or cosmetic surgeons sometimes extract huge fees from these people for their services. In this case the cost of providing the service has very little to do with its price. The price is primarily based on the ability of the patient to pay. If these doctors' patients were poorer, nothing would change except the fees, which would be less unreasonable.[1]

Law

If you were wealthy and had been accused of a serious crime which could result in your imprisonment for many years, how much would you be willing to pay to have a criminal lawyer with F. Lee Bailey's reputation defend you? What are your alternatives, or your opportunity costs? Many years in prison. And you would pay any price you could afford to avoid that.

Or imagine you are the president of a large corporation and are involved in an antitrust case that might cost your firm $200 million. How much would you be willing to pay the law firm that you felt had the best chance of winning your case? A lot. Your opportunity costs are $200 million. Are you beginning to understand why some professional people are paid huge fees?

In these examples taken from the professions of law and medicine, you can see that fees are determined by the customer's opportunity costs and ability to pay. You can also see that it's the doctor's and the lawyer's reputations that allow them to charge high fees. The customers don't know, but they think and believe these professionals are the best there are. If you enter a professional field, your reputation will be your most valuable asset. What you will be able to charge your clients will depend on what they feel your services can do for them and how much they can afford to pay. What you can charge may have little to do with how much effort you must put into any particular job. You may work harder and longer for a poor client to earn the same fee you could charge a wealthy client for less work.

Managers and Other Key Personnel

Most businesses and institutions are structured like pyramids. Authority and responsibility are concentrated at the top in the hands of the managers, the bosses, and other key personnel who direct the whole show. Because they guide and direct the efforts of the entire firm, they are the keys to its success. Their wise and prudent decisions are multiplied many times over as they are reflected in the activities of the hundreds or thousands of people they direct. Conversely, a single foolish decision by a person at the top can be ruinous to the entire firm. Bankruptcy is the firm's opportunity cost of not hiring the top executives who can keep it healthy. And bankruptcy is just as unacceptable an opportunity cost for the firm as death is for the wealthy person.

Because the consequences of their efforts are multiplied hundreds and thousands of times over, top executives can truly be worth a six-figure income. In fact, it's just plain foolish—penny wise and pound foolish—to quibble over the salary of the top executive of a very large corporation. Even if it were millions of dollars a year, it would still be insignificant relative to the hundreds of millions or even billions of dollars of business the top executive directs. Quibbling over the amount of the top executive's salary makes about as much sense as a restaurant's quibbling about the amount of salt its customers put on their steaks. The decision to hire top executives should be based primarily on their ability to do the job well. How much they are paid is a matter of secondary importance and becomes more so the closer they are to the top of the pyramid.

Let's call the principle we've outlined in the last paragraph the "key ingredient principle." There are much less obvious examples of this key ingredient principle that lie outside the field of management. We'll discuss one taken from the field of advertising and touch on another in the field of architecture.

Roughly 90 to 95 percent of the total costs of an advertising campaign are for radio and television time. Since the broadcasting stations determine the price of their time, these costs will be the same no matter which advertising agency is used. Nevertheless, the agency that is selected can make all the difference because it creates the commercials, and these are what will make or break the entire campaign. If the commercials are poorly received, the entire campaign is a failure.

If clients have confidence in an advertising agency, therefore, they should be very reluctant to switch agencies just to save on agency fees. What they might lose in an unsuccessful campaign is 20 or more times greater than what they might save in agency fees. If you felt certain that an agency could direct a successful campaign for you, you'd probably be smart to pay double or even triple the normal fee to buy its talent.

An advertising agency's fee typically represents only 5 to 10 percent of the total amount spent on an advertising campaign. Thus if $1 million is spent on a campaign, the agency would get only $50,000 to $100,000 of this amount. Assume that you had decided to spend $1 million to advertise your products. Since you've already committed yourself to gambling with $1 million, wouldn't you be smart to throw in an extra $50,000 or $100,000 to hire the agency you

Oh Harry, the Alka-Seltzer.

were convinced could make the whole gamble pay off (that is, pay $100,000 or $150,000 even though you could get away with as little as $50,000 at another agency)? In this example, the opportunity cost of trying another advertising agency is the possible loss of most of the million dollars whereas the possible gain is a saving of only $50,000 or $100,000.

Architects also qualify as key personnel. Their fees, which depend on a building's size, complexity, and the reputation of the architect, typically amount to only 3 to 12 percent of the total cost of the buildings they design. Although their fees are a very small percentage of the total cost of a building, their talents nevertheless determine its beauty and functional usefulness. Do you see why it would be well worth it to pay an architect twice the normal fee if you felt his or her talents would increase the value of your building by even as little as 5 or 10 percent? Are you beginning to grasp the significance of the opportunity cost principle?

The Bread Breakers
Some professional people, especially those in advisory positions, earn large amounts of money by selling the same idea over and over again to many

different people. Like Christ in the biblical parable in which He broke five loaves to feed a multitude, these professionals, whom we shall call "bread breakers," sell the same ideas to a multitude of clients. In effect, bread breakers are paid many times over for a single task.

People who have made or inherited large amounts of money often don't know how to invest it wisely. Some of them hire investment advisors to do this for them. Investment advisors specialize in finding attractive investments in common stocks, bonds, real estate, etc. They charge clients a fee based on the amount of money they manage and/or a percentage of the profits they earn on the money they manage.

Investment advisors usually have a minimum amount, often over $100,000 but sometimes as low as $25,000, that they will agree to manage. They usually charge an annual fee of less than 1 percent of the sum they manage. However, very successful advisors are able to charge much higher fees. Some of them even arrange to share in the profits they earn on their clients' investments. Do you see why a wealthy person might be willing to cut an investment advisor in on one-fifth of the total profits if the advisor could increase the total profits by 10 or 20 percent? Imagine how much the advisor could earn from even one millionaire's investments! And that's only part of the story.

Investment advisors sell an unusual type of product: knowledge of attractive investment opportunities. They spend most of their time discovering and evaluating investment opportunities. Once they have assembled this knowledge, their work is largely finished. They can pass it on to one client or dozens of clients at about the same cost to themselves. That is, the investment advisor's additional costs of passing on the same knowledge to many other clients is almost zero. Nevertheless, each additional client is willing to pay the same fee as the first because he or she faces the same opportunity costs as the first. The opportunity costs of not hiring a good investment advisor are far greater than the fees that are involved.

You've probably realized that investment advisors are "key personnel" as well as "bread breakers." The total fees an advisor earns depends on how many times the same key knowledge can be resold. In the past many of them have been able to earn well into a six-figure income. Like other professionals, their reputation is their most valuable asset. It takes years to develop a good reputation as an investment advisor. Without a reputation, it's difficult to get clients to trust you with the management of their funds. However, without funds to manage, you can't develop a reputation. This vicious circle can be circumvented by developing a reputation as an employee of an established investment advisory firm. Then when you strike out on your own, you can take some of your former employer's clients with you.

Consultants of all types may be bread breakers to some degree. Consultants in the computer industry, for example, may sell the same program with only slight modifications to many different customers. Lecturers, trainers, and public speakers of all kinds are also bread breakers. Although the audience changes, their message often doesn't. It's a big job plus to be able to earn more and more with very little additional effort.

Although there are other special situations, we've covered the ones that explain how most of the Big Money Game's participants get into the game. Virtually all of these lucrative special situations can be explained by an analysis of the employer's and the employee's opportunity costs.

Tickets to the Big Money Game

The general principles that allow the Big Money Game's participants to earn such large amounts can be summarized as follows:

1. Provide services to wealthy clients who have a vital need for them.
2. Be a key person who directs a pyramid of other employees.
3. Charge a multitude of clients for the same service.

If you intend to work for the government or another non-profit organization, you may have found much of the material in the last two chapters largely irrelevant to your needs. This is not an oversight on our part. The wage levels paid by non-profit employers are much more significantly affected by the particular circumstances of the individual employer, which makes it very difficult to formulate useful generalizations. Generalizations can be made, however, about the relative level of an individual's wages in this context: the wage levels of individuals who work for non-profit organizations depend primarily upon their seniority and position within their organization's hierarchy.

Moreover, we can also make additional generalizations regarding what determines one's position within this hierarchy. Thus we can at least draw helpful indirect inferences that will enable those who work in a non-profit organization to exercise a measure of control over the level of their future wages. The following section, which spells out these generalizations, does not fit into our discussion of the Big Money Game. This too is not an oversight. The fact is that this section is our "displaced person." It belongs with the discussions of Chapters Six, Seven, and Eight, but it fits into none of them. So we've just tacked it on here at the end.

WHAT DETERMINES WHO MOVES UP WHEN PRODUCTIVITY IS HARD TO MEASURE?

No matter what an organization's criteria for employee advancement are, it is mandatory that its employees view them as generally fair and equitable. Employee cooperation and effectiveness require that this condition be met. It is also mandatory that the criteria for advancement serve the needs of the organization. The organization's survival requires this. These requirements help explain the very different natures of the employee advancement criteria found in business firms as opposed to governmental and other non-profit institutions.

Most business enterprises have a clearly defined objective: the maximization of profits. In these cases the performance or productivity of employees can be directly related to their contributions to their firm's objective of maximum profits. It's not hard to measure the productivity of salespeople: how much has been sold? It's easy to tell who's doing well, and promotions can be based on a merit system that's linked to the employee's contribution to the firm's profits. This merit system is viewed as necessary to the firm's survival and is accepted therefore as a fair criterion for advancement.

Productivity is much more difficult to measure if you are employed by the government or another non-profit institution. The objectives of such employers are less clear, harder to quantify, and sometimes even impossible to measure. Consequently, it's much harder to tell how well employees are performing their jobs. Evaluations are inherently more subjective and much more a matter of colleague judgment. Such judgments are more difficult both to make and to accept as fair.

Those of you who are contemplating working in fields in which productivity is difficult to measure will face special problems. Most of these relate to the fact that you will have less direct control over your career advancement. The kind of academic and other training you get and where you get it will be of much more lasting significance to your ultimate career advancement because they will be among the few measurable aspects of your qualifications.

Your "political" skills will also be especially important to your career advancement. Exposure to those who can "make" your career is going to be doubly important to you. And you're more likely to have reasons to feel you've been judged unfairly. Can you cope with such feelings? If your talent is not recognized, rewarded, or appreciated by your colleagues, will you be crushed? Can you accept having so little control over your career advancement? You would be wise to consider if this type of evaluation system is right for you.

When productivity is hard to measure, career advancement depends upon qualitative measures of one's ability to do a job. Here is a list of the most important of these qualitative measures:

1. *Degrees.* The type of degree you have and where you get it are very important determinates of career advancement for those who work in non-profit organizations. Because it is so difficult to measure one's performance, one's preparation for the job takes on greater significance. The type (English, math) and level (B.A., M.A.) of degree one has determine the type of work one is considered qualified to do. Where one gets a degree often explains who remains an Indian and who becomes a Chief.

2.   *Seniority.* When performance is hard to evaluate, seniority often replaces it as a criterion for advancement. Promotion criterion must be viewed as fair by the majority of the people whose advancement depends upon them. Consequently, when it's hard to tell who's better it's considered fairer to promote the most experienced. When promotions cannot be justified on a more objective basis, seniority is sometimes considered the least arbitrary and therefore the fairest basis.

3.   *Previous Associations and Experience.* No matter what your field, the reputation of your former employers will follow you around and become part of your own. The principle we talked about earlier in discussing college labels applies here as well. Your previous employers are better known than you are. "Former employee of Plain and Fancy, Inc.," is a more informative, reliable, and useful label than "Jim Detrixhe" or "Donna Burgess." When productivity is hard to measure, the reputation you gain through your previous work associations is doubly important.

The kind and extent of your experience will also become part of your label. Depending on the kinds of experience you've had, you'll be labeled a "generalist" or a "specialist." The extent of your experience will affect your career opportunities in much the same way as your seniority. When productivity is hard to measure, experience and previous associations take on greater significance because they are two of the relatively few identifiable indicators of your preparation for and ability to handle the work.

4.   *People Power.* This invaluable skill, which we discussed earlier in Chapter Three, certainly bears repeating. Time and again those we've interviewed have listed the ability to deal with people, or "people power," as the most important career success factor. One man, who spent his life placing top executives in many fields, postulated that people power explains who becomes acknowledged as a field's leader. He claims that every field has a large number of practitioners of roughly equal technical competence. In addition to being technically competent, those who ultimately become known as the field's leaders are also able to promote themselves. They become the acknowledged leaders because they can also communicate with others and promote their work through themselves to others. He referred to them as their field's "salesmen."

His theory seems plausible enough. After all, people do make all of the world's decisions, including those that affect our careers. Being sensitive to others needs and feelings allows you to work with and through others to serve your mutual ends. People power is perhaps most important of all in fields where productivity is hard to measure. When evaluations are largely subjective, you simply must have the goodwill of others in order to advance in your career.

The only happy man is a man whose work permits him to function to the full extent of his ability.

                    Oliver Wendell Holmes

THE RELATIVE IMPORTANCE OF JOBS TO YOUR CAREER
Plan to Grow In and Then Out of Your Jobs
Should You Switch Rather Than Fight?

THE STRATEGIC CAREER CONSIDERATIONS
Exposure—Choice Not Chance
Visibility—It's Who Can See You and Your Work That Matters
Growth—The Right Place at the Right Time
Training—School's Never Over
Mobility, Or "Career Insurance"
Fringe Benefits and Opportunities to Earn Supplemental Income
Security of Employment
Opportunities for Women and Minorities
Opportunities for Self-Employment

CHAPTER NINE

POSITION ANALYSIS
OR
HOW TO PLAY
CAREER LEAPFROG

Selecting a career field is obviously the most important of your early career decisions, but it's only the first step. Your choice of a career field merely defines where your career path will start. Where your career will ultimately lead you—how far and how fast—will depend upon the positions (jobs) you occupy within your career field. It may seem incredible, but it is true, that certain positions can give you a 5- to 15-year career jump over the average position in the same career field. Hence the term "career leapfrog."

In many ways, knowing how to choose career positions is even more important than knowing how to choose career fields. Whereas you may choose career fields only once, you'll choose career positions or jobs many times. Understanding Position Analysis—how to identify and enter a job position that has superior advancement potential—will benefit you dozens of times during your career. You'll need the analytical tools of Position Analysis each time you're presented with a job offer or are contemplating a job change.

Our discussion of Position Analysis includes an analysis of the strategic value of a job and a discussion of the likely effects of a job on an employee's life-style and family relationships. Before we begin these discussions, however, we must first focus on the general importance of your future jobs to your overall career development.

THE RELATIVE IMPORTANCE OF JOBS TO YOUR CAREER

No matter what career field you enter, your career will be made up of many smaller pieces called *jobs*. Each of these job positions is very important because collectively they will determine what you will see, learn, and become considered qualified to do later in your career. Each of these jobs will also link you to others who, depending upon the positions they occupy, will be able to further your career interests. Consequently, choosing jobs is extremely important. Whenever you choose a job, therefore, you should expect it to make an integrated contribution to your long-run career development. Every time you choose a job, your decision should be based primarily upon this criterion of your long-run career development because your focus must remain on your career, not on a single job.

Most of us have had some trouble loosening our family ties as we grew into adults. It's difficult at first to assert your independence and develop your own identity. While I was making the awkward transition from Dad and Mom's son to Chuck, somewhere I came across this expression: "The love between parent and child is the only love that should grow towards a separation." This phrase has made a lasting impression upon me, because I believe it's true. We at the Institute believe you should also feel the same way about any job you consider or accept.

Plan to Grow In and Then Out of Your Jobs

One of the risks you want to try to minimize is that of becoming bored with your

life. Many folk proverbs refer to the common human tendency to become dis-
satisfied with more of the same and cite our need for variety, freshness,
change. When people say they would like to remain young forever, they mean
they would like to remain healthy and full of energy. They don't really mean
they would enjoy being the same age and having the same experiences forever. It's the same with a job, almost any job. After a while, it's likely to lose its
challenge and become routine, stale, and perhaps boring. This is why a job is
something you should plan to grow in and then expect to grow out of. Your job
should challenge you and stimulate you to discover and develop more of your
unique talents. You should find self-expression through your job, and ultimately it should prepare and make you want to go on to express yourself in new
and different ways. This means your job will have to grow with you or you will
have to get another job—perhaps with the same employer, perhaps not.

The primary reason most of you should plan to grow out of your jobs is
because you're likely to be happier if you do. Not because you'll make more
money. This will happen automatically if your job has allowed you to grow and
develop more of your skills and talents. You'll be paid more because you'll be
able to do more.

When your job loses part of its challenge and freshness, you are also more
likely to start failing at it. While you were growing into your job, you were
experimenting. You had to find solutions to problems that were new to you.
Your mind was open, and you had innovative ideas. You got to try some of
your ideas, and a few of them were right for the times. They became your big
successes.

Times are always changing; people, however, frequently fail to change
with them. Often they continue to apply the solutions that worked in the past.
But many times these solutions don't work as well as they did when they were
fresh solutions. If this happens to you, the job you once found challenging may
become threatening. You may fear the loss of your job because you are not
doing it as well as you used to.

The positive reasons for wanting and planning to grow out of jobs are far
more important than the negative ones, however. A series of new and different
jobs allow you to continue to realize more of your potential. New people,
places, and experiences enrich your life. Along with them come new opportunities that, in turn, lead you to still more people, places, experiences, and more
opportunities. You get the chance to apply the knowledge and experience you
have gained. You are able to help more people while you enrich your own life
and discover greater opportunities for yourself. You continue to have reasons
for wanting to get up in the morning to go to work. And since most of us must
work anyway, this is probably the best reason we can have for growing out of
our jobs.

Some of you may find this attitude toward work a bit too idealistic. Let me
ask you, "What is your alternative?" Both you and I live but once, and both of
us must spend a large part of our lives working. Don't we owe it to ourselves to
make the best of it? Don't the potential satisfactions make it worth the trouble

to search intelligently for jobs that we might really enjoy doing? It is possible to find meaningful self-expression through your work. We have interviewed many people who have found it, and there are millions more who enjoy and even love their jobs without going overboard to the extent that they become work freaks.

Yes, it is true that millions more are not as fortunate. If you don't plan to avoid job dissatisfaction, it probably will be your lot too for about 35 percent of your life—until you die or retire. Don't you think it's unacceptable to spend 35 percent of your life doing something you don't like? Wouldn't you be wiser to keep changing jobs or careers until you found work you'd like to spend one-third of your life doing? If you're losing that much of your life working at something you don't like, how could you lose any more by trying something else?

Should You Switch Rather Than Fight?

Before you stick with a job or career you dislike, consider your alternatives. If you try something else, you may like it and, in a sense, regain a third of your life. If you don't like your new job, you're no worse off than before. Finally, if the worst happens and you can't find any job at all, the state will feed you—at least temporarily. And you'll have lots of time to do the things you enjoy that don't cost much money. Any way you look at it, doesn't it appear more reasonable to switch rather than fight a job you really don't like?

Some of you will want to know how frequently you should expect to grow into and out of a job. Usually every two to five years, but there is no hard and fast rule. Jobs and people differ greatly in the amount of variety they provide and require. The point to remember is that jobs usually become tiresome after awhile. Therefore, when you accept a job, you should be sure it has the potential to lead you into something else. Then by the time it starts to lose its luster, it will have prepared you to move on to another interesting job.

Those who understand the true importance of jobs realize that the first consideration in choosing a job is its potential to lead them ahead in their career development. These individuals carefully choose each of their jobs to serve their specific long-run career objectives. They realize that each job is preparing them to take their next step (their next job) along their career path or up their career ladder, of which their jobs are the individual rungs. They envision each job as a launching pad to the next; and while they enjoy their jobs, they consciously plan to leave them before they become routine and boring. Consequently, these people are happier as well as more successful.

In a few instances, the same job may provide enough variety and change to keep it fresh for a lifetime. For example, trial lawyers never deal twice with the same case, and careers in book publishing offer constant change. What you must do is leave your job when it begins to stifle you. If you have chosen your job carefully, it will have contributed to your career development. Therefore, you will be a more capable, experienced employee than before, which will make it easier for you to find the next job in your career.

Finally, those of you who have or may develop specific career goals will also have specific objectives in mind when you select and change jobs. For example, if Henry Kissinger were your idol and you wished to pursue a career similar to his, you could select a diverse series of jobs to provide you with the background of understanding you would need. You could select a series of jobs to gain expertise in domestic and international politics, diplomacy, national defense, history, economics, and the art of negotiating. In cases like this, you have more narrowly defined career goals in mind when you choose a job. Rather than select a job because it offers a broad range of strategic advantages that can lead you into many attractive situations, you select a job because of its specific advantages. This can be done, of course, only if you've defined and set specific career goals for yourself. Therefore, besides a general desire to progress and remain interested and happy with your work, you may also have some specific reasons for expecting to grow out of your job.

THE STRATEGIC CAREER CONSIDERATIONS

We have seen why your first consideration in choosing a job should be its potential to lead you ahead in your career development. The first strategic principles we shall study—exposure, visibility, growth—are the best measures of a job's potential to do this. We shall illustrate each of these principles with examples of jobs that offer these important advantages. Each time you go through the job selection process, you would be wise to evaluate your alternatives in terms of these key considerations.

Exposure—Choice Not Chance

Let's face it. When you first start working in a career field, you really don't know much about the specific opportunities it offers. This will be true no matter how carefully you've done your research. You still haven't tried to do any of the many different tasks that must be done by those who work in your chosen field. You don't even know which of these you would enjoy and could do best. Therefore, it would be very advantageous if you got a job that familiarized you with the many kinds of work that are available in your field. It would be even better if, in addition, your job gave you the chance to try your hand at a lot of these various tasks. Then you'd be able to find out what your talents and interests made you best suited for, and happiest doing, that much sooner.

By *exposure* we mean the ability to discover and sample the various types of work that exist in your field. Having a job that offers you exposure is like being on a high tower in your career field. Your career field lies exposed beneath you, open to your investigation. You can witness what's going on in your field, sample some of the work that you think looks most interesting, see if you really enjoy it, and find your career path that much more quickly and surely. We shall demonstrate these advantages with a particularly lucid example.

Imagine you had carefully considered your preferences and personality—those things we discussed earlier in Part I—and decided to follow a business career. You've held various summer jobs in business; but even now, as you leave graduate school with your M.B.A. (Master of Business Administration) degree, you're uncertain. You still do not know exactly what you want to do in the business world. You majored in finance in graduate school, and now you have two job offers. One with the financial department of a large oil company and another with a leading management consulting firm. Let's see how these jobs differ in terms of exposure. Let's see how much more you'll know about what you want to do with your career three years from now if you take one or the other of these jobs.

If you take the job with the oil company, you'll spend the next three years learning about the financial details of the oil industry. You'll meet and deal largely with others in the oil industry. You'll learn of the career opportunities in the financial end of the oil industry. But the knowledge and experience you'll acquire will be limited almost exclusively to the oil industry and your firm's specific financial operations. This experience *may* help qualify you for financial work in other industries. It *will* specifically train you for other financial work in the oil industry.

If you take the job with the management consulting firm, you'll see and learn much, much more about your career opportunities. Management consulting firms act as the "doctors" of corporations and government. When a firm or a branch of the government can't solve its own problems, it calls in one of these firms for help. If you spend the next three years working for such a firm, you'll get to try your hand at many different types of problems in many industries.

Typically you'll spend an average of two to three months working on each project. You'll have worked on 12 to 18 different problems in different industries at different locations all within three years. This type of exposure will provide you with a fantastic early introduction to a very broad range of the career opportunities available in the business world. You'll probably have a chance to work on production, sales, organizational, personnel, and marketing, as well as financial, problems. You'll be much more certain about what you like and can do best. You'll have seen the opportunities that exist in many fields and will have learned of many more from your coworkers who have been working on other projects. You will know more about yourself, will have developed more of your talents, and will have discovered many, many more career opportunities than you ever could have in the oil industry job.

Konrad Adenauer, West German's political statesman during the reconstruction years after World War II, was once criticized for reversing himself on an important matter. He replied with words to this effect: Should I not change my mind today, now that I am wiser because I have better information as regards these matters? Your career is certainly an important matter about which you can never have too much information. Exposure is not just something that should concern Raquel Welch and Burt Reynolds. The amount of exposure a job offers you should always be a key consideration in your choice of jobs. Stay far away from jobs that put you in the "career closet," where you lose sight of what's going on in your field.

Visibility—It's Who Can See You and Your Work That Matters

Being visible to others—especially those outside your firm—is the second big job plus. Visibility is stamped on the other side of the career coin that has exposure on its face. Whereas *exposure* refers to your ability to see what others in your field are doing, *visibility* refers to the ability of others to see you and become familiar with your work.

Although you may deserve your career breaks, others will still have to give them to you. No matter what position you're interested in, people must hire you for it. They can't hire you if they don't know of you and can't find you. They'll be much more likely to hire you—in fact, they may even come looking for you—if they already know you and your work. Through exposure you learn what the Career Game in your field is all about. Through visibility you get invited to play in it.

Visibility has to do with positioning yourself so that you become visible to, and establish contact with, those who can advance your career interests. There are three things to remember about visibility.

1. You must be visible to the right people—those who can hire you for the job you want.
2. Being visible to those outside your firm is especially important because most of your potential career opportunities lie outside your firm.
3. Remaining visible is an ongoing responsibility. You never know when an opportunity you may like will come up or when you'll need a new job. Therefore, you always want those who can hire you to keep you in mind.

Earlier in discussing educational barriers, we noted that firms prefer to limit their risks by hiring experienced workers who have shown they can do the work. Once you've entered your career field, therefore, you should identify those who can advance your career and devise a plan to get examples of your best work in front of them well before you need a job change. Then when they must hire someone, your name can come to mind. They're likely to feel they're taking fewer risks by hiring you because they already know you and your work.

It's always an advantage to hold a position in your firm that requires you to deal with others outside your firm. Through dealing with your firm's clients or suppliers you come to know and be known by more people. Each person you meet is a potential source of career information, job referrals, and even job offers. A job with the right kind of visibility plugs you into the people who are likely to need your talents. Let's look at our example.

The example we used for exposure is equally as good, if not better, for visibility. If you worked for the large oil company, you probably would not represent it to any important outsiders for many years. Furthermore, you probably wouldn't even get the chance to speak directly to the financial vice president of your oil company either for many years.

By contrast, if you took the consulting job, you would be working directly with the top-level executives of the firms whose problems you were trying to solve. The decision to hire an outside management consultant—call in a "doctor"—can only be made by the firm's top personnel, who then work directly with the consultants they bring in. The difference in the level of visibility offered by the consulting job can be dramatized by imagining that the oil company hired your consulting firm to work on one of its financial problems.

If you worked for the consulting firm, you would get the chance to work directly with the oil company's top executives. Perhaps even the financial vice president would learn of you and your work. You could show what you were capable of doing and your broadly based experience might impress your clients. In any case, you would be working with much higher level executives than the person in the oil company position, whose job you were offered but rejected. If these top executives have a job opening, they're much more likely to think of you than the person in the job you rejected because they still don't know that person or his or her work. Are you beginning to grasp the significance of position analysis?

Being visible—especially early in your career—to the people who can advance your career is a tremendous advantage. If you prove your ability, such visibility may enable you to spring directly into middle-level management 5 or even 15 years "ahead of your time." That's what we call "career leapfrog." Visibility should be right up at the top of your Career Shopping List. Stay away from jobs that isolate you from those who can give you the career breaks you desire.

Growth—The Right Place at the Right Time

How would you like to get a 10- to 25-year career jump on most of your friends, be more experienced than 80 percent of your firm's employees, and therefore step into a position of great responsibility and high pay before you're even thirty? Well, it's been done by thousands of fortunate people who have worked in rapidly growing industries and firms. Growth has been emphasized over and over again throughout this book. Perhaps you're getting tired of it; the important thing is not to forget it, and you won't once you understand the implications of Table 9–1.

Earlier, in Chapter Seven, we discussed in detail why firms prefer to hire experienced workers. Experienced workers make fewer mistakes because they've already made most of their mistakes and learned from them. We also noted why firms in rapidly growing industries hired relatively inexperienced workers to fill important positions. They have no alternative. Their very success makes it impossible for them to find enough highly experienced personnel to fill all their important positions. A firm that's growing at 20 percent a year experiences more than a six-fold increase in size in less than 10 years! Such firms usually cannot find enough experienced personnel to fill all their important positions. Instead, they must fill them with the most experienced personnel available.

Table 9–1 gives you a rough idea of how your firm's growth rate will affect your status as an experienced employee. If you have just left school and started working for a firm, you will be its least experienced employee. If the firm continues to grow, however, it will need to hire more new people and your status as its least experienced employee will then change. Gradually, as more and more new employees are hired, you will become one of its more experienced employees. The speed with which your experience status changes from least experienced to ultimately one of your firm's most experienced employees will depend on how rapidly your firm grows.

Table 9–1, which shows your experience status as a function of your firm's growth rate, dramatically illustrates the fact that you quickly become one of your firm's most experienced employees if it is growing rapidly. Surprising as these figures are, they actually understate our case because of the conservative nature of the assumptions used to construct Table 9–1. The figures shown assume that: everyone hired after you will be without previous experience; that your firm will retain 100 percent of its employees; and that the number of employees in your firm will grow at the same rate as your firm's sales.

These assumptions are particularly good in the context of rapidly growing firms, which is the case we wish to illustrate. Rapidly growing firms are usually found in young, rapidly growing industries. As the firms in these industries expand they must hire inexperienced workers and train them because experienced personnel are not available. The assumption that the firm will keep 100 percent of its employees is also close to being accurate because firms prefer to hire and train young employees: they're cheaper, easier to train, and have a longer useful lifetime for the firm. Consequently, most of a rapidly growing firm's employees will be young, and its work force will suffer little attrition because of retirements. Obviously, some people would leave such a firm, but that would only strengthen our case, which is therefore understated somewhat as shown in Table 9–1. Finally, the third assumption is perfectly valid. There's no reason to assume that the firm's work force should not grow in step with its sales.

To read Table 9–1, first look down the far left column until you find the number representing the years you've worked for the firm. Then look at the numbers that stretch out in a line directly across the page from left to right. Each of these numbers tells you the percentage of your firm's employees that would have been more experienced than you had it grown at the rate listed at the top of that column. For example, suppose you've worked five years for a firm that's grown at 12 percent a year. Looking down the far left column to 5 and across three columns to the one headed by 12 percent at the top, we find 57 percent as the answer. That is, after five years with a firm that is growing at

TABLE 9-1

HOW GROWTH AFFECTS YOUR STATUS AS AN EXPERIENCED EMPLOYEE

YOUR EXPERIENCE IN YEARS	PERCENTAGE OF YOUR FIRM'S EMPLOYEES WHO HAVE MORE EXPERIENCE THAN YOU ASSUMING YOUR FIRM GROWS AT A COMPOUND RATE OF GROWTH OF:						
	4%	8%	12%	16%	20%	24%	28%
0	100	100	100	100	100	100	100
1	96	93	89	86	83	81	78
2	92	86	80	74	69	65	61
3	89	79	71	64	58	52	48
4	85	74	64	55	48	42	37
5	82	68	57	48	40	34	29
6	79	63	51	41	33	28	23
7	76	58	45	35	28	22	18
8	73	54	40	31	23	18	14
9	70	50	36	26	19	14	11
10	68	46	32	23	16	12	8
11	65	43	29	20	13	9	7
12	62	40	26	17	11	8	5
13	60	37	23	15	9	6	4
14	58	34	20	13	8	5	3
15	56	32	18	11	6	4	2
16	53	29	16	9	5	3	2
17	51	27	15	8	5	3	2
18	49	25	13	7	4	2	1
19	47	23	12	6	3	2	1
20	46	21	10	5	3	1	1
25	38	15	6	2	1	0	0
30	31	10	3	1	0	0	0

12 percent, only 57 percent of your coworkers would be more experienced than you. If your firm's growth rate had been 20 percent, only 40 percent of your coworkers would be more experienced than you after 5 years.

Table 9–1 also shows how many years you'd need to attain the same experience status in firms that were growing at different rates. For instance, you might want to know how many years it will take you to become more experienced than the majority of your coworkers. To discover this, look down each column until you find the first number smaller than 50. The number of years this will take is shown in the far left column on the same line. If you do this, you will note it takes 18 years if the firm is growing at 4 percent, 7 years at 12 percent, 5 years at 16 percent, and only 4 years at 20 percent.

It is an incredible advantage to work in a rapidly growing industry. The firms in such industries are profitable and can pay you well. Since they can't hire enough people with experience, they must give their employees responsibilities, promotions, and higher salaries long before they could hope for these in less rapidly growing industries. Growth truly is the fast track. If a career in a growth industry meets your other requirements, it probably represents your most promising career option.

If you truly know yourself and your needs and you've found a position that has growth, exposure, and visibility, you have very good reasons to be optimistic and confident about your future. The growth factor alone will take your career a long way—you're in the right place at the right time, so to speak. Exposure will help you continue to find the right place, and visibility will keep you connected to the people who can keep putting you into the right place at the right time. Remember these three principles. They are among the most important principles in Part II.

Training—School's Never Over

Visibility may fail to bring you job offers, exposure may only lead to envy, and failure is possible even in the context of growth. When your contacts refer and/or recommend you, they put their own reputations on the line. This they will not do unless they're convinced that you're adequately trained to do the job. Even if you fool them and their recommendations help get you into that right place, you'll be right out of it again if you prove unprepared to handle it. And your reputation, your most valuable asset, will be tarnished, if not ruined. Exposure, visibility, and growth cannot guarantee your success, they merely increase your chances of being placed in a favorable position. Training prepares you to do something with a favorable position once you're in it, prepares you to prove yourself. Ultimately, therefore, training is more important than anything else.

Dunn & Bradstreet has attributed 91 percent of business failures to management incompetence.[1] Conversely, managerial competence is often cited as the major cause of business and institutional success. Because so much of what you need to know cannot be learned from books, it follows that it's of paramount importance that you choose an employer who can give you the practical training you will need to become a competent problem-solver/decision-maker. Training is especially critical at the outset of your career, be it in business, the performing arts, politics, or whatever other field you enter. You should place a great deal of emphasis on the training you'll receive from your first few employers, and you should also evaluate the training of the specific people you'll be working directly with and for. Where and how have they been tried and tested? What will you be able to learn from them? Nothing could be more promising to your long-run success than to become the protégé of some grand old masters who really know the ropes.

When you reach the final stage in the interviewing process, discuss training at length with the experienced friends you've made in your chosen career field. Ask them to help you evaluate your job offers on the basis of the training you can expect from them. Make training a key factor in your first few job choices. Training is the foundation that sets you up for the rest of your career. Certain employers are well known in their field for their training programs. Having been one of their trainees is a credit that will follow you around for the rest of your career and become part of your "label."

Career capabilities are developed continually over your lifetime, and you alone are responsible for the development of those you'll need to implement your career goals. You can best achieve this development by focusing on the skills that are needed by those on the next, and the next above that, level of responsibility into which you plan to move. *That is, you should maintain a forward focus and continually seek to develop those skills you'll need to perform in your future job functions.* Train yourself to develop the habit of becoming interested in and informed about the problems of those who have greater responsibility than you. When the opportunity presents itself, discuss their problems with them. Learn what their biggest problems are, how they go about solving them, and the skills needed to do this. Work on developing these skills; and when you have come up with a possible solution to one of their problems, ask to discuss it with them. Make it clear, however, that you're primarily interested in learning from their evaluation of your possible solution. Don't push yourself on them or maintain that you have a solution. That is, assume the manner of a student who is interested in learning from them and who may only possibly have something of interest for them.

Finally, a very important word of caution. If you aren't already familiar with *The Peter Principle,* read this witty little book and take its message very seriously. In this runaway bestseller, Dr. Peter explains the rampant incompetence that permeates our institutions as follows:

1. Promotions are granted to those who have performed well on the immediately lower level in an organization's hierarchy.
2. Quite different skills and personality traits are required at each level, however, and it is this fact that results in untold personal tragedies.
3. Successful individuals are continually promoted until they are finally promoted into their level of incompetence, which is a level for which they lack some of the required skills and talents. There they spend the rest of their careers as unhappy failures, struggling with work that is not right for them.

Thus, the Peter Principle brings us around full circle to where we began, with the Ancient Greek dictum: "Know thyself." Please, before you accept or seriously aspire to any position, try to realistically evaluate its rightness for you. And if you do get into the wrong slot, respect yourself enough to return again to your own turf.

Mobility, Or "Career Insurance"
There is at least one fundamental, unchanging fact about the circumstances you will face during your lifetime: they will be continually changing. You should

never lose sight of this simple truth. It should be incorporated into all your plans, especially your career plans. If you follow this advice, it may do more to minimize the potential consequences of the hardships you will face during your life than any other single piece of advice anyone could give you.

The principle of mobility is highly respected in many fields of human activities. Its essential merits are captured in the familiar expression, "Don't put all your eggs in one basket." In business and finance it's called *diversification*. In military circles it's called the *principle of dispersion*. In career planning we're going to refer to it as the *principle of mobility*. Mobility, in the sense we use this term, is similar to flexibility, adaptability, and transferability. Our very success as a species has been attributed to our adaptability, our ability to adjust successfully to the changing conditions that confront us. Likewise, your career success will depend largely upon your ability to remain mobile or flexible so that you can change jobs or careers with relative ease if you have to or want to. Mobility is most important when you're "uncertain" about what you really want. All of us would be wise to consider ourselves as "uncertain" when we first begin our careers, because there's really no way of knowing if we'll like our work and be able to do it well until we've actually done it for some time.

Our discussion of mobility and the issues that surround it will be brief because the next chapter addresses these issues in greater detail. There are three types of mobility we shall touch on here. Mobility within your career field, mobility between career fields, and geographic mobility.

Mobility within one's career field should be maintained by everyone. Positions that offer exposure and visibility provide career-field mobility. There's no excuse for not keeping yourself mobile within your field. You should do this in order to be sure you discover the career opportunities you want and that "they" discover you. Then, if you encounter personality conflicts at work, lose your job for any reason, or simply want to change jobs, you'll have the mobility you need to find another job in your career field. You can best maintain your career-field mobility by keeping your eye on your field and your name and work in front of those who can hire you—that is, by practicing the principles of exposure and visibility.

Mobility between career fields is much more difficult to achieve in our age of specialization. The more technical your specialization, the less mobility you have. People in the field of medicine, engineers, and technicians of all kinds are less able to move into other fields. Their skills are generally not transferable into other fields because they are not very useful in other fields. General skills like the ability to deal with people and communicate ideas, administrative and managerial skills, and sales and marketing ability are much more transferable from one industry to another.

Managers, salespeople, and people in finance and marketing perform functions that must be performed in many industries. Although most of these people happen to stay in one industry, they could perform their function in other industries as well. The bulk of their skills are transferable. In most cases they need only familiarize themselves with the new industry's products, markets, organizations, etc. Managing is managing and selling is selling, no matter what the industry. In effect, it's more accurate to say that these people follow careers in management or sales rather than careers in an industry.

When you've progressed to the point that you're seriously considering a specific field and are interviewing people in it, ask them directly about mobility into other fields. These people are probably your best source of information on this subject. Ask them if they have had colleagues who have entered other fields and how many problems they had making these transitions. Ask them what they themselves believe they could do if they wanted to leave their field.

Geographic mobility is relatively less important, but it may become very important if you or someone in your family must relocate for reasons of health. The issues surrounding geographic mobility and preferences are discussed at length in Chapter Five. To summarize this section: for the same reasons you keep fire, ambulance, and doctor's numbers handy, you want to develop and maintain career options or alternatives. You hope you'll never need them, but you must be ready to move into something else if you have to or if you change your mind and want to. Your career is too important a part of your life: you must have contingency career plans. You can't afford to get trapped in and be forced to spend one-third of your life working in a career you don't find satisfactory.

Fringe Benefits and Opportunities to Earn Supplemental Income

Non-salary benefits such as stock options (chances to buy your firm's stock at big discounts), bonuses and profit-sharing plans, a company car, club memberships, generous expense allowances, travel benefits, legal aid, discounts on your firm's products and services, as well as the traditional health and life insurance benefits—all these should be evaluated and compared when you are choosing between employers. A company car, along with gas and parking, for example, may save you as much as $3,000 a year. This could easily be the equivalent of $6,000 in before-tax income, depending on your tax bracket. You should determine how much such fringe benefits are worth to you and add this amount to your salary before you compare your job offers on the basis of how much they pay.

You should also consider special knowledge and information that you obtain through your job which may help you invest your savings more wisely. People in the real estate business sometimes gain access to especially attractive investment opportunities. The same is true for those who work on Wall Street and in several other fields.

Finally, there are many important advantages associated with being able to moonlight in a consulting capacity. This is an excellent way to attain exposure, visibility, and mobility and to develop additional career options. The ability to supplement your income may be especially important if you have extraordinary expenses. Moonlighting also provides an avenue through which you may ultimately enter business on your own in a free-lance capacity. It's very nice to have the option of moonlighting in a consulting capacity.

Security of Employment

Obviously, the amount of job security offered by your field in general and your employer in particular is of strategic importance. Review the discussion of job security in Chapter Six and size up your career alternatives along those lines. In addition, you may wish to consider how your age will effect your employment security later in your career. A few fields, such as advertising, in which relatively few middle-aged people are found, seem to be young people's fields. It's not exactly clear why this is the case, but it is obvious that advertising does not offer much job security to people over the age of forty-five or fifty.

Age generally becomes a handicap in most fields for those over forty-five or fifty who become unemployed. Although these individuals are qualified by experience, their potential employers look upon their being unemployed with suspicion. Employers generally hesitate to hire anyone for less than they were previously earning because doing so usually results in employee dissatisfaction. Employers fear these older people might have become unemployed because they weren't worth their high salaries; and, since they usually won't offer them less, it's hard for these older people to find reemployment. Furthermore, firms are reluctant to hire older people because their pension benefits mature much sooner. For these reasons, job security declines after age forty-five or fifty in most fields. There are exceptions however.

Lawyers, for example, improve with age like wine. The older they get, the more experienced they become, which makes them more employable because law is a life of continual study and learning. As a general rule, however, it would be wise for you to have secured the position you hope to retire in by about age fifty. You'll have plenty of time between now and then to research these matters in greater detail.

Opportunities for Women and Minorities

You should attempt to learn how your career opportunities may be affected if you are a woman and/or a member of a minority group. Fortunately, the past often serves as a poor guide to the future on these matters. Recently, career opportunities have improved and expanded dramatically for women. And, of course, laws exist that are designed to give every individual equal access to jobs. But if you're a woman and/or a member of a minority group, you don't have to be told that there are many ways the spirit and intent of the law can be ignored and circumvented.

In order to check out the specifics of the employment scene in your field, we suggest you talk with people who are working in the field that interests you. Speak directly with the members of your minority and with women in the field. Try to determine the trend, whether it's likely to change and why, when, and how. These people are likely to level with you. You'll find some helpful questions to ask them in Chapter Eleven.

Opportunities for Self-Employment

Finally, if you hope to ultimately open your own business, you'll need two things in order to be successful: money and a knowledge of the business you hope to enter. You can acquire the knowledge by working as someone's employee for at least three years in the business you hope to enter. As we noted earlier in Chapter Seven, you should overestimate rather than underestimate your financial needs. Financing has typically been the Achilles' heel of many an infant business. When you're constantly fighting off the financial wolf, you have no time left to manage and develop a young business. So before you start acquiring knowledge about a field, be sure you stand a good chance of being able to afford to enter it.

Before you start your own business, you should analyze 20 or more small business failures. Read everything you can about small businesses. Also investigate the personal life of small business people to see if you are willing to make the necessary personal sacrifices that are required, especially during the difficult start-up years. Finally, work and rework your marketing plans before you actually open your doors. Marketing is the second Achilles' heel of infant businesses. If you still feel you want to do your own thing after all this, think positively, continue to pray, and do it.

*"Who are you?" said the Caterpillar.
. . . Alice replied, rather shyly, "I—I
hardly know, sir, just at present—at least I
know who I was when I got up this morning,
but I think I must have been changed
several times since then."*

Lewis Carroll

CHAPTER TEN

I'M UNDECIDED. WHAT SHOULD I DO?

I'll bet a few of you who are especially nervous have picked up this book, skimmed the table of contents, and turned quickly to this page, hoping to somehow find an immediate solution to your career problems. Your feelings are quite understandable, and you can be sure that you have lots of confused company. But slow down: let's approach making this important decision calmly.

Your career will occupy at least one-third of all your waking hours—more of your time than you'll spend on any other single activity. The career you choose will determine how much time you'll have for your family and other interests, prescribe the life-style you'll be able to afford, and affect where you'll be able to live and find work. With so many things to consider, there really can't be any simple answers, only simple questions. Accordingly, the strategies outlined in this chapter build upon and represent the culmination of the concepts and analyses developed earlier, especially in Part II. You'll simply be missing too much of their important message if you start reading here at the end of the story.

This chapter has two objectives. By demonstrating why flexible career plans are both necessary and desirable, it tries to persuade you to build flexibility into your own career decision-making. Secondly, it explains how you can formulate flexible plans to protect yourself from the uncertainties of tomorrow's changing occupational environment. Our Minimax Option Approach to career decision-making is developed, explained, and integrated into the many separate pieces of Parts I and II that are summarized and pulled together here. This approach emphasizes the strategic value of flexibility and formally introduces it into career decision-making.

Career Options Determine Your Occupational Freedom

The word *option*, as used here, is synonymous with the word *alternative;* and a *career option* shall be defined as any job position that you are formally offered or could possibly be offered because you have developed the skills needed to qualify you for it. Options are the basic ingredients that make decision-making—and indeed all other circumstances that allow us the freedom to choose—both possible and necessary. When you have but one option, you cannot choose. Consequently, the extent of your occupational freedom is directly related to the number and nature of the career options you can exercise.

When you have but one option, you've got all your eggs in one basket, so to speak. That can turn out to be very good, very bad, or anything in between. In any case, it's especially nerve-racking to be without career options. Your career is too important to allow yourself to become boxed in without alternatives. Most of us insure our valuable possessions, such as our homes and cars, because we realize we cannot afford to lose them. Don't we have even more imperative reasons for trying to "insure" our careers from which we earn the cash to pay for these possessions, as well as the insurance premiums we place on them? Viable career options constitute the only true source of career security, the only source of genuine career insurance.

Let's assume that you had developed sales ability, ability with numbers, a knowledge of German, and supervisory skills. You would then be qualified for, and therefore have career options in, a variety of positions that required these skills separately or in combination with one another. For example, you would be qualified for positions as a salesperson, an insurance salesperson, an insurance salesperson dealing with German-speaking immigrants, and a supervisor of insurance sales people dealing with German-speaking immigrants. Each of these jobs would use a progressively larger combination of your separate skills. You would also be qualified for a position as a German-speaking tour guide as well as for many other jobs that may not ever interest you now or in the future. Now that you understand what career options are and the relationship between them and occupational freedom, we're prepared to begin our investigation into the need for flexible career planning.

WHY FLEXIBILITY IS ESSENTIAL
TO GOOD CAREER PLANNING

Career planning involves making decisions now that will affect the alternatives we will face in the future. All we know about the future, however, is that conditions will be different. Since we do not know specifically what will change, we also cannot anticipate the alternatives we will prefer in the future. We need flexible career plans, therefore, to help us cope with these changes, whatever form they take. Important changes will occur both within us as well as in the world around us.

Flexibility Because You Will Change

The need for flexibility is best comprehended if we step outside ourselves, observe who and what we are, and consciously seek to understand the influences that shape us. In Part I we did this. We came to the realization that our consciousness, which is our essence, reflects the multidimensional environmental influences that we have experienced. Since we "become our environment," which is itself continually changing, we will "become someone else" in the future. That is, the new people and experiences that the future will introduce to us will forever change our consciousness, and this further complicates the planning process. As if knowing thy present self were not difficult enough, we must somehow attempt to formulate farsighted plans for the unknown future stranger into which we will evolve.

Eventually you will make plans to enter one career field or another. Until you've worked in that field, however, you can't possibly become familiar with

all the career options it offers. Once you enter your field, you may discover and want to follow an option you overlooked completely. Or through your work you may discover and wish to pursue an opportunity in another field. And finally, there's always the possibility that you'll just change your mind. Do you remember the career fantasies we had as children? Those were the unliberated days when little girls were going to become nurses and I was going to be a big, tough fireman. Oh yes, and what was that you were considering last summer, last week? Adults change their minds too. For whatever reasons, you may just grow to want something different from your work and life. These are some of the things about yourself, your likes and dislikes, and your aspirations that will change in the future. They constitute only a few of the examples of why flexibility is essential to good career planning.

Flexibility Because the World Will Change
Although we may have some control over the changes that occur within us, we have almost no control over the direction and amount of change that occur in the world around us. For this reason alone, we would be wise to build flexibility

into our career plans because none of us fully controls the circumstances that would make making permanent career plans sensible. Technological change or changes in business or institutional structures may severely reduce or eliminate employment opportunities in your career field. In the future you may face circumstances similar to those faced in the past by blacksmiths, streetcar operators, icemen, and the corner grocery store. You may not be able to find work in your chosen field. Consequently, you should give serious consideration to the career options you could fall back on if you cannot, or would rather not, pursue your original career plans. This is the essence of what we mean by flexible career planning. Prudent career planning must include a detailed evaluation of the options you would face if your original plans fell through for any reason. Thus, although you cannot control the circumstances you will face in the future, you can, and you should, investigate and attempt to limit the potentially adverse consequences of any career decision you make.

The need for flexibility in career planning can be summarized as follows: Not only must you design plans for an unknown future world, you also must make them for a stranger, for the "someone else" you will become. On the one hand, you don't know how changes in the world around you will affect what you will be able to do careerwise in the future. On the other hand, you don't know how changes within you will affect what you will want to do careerwise in the future. Consequently, you don't know which career options you'll be able to, and/or want to, exercise in the future. It follows that you also cannot know which of your present options will be unnecessary, and thus could be discarded now without adversely affecting your future position. You'd be wise, therefore, to guard all your career options and develop new ones, provided the cost isn't too great. This represents our Minimax Option Approach in a nutshell.

**The Minimax Option Approach to Career
Decision-Making: A Formal Outline**

FOCUS: The Minimax Option Approach emphasizes the strategic value of making flexible career plans, and therefore explicitly introduces flexibility as a key ingredient of career decision-making. Flexible career plans are needed in order to accommodate predictable, albeit specifically unforeseeable, future changes that will result because:

1. The world around us will have new and different needs. Different tasks will need to be performed in the future. Therefore, new and different employment opportunities will arise, and some old ones will disappear. Consequently, what we are able to do careerwise will change in the future.
2. Our awareness of career opportunities will change in the future. We may wish to follow a career path we may overlook or find unattractive now.
3. We will evolve into different people with different career objectives, aspi-

rations, and motivations. What we will want to do careerwise may change in the future.

Although we are able to anticipate that change will occur both within and around us, we are unable to predict the specific forms it will take. We are also unable to control the circumstances that produce these changes. Since we expect change but cannot define or control it, about the only rational way we can accommodate it is by building flexibility into our career plans.

OBJECTIVE: The Minimax Option Approach builds flexibility into career planning by maximizing the number of career options the individual has to choose from both now and in the future. This strategy, which is designed to increase occupational mobility and freedom of choice, is implemented by:

1. *Minimizing* the number of potentially useful career options you forfeit when you make career-related decisions. Provided the cost of doing so is reasonable, you are advised to remain proficient in all your developed occupational skills because you may need them later in your career.
2. *Maximizing* the number of new career options you develop when you make career-related decisions. You are asked to consider how each of your career-related decisions will contribute to the development of your stock of useful, or marketable, occupational skills. That is, your career decisions are to be evaluated in terms of how they will affect your occupational mobility and freedom of choice in the future. What will the jobs' you're considering train you for, what career opportunities will they expose you to, to whom will you become visible, etc., if you accept them? The answers to questions such as these will reveal how accepting this or that job will affect your future career options.

The Minimax Option Approach constitutes the final part of our overall game plan, which is designed to minimize the chances of your making an unsatisfactory career decision. Thus, the key elements of the comprehensive approach proposed in this book can now be summarized as follows:

1. *Integration:* We stress that the career you choose will generate important effects on the rest of your life. Ideally, therefore, all your important life decisions—such as those that involve your career, marriage, choice of a life-style, and the location in which you'll live—should be integrated because each of these aspects of your life interacts in important ways with the others.
2. *Definition:* As a first step, you identify what is most important to you and thereby decide what you want most out of life. You should learn everything you can about yourself, especially as regards your revealed per-

sonality and talent traits. You should consider how your career decision will affect the amount of leisure time you'll have and where you'll be able to live. As they occur to you, record all your tentative preferences on your Career Shopping List that is found at the very back of this book. With the aid of this list, you can begin to define what you would consider to be an ideal career choice, based on all these integrated considerations. While this is not a simple assignment, it is a much less unpleasant and difficult task than having to live with, or attempting to undo, the distructive consequences of inadequate career decision-making.

3. *Evaluation:* As a second step, you evaluate career options as they exist in the real as opposed to your ideal world. You learn to evaluate career fields on the basis of such criteria as job security and earnings potential. The tools of Position Analysis will help you identify the job positions within your chosen field that offer the promise of allowing your career to develop along the lines and at the pace you prefer. In making all of your career decisions, you should place a premium on career flexibility in order to accommodate the unknown changes you must anticipate in the future. This is where the Minimax Option Approach enters our overall game plan. With the aid of these analytical tools, you can seek the career option that most closely resembles the one you defined as ideal for you. In other words, our approach encourages you to enter the realm of dreams where you are asked to find yourself and define your career dream. Then through analysis it provides you with the tools that can help you find and realize more of your dream when you return again to the realm of reality.

4. *Implementation:* At this point, all you need in order to implement our basic program are Chapter Eleven's Questions. With the aid of these questions, you'll be able to secure the career information you need to implement our program. You'll get this information directly from those who are presently working in the fields that interest you. It will be up-to-the-minute and as detailed as you want it to be. And, most important of all, the analytical tools you've learned about in Part II will make it meaningful and, therefore, useful. You'll have overcome the career information barrier.

FORMULATING FLEXIBLE CAREER PLANS TO DEAL WITH UNCERTAINTY

The task of formulating flexible career plans is facilitated by several definitions and concepts that lend structure and organization to the search for the strategic advantages of flexibility. These conceptual aids, which help us pinpoint and better understand the origins of flexibility, also help us further refine our arguments concerning the strategic principles of Position Analysis.

Position-Generated versus Function-Generated Career Options

We shall define *position-generated options* as those options that passively accrue to you as a result of your position. Position-generated options are the result of exposure, visibility, being in a growth industry, or any of the other principles of Position Analysis. For example, because you represent your firm to its clients and suppliers, you and your work are visible to many potential employers. These outsiders are a very fertile source of job offers, which we defined earlier as *career options*. As your firm's representative to the outside world, you also enjoy exposure, which is another rich source of position-generated career options. You see what's going on and where the attractive jobs are being offered. If you're working in a rapidly growing industry, more job offers are likely to come to you simply because people with your experience are relatively scarce and in great demand. Position-generated career options occur as a result of where you are working.

Function-generated options, on the other hand, occur as a result of what you are doing and the skills required to do it. For example, if you were a supervisor of social workers, in order to function at work you'd have to develop and maintain the following function-generated skills: supervisory skills, administrative skills, writing and reporting skills, and the skills needed to deal with people. As long as you function as a supervisor of social workers, your work will require you to maintain these skills. Consequently, you will be qualified by experience for other jobs that require these skills. These potential jobs are the function-generated career options your job as a supervisor of social workers would develop and maintain for you.

The additional costs of developing and maintaining most career options are small or nil because you must develop and maintain these options anyway if you want to hold your present job. You should become concerned about the cost of career options only if you must deliberately go out of your way in order to acquire or maintain them. For example, you're only "paying" directly for the position-generated benefits of visibility if you consciously choose job A because of its better visibility rather than job B which you would otherwise prefer. If you would have preferred job A anyway, its position-generated career options are yours at no extra cost. Likewise, if you don't go out of your way to develop or maintain function-generated options, they too are free. Maintaining your writing skills and the function-generated options of doing so "cost" you something only if you'd rather take job D but accept job C because it forces you to maintain these skills. Similarly, if you took job D in this case and then went out of your way to request assignments that helped you maintain your writing skills, you would also be "paying" for function-generated options. If you preferred job C anyway, it would cost you nothing extra to maintain your writing skills so that you could continue to qualify for jobs that required writing skills.

The maintenance of function-generated options is very much at the heart of the decision to specialize or remain a generalist. It's much easier for generalists to maintain and develop a large number of skills. They can use a broad range of skills and thereby remain proficient in them. Ours, however, is an age of increasing specialization. Because the demand for generalists is rather limited, most of us will have to become specialists in order to advance in our careers. But by becoming specialists, we run the risk of boxing ourselves into career situations we may later regret. We suggest, therefore, that you resist becoming overly specialized until you're so sure you're in the right field that you're willing to consciously trade the benefits of flexibility for those that specialization offers you.

The "T-Shaped" Individual

The concept of the T-shaped individual is useful in depicting the relationship between general and specialized skills; this concept also helps illustrate the advantages of both these types of skills. The top of the T represents the breadth of the individual's general skills whereas the stem refers to the depth of his or her specialized skills. The successful person often needs both types of skills: a breadth of general skills (wide top of the T) to deal with a range of problems, and a depth of specialized skills (long-stemmed T) to produce really solid results and accomplishments. It is possibly interesting, but also rather risky to have a T that is a mile wide and an inch deep—you're likely to hang on everything but stick in nothing. It is probably boring as well as risky to have a T that is an inch wide and a mile deep—you'll hang on nothing and get vulnerably stuck in your narrow speciality. Ideally, your T should allow you to hang but provide you with a specialty that has enough depth to allow your feet to reach the ground—a less risky, more comfortable position. Some financial positions offer examples that fit this ideal T.

Financial people are specialists who nevertheless enjoy the advantages that normally accrue to generalists. The financial function they perform is needed by virtually all types of organizations. Consequently financial people have excellent mobility across industries and across governmental and other non-profit fields as well. Their career is in their function rather than in an industry. Because their specialized function is in general demand, their career field offers excellent mobility and their career plans are therefore inherently flexible. Others such as those whose careers are in sales, marketing, accounting, personnel work, and general management enjoy a similar, although lesser, degree of mobility across industries. Fewer of these functional specialists are as successful as financial people in carrying over and making use of their previous contacts and knowledge when they move to other industries, etc.

Incidentally, the terms flexibility and mobility, as we are using them, are nearly synonymous. Flexibility is the more inclusive of these terms, but this difference is inconsequential.

A Special Strategy for Your First Job

Let's face it. When you enter a new field you can't possibly be sure that you'll like the work and be able to do it well. This will be the case no matter how carefully you've investigated the field, your job, and yourself. Consequently, when you accept a job in a new field you should view it as a continuation of your investigation of that career field. Since this is especially true of your very first job, you should choose it accordingly.

When you enter a new field you should consciously stress the point to yourself that you're still looking for work—for a career that truly interests you. Your first job in a new field simply provides you with an inside view of a career field you hope may be right for you. In finding it, you *have found* an opportunity to check out a career field. You only *may have found* your future career field. Consider yourself as only *testing* at this point.

The strategic principles of Position Analysis should be reviewed and given top priority when you're choosing your first job. It's not that these principles are only important when you choose your first job—they're always important. It's just that getting started is always the hardest part; and when you know so little about your field, you need every advantage you can possibly get out of exposure, visibility, mobility, and the other principles we formulated. You'll need exposure to help you discover the field's opportunities and attain the niche that's right for you, visibility to help you be discovered by the right people who can get you on the "fast track," and mobility so that you can switch tracks if you find out your choice wasn't right for you.

The additional strategies that follow are also particularly helpful in dealing with the circumstances you face when you choose your first job. Most of them are specific formulations of the general principles of exposure, mobility, and visibility.

Develop Your General Skills While You Decide

It's almost always the case that greater specialization results in less career mobility. Therefore, until you're rather sure you're in the right field you should avoid becoming specialized as much as possible. Specialized skills are frequently of little value to employers outside the field you learn them in. Consequently such skills won't increase your career mobility.

General skills that are needed by employers in every field are transferable and will therefore increase your career mobility. Function-generated skills like the ability to deal with people, general administrative skills, the ability to communicate orally as well as in writing, and all types of analytical and problem-solving skills—these skills are all directly transferable into any industry or occupation you may subsequently wish to enter. You'd be wise to choose a job that helps you develop general skills like these while you're trying to decide on a career field. These skills will increase your mobility by making you more attractive to employers in any field you ultimately decide to enter.

Maybe You Should Choose a Small Firm

Those who prefer working for small firms (those with hundreds rather than thousands of employees) maintain that their work is more varied and therefore more interesting. They also claim it's easier to grasp the whole picture of what they and their firm are doing, which helps make their work more meaningful. Since small firms are less formally structured, it's easier to find yourself and feel that you count. Most of these acclaimed advantages of working for a small firm can be expressed in terms of our principles of exposure, mobility, and, to a lesser extent, visibility.

Because small firms are usually less specialized, if you work for one you'd probably be involved with a broader range of assignments, which means you'd enjoy greater exposure. This would also increase your mobility because you'd have to develop a broader skill base in order to deal with a broader, less specialized set of problems. Some of these diverse problems might require you to represent your firm to its customers and suppliers. In this way you'd also get visibility as well as exposure and mobility. These are the reasons why working for a small firm may help you discover what you want and can have as a career.

Represent Your Firm to the Outside
This straightforward strategy was suggested earlier as a technique to gain visibility. But this turns out to be a multipurpose strategy because by representing your firm to the outside, you also gain the advantages of exposure. Learning more about what's going on in your career field can help you decide what work is best for you. The more people you contact, the more you will learn about career possibilities and the more likely you are to discover one you like and want to pursue. It's that simple.

Maybe You Should "Buy" a Springboard Position
The strategy of "buying" a springboard position, which deals with the trade-offs between present and future objectives, has a variety of important applications. Each of these involves making present sacrifices, if necessary, for the benefit of future goals. When you're uncertain about your career direction, this strategy suggests that you rank a job's potential for helping you find yourself above the salary of that job. That is, it suggests that you reject a higher paying job for one that pays somewhat less but is more likely to help you discover what you'd like to pursue as a career.

In effect, this strategy suggests that you "buy" a position which offers greater exposure, visibility, and mobility, even if this means accepting less pay. This policy is almost certain to be much more lucrative in the long run however. The sooner you find yourself, the sooner you'll begin reaching your ultimate career objectives; and this, of course, is far more important than the salary you earn in your first job. A somewhat lower initial salary may be the price you have to pay to position yourself on the springboard from which you hope to spring onto your career path.

Sample "Hard-Exit Occupations" Before Entering

The term "hard-exit occupation" is not meant to be derogatory. It is used here to emphasize the added riskiness associated with entering fields in which occupational mobility is extremely limited. Professionals who enter the health services fields, for example, encounter added risks of occupational immobility. The training they receive is narrow and specific. It imparts knowledge and develops skills that are limited almost exclusively to the fields of health services. These are "hard-exit occupations" in the sense that the training for them prepares you for a very narrow set of alternatives: it leads you down one specific career path. If you change your mind later, you're left at a dead end. You must begin your career all over again because very few of the skills you learned are useful outside your profession. Consequently, if you decide to enter training for such a field, you should be doubly sure it's the right field for you.

The specific reasons why individuals in technical fields lack occupational mobility become apparent when we consider the nature of the training they receive. Students of commercial arts, the fine arts, the performing arts, and nurses and other medical technicians are taught to develop specific skills that require a great deal of practice. Whereas most college curriculums stress the development of analytical and communicative skills, the curriculums of students in these creative and technical fields stress the development, practice, and perfection of their particular art form or skill. Whereas most college students spend their time reading, researching, and writing exams and term papers (among other things), students in creative and technical fields spend their time practicing their arts and skills. This more specialized training that students in creative and technical fields receive is generally useful, however, only as long as they remain in their specific fields. If they change careers, they typically suffer because their formal education has not stressed the development of general verbal and analytical skills. This handicap is one of the disadvantages of their more specialized training.

If you're drawn to a "hard-exit occupation," realize that you're gambling with as many years of your life and as much money as your training will cost you. These years and money may be almost completely wasted if you leave the field. Raise as many questions as you can, pursue the roots of all your doubts, and do everything you can to determine in advance if you're headed toward the right field. Among other things, you might do the following:

1. Talk with the people in the field; see what their typical day consists of, and project yourself into it.
2. Tell your friends and relatives what you're considering, ask their opinions, listen carefully to their answers, and evaluate them at length.
3. Visit the places where you would be working and work in them if you can.

4. Try to get part-time work that will give you a foretaste of and insight into the realities of working in the field. For example, if you're considering a health field get a job in a hospital, even if you must volunteer your services.

5. If you're interested in a creative or artistic field like commercial art, have your talent evaluated by several people in the field. If, after taking these and all the other precautions you can think of, you still appear to be cut out for the field, enter training with a positive attitude. But continue to check out any doubts or indications that suggest you may have made a mistake.

All my life, when I have been faced with a particular problem, I tried to find the man who knew more than anybody else about that problem. Then I have asked his advice. After I get the best advice available to me, I try to follow it.

Lyndon B. Johnson

Notice: *The 16-page* Career Information Questionnaire *referred to in this chapter is included only with the hard cover edition of this book. Single copies of this questionnaire which includes a letter of introduction to the person being interviewed plus a restatement of the 40 questions that appear on pages 183-200 can be ordered direct from the publisher, The National Institute of Career Planning, 521 Fifth Avenue, New York, NY 10017, for $1 each* prepaid.

CHAPTER ELEVEN

THE CAREER INFORMATION QUESTIONS

This is the payoff. Get ready to go over your Career Shopping List and order your preferences: we're putting it all together.

Five years ago, when I first began doing research on career decision-making, I told my students to interview people working in the fields that interested them. My students usually had nice chats with these people, but they didn't learn much because they didn't know what questions to ask. Their interviews lacked direction. It's taken five years of research, NICP's support, the generous cooperation of several hundred people, and finally this book to correct that problem. The answers to the questions in this chapter will provide you with the current career information you will need to make a wise decision. Because the earlier chapters have prepared you to analyze these answers, you will now be able to act independently as a fully informed, self-reliant career decision-maker who is able to hurdle the career information barrier.

In this chapter we review and illustrate our step-by-step career selection process of integration, definition, evaluation, and implementation by actually going through this process with someone. We'll see how this person begins by finding out who he is and, based on this, what the characteristics of his ideal career position would be. Then we'll see how he applies the analytical tools of Part II to the career information he collects first-hand from people who are working in the fields that interest him. You'll learn what questions to ask, how to find the people with the answers you need, and how to enlist their willing cooperation in giving you these answers.

PROGRAM REVIEW IN PREPARATION FOR INTERVIEWS

In covering so many different subjects, you may have lost sight of how they are all related. The following step-by-step review, which you should refer to when you are making your career decision, will help you pull the many separate pieces of our program together. Essentially what we are doing is having you identify your skills and personality traits, define your career preferences, evaluate the career alternatives that appear compatible with your abilities and preferences, and select the alternative that you feel is the best match. The hypothetical individual who is speaking is a young man named Lee who is beginning his junior year in a liberal arts program. These are the thoughts that come to Lee's mind as he reviews the notes he has made on his Career Shopping List.

Integration: As I begin to formulate my career plans, I must seek to make them consistent and compatible with the rest of my preferences and life goals. I must realize that my career decision will affect where I'll be able to work, the life-style my family will be able to afford, and the type of people I will meet and be likely to socialize with. Moreover, my career decision will affect when and how much time I'll have to spend with my family and on my other interests.

Consequently, I must attempt as best I can to integrate my career decision with my decisions about marriage, life-style, and where I want to live.

Definition: Well, let's see, what do I know about my strengths, weaknesses, and preferences? I've never had any real difficulty in school or felt significantly less gifted than my classmates and friends. My IQ was measured twice as being in the mid-120s, so I guess I'm smart enough to follow almost any career I enjoy and put my mind to. My teachers, friends, and family have said I'm imaginative, curious, self-disciplined, persuasive, industrious, and ambitious. I know I get bored easily and that I just can't stand being bossed around or working under close supervision. While I no longer want to enter the ministry, there still is a streak of altruism in me and I derive a tremendous sense of satisfaction from knowing that people need me.

As far as the major three-way classification of work subjects is concerned, I prefer working with them in the order of people, data, and—least of all—things. On the other hand, I often become impatient with slow or careless people, and I can be somewhat of a snob at times. On Dr. Holland's Self Direct Search Test, I came out as enterprising/investigative/social, which I believe are fairly accurate results in my case. I'm definitely an analytical left-minded type. However, since I'm also graphically oriented and love music, I believe I rely on my right mind quite a lot too.

I'd like to be comfortable, but would prefer being rich if that didn't require sacrificing too much of my time. I really don't want the things as much as the freedom and independence that money can buy. I would prefer to be able to adjust my income to my needs, and I'm only moderately risk-adverse. Job security, therefore, is not that important to me but may be more so when I have a family.

Although I've never tried it, I don't want to have to live in a large city. I've grown up in a small city, and I prefer living near the fresh air of the country. Ideally, I'd like to live near both the sea and the mountains; but, of course, I expect I will have to compromise on this front. Wherever I live, however, there must be a hot summer and access to outdoor forms of recreation for most of the year. I've really enjoyed scouting, hunting, fishing, and camping. Therefore, whatever I do, I insist on having time to enjoy my love of nature. My parents took time to enjoy life, whereas my uncle became rich at the expense of becoming unbalanced in his interests and a bit of a "work freak." I'm willing to work hard for long hours if I can compensate for this by taking days off frequently. I really value a flexible time schedule highly.

Let's see now, what did I learn about my work preferences through my part-time and summer jobs as a camp counselor, hotel receptionist, park ranger's assistant, and encyclopedia salesman. The one thing I liked about all these jobs was the contact I had with people, which was of a different nature in each of these jobs. I liked the people I met in the hotel best. I really liked the tremendous variety of people who attended the hotel's conventions, but I never got to know any of them well. That's what I liked about being a camp counselor—you really can get to know a lot about a kid, even in two weeks. It was great fun being a park ranger except for the constant need to discipline and hassle all those fun-loving campers about putting out their fires, hauling away their trash, etc. I hate giving orders and being pushy, which, come to think of it, is what I didn't like about selling encyclopedias.

On the other hand, I really think I enjoyed selling most of all, especially when I met a family that really needed encyclopedias. I guess I just love being persuasive, building a case and proving it to customers when I realize they can use the product. I guess I learned a lot more about myself than I realized from those part-time and summer jobs. The sales job seems to have had the most advantages for me: contact with people, the chance to help people when they needed encyclopedias, challenge, and I could adjust my income and hours to my needs by working a little harder or taking off for a day or two if I wanted to.

OK, now I must organize all this information I've collected about myself and my preferences. I'm going to classify my career characteristics in three ways as mandatory, strongly preferred, and preferred and make a separate list for each of these categories.

Mandatory Career Characteristics
No matter what career I follow, I intend to insist that the following seven conditions are realized. The order in which I've listed them is not very important because all seven of them are "musts." Although I am single now, I expect to be married eventually and to have two children and I am making an allowance for this in my plans.

1. *Freedom from Close Supervision.* I simply cannot function under close supervision and, therefore, must have the freedom to do what must be done my own way. I am a very independent, responsible, self-disciplined, "self-starter"—orders drive me mad. I'd prefer to run my own show; but if that's not possible, I must at least have the freedom and discretionary authority to organize and conduct my work as I choose. I'll consent to allow my employer to tell me what I must do, but not how I must do it.

2. *Flexible Time Schedule.* I refuse to be locked to an inflexible time schedule period. I'm willing to work long hours, but I want the freedom to make my own schedule, which will allow me to take time off when I want to attend a particular event, visit with a friend, or just get away for part of the day. Besides, I just can't accomplish much when I'm not into my work. I also perfer to work hard for several weeks or months and then take off for several days or weeks at a time.

3. *A Comfortable Income.* Money is far from the most important consideration in my life, but I don't want it to be a constant consideration either. I

do not want my wife and I both to have to work once we have children. I want to earn enough, therefore, so that my salary alone can support our family if my wife and I decide that she will assume the primary homemaking role. Once I become established in my career (after five to ten years), I want to earn at least the equivalent of $25,000 in 1976 dollars. I want my family to have pleasant summer and winter vacations, some travel, and a good college education.

4. *A Permanent Home.* Once we have children, I want to remain in the same community. The nomadic life of so many corporate managers is an unacceptable way of life for me. To the extent it is possible, I want our children to grow up with an unbroken circle of close friends, and I want the companionship of many lifelong friends in my old age.

5. *Working with People.* While I do not dislike working with data and things, I must work with people because I simply enjoy them too much to cut them out of so important a part of my life as my work. People are a source of infinite variety and challenge. I also have strong preferences as to how I would like to work with people, but these are less important than my need to work with people, period.

6. *Variety, Change, and Freshness in My Work.* This is not so much a preference as a necessity for me. I become depressed and fail miserably when my work becomes repetitive. It's probably the other side of my curiosity that makes me incapable of doing routine, repetitive work.

7. *Hot Summers.* I guess I like the changing seasons, but I love summer— and would never give it up. I'll compromise quite a bit on climate, but I won't give up hot summer days and those warm summer nights under the full moon.

Strongly Preferred Career Characteristics

I am reluctantly prepared to compromise on several of these strongly preferred career characteristics if I must. Again, the order in which they appear does not reflect their importance, which is roughly equal in all cases.

1. *My Own Show.* Ideally, I think I would prefer to be self-employed, which would allow me to be completely independent, use my imagination to the fullest, and become financially independent. However, I would have to consciously avoid becoming a self-employed slave or work freak. I'd have to work a lot more earlier in my career, but I could compensate for this with longer vacations and greater personal and financial freedom later.

2. *Adjustable Income.* I would strongly prefer to be able to adjust my income to my needs by working a little more or less depending on my family's financial needs. This would allow me to avoid having money become a big consideration because if illness or educational needs pressed the family budget, my income could be adjusted to meet these needs.

3. *Permanent Working Relationships with People.* The job as a camp counselor showed me that I prefer in-depth, ongoing relationships with people. Whatever work I do, I hope I'd deal with the same customers or clients over and over again so that I would be able to develop a personal rapport with them and include some of them in my private life as friends as well.

4. *Manageable Sized Community.* I'm almost sure I wouldn't enjoy living in New York City or Los Angeles. Wherever I live, I want to feel that I can help shape the community I live in. I don't want to feel that the community controls me and dictates most of my life-style options.

Preferred Career Characteristics

1. *Tangibly Helping People.* This used to be much higher on my list of priorities until I realized that most kinds of work directly benefit people. It is rather silly to maintain that social work is somehow more worthwhile than being an architect because it helps people more. People need both social workers and houses and factories. In fact, aside from the important exception that advertising creates artificial needs in us, people must believe they are served by anything they willingly spend their money for. What's more important than the boost our spirits can get from an entertainer, for example? Although I believe intellectually, therefore, that almost all types of work benefit people, emotionally I still feel more needed when I can see that others realize how much they need my work. Consequently, I'll probably enjoy my work more, do a better job, and be somewhat happier if I respect my hang-ups and find work that allows me to tangibly help others.

2. *Frequent Little Victories.* Another of my personality quirks that I realized as a salesman is that I enjoy the challenge and immediate reward of making a sale. I've always done well in school, but in a strange way I enjoyed taking exams because they "measured" my progress. Between exams I often felt uncertain of what I was accomplishing, where I was. So it would be nice if I had work that frequently showed me how well I was doing my job. Maybe I lack a little self-confidence and, therefore, need to have a little victory now and then to keep my spirits up.

3. *$50,000 a Year in 1976 Dollars.* I've seen the life-style that a family of four can enjoy with this much income, and I like it. Beyond $50,000, money loses most of its attraction to me except for the added independence and security that wealth commands. I don't think I'd want to spend much more than $50,000, and I'm sure I wouldn't be willing to trade additional time to earn more for my own family's financial needs.

4. *Six Weeks of Annual Vacation Time.* This would be one of the important uses of the $50,000 income. Vacations are important to me, and I would in any case insist on four weeks a year. As my income increases, I would spend more on vacation trips for the family to overseas locations, etc.

5. *Ideal Climate and Location.* These preferences fall into the "frosting on the cake" category. Among the things I love are warm seas, snow-covered mountains, sunshine, mild climates, good hunting, fishing, camping, and fresh air. I'll try to put as many of these as possible into my environment.
6. *Some Work-Associated Travel.* I would enjoy two to four overnight business trips a year. Beyond this, however, travel would start to become the routine rather than a break in the routine.

At this point Lee is prepared to leave Part I and begin the evaluative processes we learned about in Part II. With his reorganized Career Shopping Lists in hand, he is leaving the ideal dream world atmosphere of Part I to begin touring the real world of work in search of the career alternatives that most closely conform to the ideal characteristics he has outlined on these lists.

Career Field Evaluation: Since he began to read this book, Lee has been asking the adults he meets or knows about their career work. With brief exploratory questions, he's been warming up for the in-depth interviewing process we're finally ready to explain. In reviewing what he's learned from these discussions and in looking over his reorganized lists, Lee concludes that a career in one of the professions seems most appropriate for him. He rules out working for a large corporation because he can't take orders well, doesn't want to move from city to city, and feels he would probably have to do some of both if he worked for a large corporation. Lee also rules out going into his own business because he doesn't have any capital, business experience, or ideas at this point. He begins to evaluate career field alternatives by listing ten different professions that he feels might possibly meet his mandatory career characteristics. The career fields he selects for further investigation are: law, medicine, high school teaching, life insurance, psychology, stock brokerage, public accounting, social work, real estate brokerage, and banking.

SETTING UP THE INTERVIEWS

We are now entering the first phase of the *implementation* process. If you're afraid it will be hard to find people to interview, rest assured that this is the easiest and most interesting part of our program. Three separate steps are involved: finding the people to interview, gaining their willing cooperation, and asking them the right questions.

Finding the Right People to Interview

Although you can interview complete strangers whom you just happen to meet somewhere, you'll have a larger measure of success if you work through personal referrals. First of all, go over the list of friends you already know well through your family and social groups, etc. Choose a few of these people who work in career fields that are at least slightly related to, or comparable to, the fields you feel might interest you, and conduct "dress rehearsal interviews" with them. These people will better understand and tolerate your initial ineptness at interviewing, but be sure to ask them how you might improve your interviewing techniques.

Incidently, you need not conduct all of these, or your later interviews, in person. The 70 taped interviews that are available from NICP were conducted over the telephone because it was found that people were less self-conscious in the absence of a microphone. Regardless of how you conduct them, you should also try to record your interviews in order to have a permanent record of this valuable information. An adequate cassette recorder and all the other equipment you will need to do this can be purchased for as little as $40 to $50. It's well worth considering, or you might try borrowing this equipment. Buying a recorder would be a very smart investment that you might think of as part of your "career insurance policy." Without tapes you'll be unable to draw direct comparisions between many of the important details that are otherwise sure to slip your mind. And, by the way, you can do a lot of other interesting things with these inexpensive recorders.

After several of these rehearsal interviews or when you feel you're ready, ask your friends for the names of people who are working in the career fields you want to investigate. Now suppose you draw a blank among your friends. In this case, turn to your family's doctor, dentist, lawyer, banker, insurance representative, or another professional person who serves your family. These professional people have all types of career people as patients and clients, and they are almost certain to know several people in each of the fields that interest you. All you need is the name of one person in each field because that person will lead you on to his or her colleagues. Your problem will probably not be having too few people to interview, but rather not hurting the feelings of the people you don't have time to interview.

Gaining the Interviewee's Cooperation

When you phone the person you wish to interview, use the following procedure or another tactful procedure that you find effective.

LEE: Hello, Ms. Driansky. My name is Lee Wade. Has Mr. Reynolds, who is also my family's insurance representative, told you I might be calling you?

MS. DRIANSKY: Yes, Bob mentioned that you had some questions about the accounting profession.

LEE: That's right. Quite a few questions, I'm afraid. Perhaps you would be willing to help me or be able to direct me to someone else who could answer them. Do you have a few minutes? May I explain why I'm calling you?

MS. DRIANSKY: Of course, but I only have a few minutes this evening.

LEE: That's fine if you have five minutes, because I only want to explain the nature of my request at this point.

MS. DRIANSKY: OK, what is it?

LEE: I've enjoyed the few accounting courses I've taken here at Northwestern, but I know so little about the kind of work people like you do in public accounting firms. I've seen my guidance counselor at school, and I've been following a rather comprehensive career decision-making program developed by the National Institute of Career Planning. Basically, this approach asks you to identify your talents, skills, and preferences which you then try to match with a career field for which they are desirable and compatible. This program points out, however, that the only way to get really worthwhile and current career information is by talking with people like you who are successfully employed in a field.

I've worked through the first part of this program, and I know pretty much who I am and what I want from a career. But it's such an important decision, and frankly I'm very concerned and a little scared. I mean going on to become a CPA (certified public accountant) seems like such a big step in my life, and I'm nervous about making the wrong decision. What I'd really like is some guidance from someone like you.

The Institute has prepared a list of questions that anyone working in a field is able to answer. The economist who developed these questions has found that those who are asked to answer them also benefit from this experience because it causes them to reevaluate their career field and their position in it. The career advancement techniques developed in the section called "Position Analysis" have been especially helpful to several of my parent's friends with whom I've conducted practice interviews.

Well, that's essentially why I spoke to Mr. Reynolds about you. I'm sure you are still a little unsure about what is involved so I don't want you to give me an answer now. May I just send you a list of these questions, or, better yet, drop the book off at your office? Then I'll get back to you in a week or so to see if you are willing and have the time to answer these questions over the phone. There's absolutely nothing for you to fill out or write down, but you may wish to think about a few of the answers or perhaps refer me to a colleague of yours who you feel might be better equipped to answer some of them.

Regardless of how you phrase it, you want to make the following points in these initial conversations:

1. Introduce yourself courteously as a friend of someone they know.
2. Make it clear immediately that you are in need of guidance and that someone has suggested they might be willing and able to provide it. Whatever

you do, don't flatter them and then ask for a favor. That will make you look deceitful. Make it clear up front that you're after a favor.

3. Make it clear that important matters are involved, that you are acting responsibly with a great deal of planning and forethought, and that you have very good reasons for coming specifically to them for the rest of the information you need.

4. Hold out the real probability that they too will benefit from considering your request. They definitely will benefit.

5. Be certian that you make it clear that you are not asking for a commitment at this point, and give them several outs, such as saying "no" later or referring you to someone else. People will be frightened if you ask them to commit themselves to something they don't fully understand. Even if they do agree to be interviewed, they will resent your being pushy. Let them commit themselves on their terms.

6. Finally, we've suggested you drop off the book rather than just the questions for two reasons. If they have the book, they'll be able to read the background material for the questions and give you better answers. Secondly, if they have the book, they may get more out of the experience and, therefore, put more into it, which would benefit all concerned.

Making the Interview Appointment

Call back in about a week or whenever you said you would and introduce yourself again as the friend of the person who referred you. Let's continue with Lee.

LEE: Hello, Ms. Driansky. This is Mr. Reynolds' friend, Lee Wade, again. How are you today?

MS. DRIANSKY: Fine thanks.

LEE: Have you had a chance to look over the list of questions I sent you (or dropped off)? I hope they didn't frighten you—there are so many of them.

MS. DRIANSKY: Yes, I got them, and I believe I can answer most of them. Would you like to meet me in my office some afternoon next week? If you get there about 4:00, you can meet a few of my colleagues and see the place in operation.

LEE: Oh, thank you very much. I'm free Tuesday and Thursday afternoon. Which would you prefer?

MS. DRIANSKY: Let's make it Thursday at 4:00, and would you please bring that book?

LEE: Fine. Where is your office, and may I please have your number there in case something happens?

MS. DRIANSKY: Yes, of course. We're located at 780 Main Street, I'm on the third floor, and my office number is 865-5886.

LEE: Thank you very much. I look forward to meeting you Thursday at 4:00.

If they hesitate, ask them why. If they haven't looked at the questions, give them some more time. If they don't want to answer some of the questions, say that's fine, but that you'd still like to discuss the others. Some people don't like to discuss salary levels, for example. If they refuse because they don't want to give you so much of their time, don't push them because they probably won't give you very helpful or thoughtful answers anyway. But do ask these people, as well as everyone else you interview, for referrals to others in their field—especially others in a slightly different position or specialty within their field—whom you might approach for an interview.

At this point we're ready to go over the two lists of questions you can ask. The short list includes only enough questions to determine if the career field meets your mandatory career characteristics. This short list can be used to screen a long list of possible career fields more quickly. The comprehensive, long list of questions is usually used only in the final stages of your career selection process. If you are willing to take the time, however, you would profit greatly from basing all your interviews on the longer questionnaire.

Questions to Screen Career Fields

If you have a long list of career fields that you feel might possibly interest you, you may not be willing to spend a great deal of time investigating each of them. Under these circumstances you may wish to contact someone in each career field and quickly go over only your list of mandatory career characteristics with them. Fields that do not meet your mandatory requirements could then be dropped immediately from your list, thus giving you more time to spend interviewing people in the remaining fields that meet all your mandatory criteria. Essentially, you would be screening a long list of career fields in order to reduce the list to more manageable proportions. For example, if Lee were to prescreen his ten career fields he would knock out high school teaching and social work from further consideration because he would learn that it is unlikely that he could earn $25,000 in 1976 dollars in these fields. The relatively few jobs that pay this much in these professions also involve more administrative work and less contact with people. Moreover, getting placed in these positions would probably mean relocating several times during his career, which is a second knockout factor in Lee's case.

Finally, you might choose to limit your questions to the list of mandatory career characteristics if your interviewee is unable or unwilling to spend much time with you. It is generally wise, however, to avoid using an abbreviated set of questions. The interviewee gains very little from your discussion when you limit yourself to a search for knockout factors. But you lose far more because you fail to develop the broad perspective that comes from evaluating a large number of career fields in depth. Each career field and each position within a career field have their own unique advantages and disadvantages. The more of these you become familiar with, the easier it becomes for you to identify the advantages and disadvantages in other fields and positions. In fact, you would be wise to conduct some exploratory interviews with people in career fields that interest you only marginally. The more in-depth interviews you conduct, the easier it becomes for you to: recognize a good thing when you see it, know where to look for a good thing, and realize what is a good thing for you.

THE CAREER ANALYSIS QUESTIONNAIRE

The career analysis questions presented in this section are the same questions on which the National Institute of Career Planning based its seventy taped career interviews. (If your school guidance department already has some of these tapes among its program materials, listening to a few of them will help you in preparing to make your own interviews.) Each section of the questionnaire is introduced by a paragraph or two that explain what the questions in the section are designed to accomplish, why, and why they have been asked at this particular point in the interview. The questions appear next, followed in many instances with explanatory notes, enclosed in brackets, to the interviewee.

Lee's list of possible career fields has already been reduced to eight. Teaching and social work were eliminated in the prescreening examples we used to show how the short list of mandatory career characteristics could form the basis for an abridged interview. Seven more of these fields were eliminated during this final interviewing process. Separate paragraphs that explain why each of these fields was dropped from further consideration follow the sections that contain the questions that eliminate them. This does not mean, however, that Lee terminated his interviews with these questions. Interviews should always be completed for the experience itself, in order to be polite, and because you might be forced in the end to even compromise on one of the characteristics you've listed as mandatory. Consequently, you may have to reconsider a field you initially reject.

The concepts that are related to each question appear in the wide left-hand margin along with the chapter number in which they are discussed. This is why it is helpful for interviewees to have the book when they are preparing answers to the questions. If they don't fully understand the question or why it's being asked, they can look up the concept involved and prepare a more direct and relevant answer. Of course, you can also use these locational references to look up concepts you've forgotten or wish to review.

The questionnaire that appears below is designed and structured to guarantee that all the information needed to make a wise career decision is collected. Those who use this questionnaire are encouraged, however, to depart frequently from its format to pursue tangential issues of interest to them. These "side steps" are recommended because they will make the interview less formal and provide anecdotes, details, and examples, etc. that will make the interviewee's work situation much more tangible. Likewise, it is often more appropriate for the interviewee to answer the separate parts of a multi-part question in paragraph form without referring to the specific parts of the question. Later you can refer back to the specific parts of the question to make sure they've all been answered in the context of your less formal discussion. Some of the questions will not pertain to certain career fields, and they may be ignored. In short, the questionnaire should be used flexibly as a guide—as a "creative catalyst."

I. Present Job Description

What we are looking for here at the beginning are broad general impressions of what the interviewee's work consists of and how it serves society. To the extent that it is possible, we are also trying to "see" the interviewees at work as they go through a typical day. And because we ultimately pursue a career in order to earn a living, we also ask the salary questions here at the beginning.

Classification of the
Good for Job
Security—6

Exposure—9

Visibility—9

Q1: Would you please begin by identifying the industry your firm is in and explaining how that industry serves society. What functions are performed by the industry you work in, and what functions does your firm perform within your industry? What is your job title, and what do you do for your firm? What are your responsibilities? Whom do you supervise, and to whom do you report? [That is, please try to place your industry within the context of the overall economy, your firm within the context of its industry, and yourself within the organizational framework of your firm.]

Q2: Please try to detail carefully what your typical work day, week, and year consists of. How is your time divided between working with people, data, and things? Can you state approximately what percentage of your working time is spent writing, reading, telephoning, reporting, researching, supervising others, etc.?
    a. How many hours do you work each week?
    b. How closely do you work with others?

Visibility—9

        1. Within the firm?
        2. How much contact do you have with people outside your firm? Who are they, and

Exposure—9

what is your relationship to them? How much authority do they have within their own organizations?

[We want to try to "see you at work" and follow you around as you carry out your typical duties. We're also very interested in meeting the people you deal with both inside and outside your firm; and we would like to know how closely you work with them, in what capacity, and how powerful they are.]

Training—9

Q3: What are the toughest problems and decisions with which you must cope? What skills and talents are especially useful and necessary to the satisfactory fulfillment of these responsibilities?

Q4: How much variety would you say there is in the type of work you do (little, a moderate amount, a great deal, etc.)?

Identity-Match—3

Please try to illustrate your answer with several examples. Is the amount of variety associated with your work also typical of those who work below you

Career Mobility—10

and are likely to be promoted into your present position? How hard must you work just to keep up with the changes that are occurring in your field?

Q5: How specialized is your work, and what bearing does your firm's size have on the variety and the

Career Mobility—10

amount of specialization associated with your work? [We would like to know how specialized your job is and whether or not someone like you could deliberately and successfully seek or avoid greater specialization by choosing to work in a particular size of firm?]

Educational and Legal Entry Barriers—7

Q6: What type of educational degrees and licenses, if any, are required of someone who presently wishes to enter a position such as your own? How long does it take to satisfy these entry requirements, and how does one go about meeting them? What types of college majors are advantageous for your kind of work?

Pay—7

Q7: Would you please try to make some rough estimates of the following annual salary levels that are presently being paid in your field?
  a. How much can one expect to earn as a starting salary in your field with an undergraduate degree, graduate degree, etc.?

b. How much can one earn at the top of the ladder in your field?

c. How fast can one climb up the ladder, and how fast do most people in fact get up the ladder? What role do advanced academic degrees play in helping one get to the top of the ladder?

d. Finally, roughly how much are people with the following years of experience and degrees of success now earning in your career field?

Years of Experience	Average success	Moderate Success	Very Successful
2			
5			
10			
15			
25			

The interviewer would like to obtain a realistic picture of salary ranges and levels in your field. Please try to indicate how you arrive at your estimates, and how current and accurate you believe they are. If you don't have this information, perhaps you could get it from a colleague who is closer to the job market or refer the interviewer to such a person. Although many people are embarrassed by such questions, salary is a central consideration in career decision-making. Please try to be as helpful as possible without getting personal, unless you prefer to.]

At this point in the interview, Lee already feels he can eliminate both law and medicine from his list. He's discouraged by the financial costs and the long years of graduate training as well as the licensing requirements one must endure to enter these professions. In addition to these financial, educational, and legal entry barriers, he has some reservations about the work itself.

Lawyers, he learns, spend most of their time with data rather than people. Theirs is a life of research and attention to fine legal details. Very few of them are trial lawyers like Perry Mason, who is a very misleading example of what it's like to be a lawyer. Since people are also frequently angry and upset when they come to lawyers, Lee wonders if he would really like to deal with people under such circumstances.

Lee has very serious doubts about his ability to deal with very sick patients. Death, disease, and blood are all things he would prefer to avoid. These doubts, when coupled with the very discouraging entry barriers, are enough to make him drop medicine from further consideration.

II. Personal Background Information

In order to lay the foundations for a more honest, willing, and rewarding interview, we want to back off the heavy questioning at this point. By showing a personal interest in the interviewee and revealing some things about ourselves, we hope to become more intimate so that it's easier and more natural for us to level with each other. In particular, we must guard against sales pitches that glamorize the interviewee's career field or position. We want to be told about, not sold on, a career field.

Now that we have some general impressions about the work, we'd like to gain some insights into the people who do it. We'd like to try to "get into their heads" when they were experiencing the life stages we've gone through. We'd like to compare our backgrounds for similarities and differences with those of the interviewee. This is our chance to get acquainted. (If you like, you may make this the opening part of the interview. At the Institute, however, we prefer to "place" the interviewee in his or her occupation first.) Comparing backgrounds will help us see how we might get into similar career positions.

Finally, the more we know about the people we're interviewing, the better able we are to "interpret" what they say. Our attitudes, opinions, and feelings about our work (as well as everything else) are inevitably colored by and reflect the uniqueness of each of our backgrounds. Understanding the interviewee's background can help us depersonalize the information we are given.

Identity-Match—3

Q8: At this point the interviewer would like to learn a little bit about your personal background. Please answer the following questions in the form of a general discussion about your life and interests as a youth. Your interviewer is trying to compare your background with his or her own. It will help if you ask your interviewer about his or her background, get acquainted, etc.

    a. Where did you grow up?

    b. What were your parents' occupations and economic class status?

    c. What interests (sports, hobbies, activities, etc.) did you have as a teenager?

    d. Where did you study? What was your major course of study, and why did you choose it?

    e. What was your attitude toward school, and how successful were you in school?

    f. How was your time divided between people, data, and things? That is, which of these received the greatest emphasis?

III. Employment Experience Prior to Assuming Your Present Position

This set of questions is designed to reveal how the interviewees got from positions similar to the one you're presently in to the ones you're investigating. Your job becomes more difficult at this point as we enter the analytical phase of the interview. Unless your interviewees have read this book, they will not realize that they are discussing the strategic principles of exposure, visibility, mobility, etc.; but you must. Try to relate everything they say to these key principles. Don't just listen. Analyze what they say and interrupt them frequently with questions if you have any. This is where you can begin to harvest the fruits of all that hard work you put in on Position Analysis.

Position Analysis—9

Q9: These questions about your previous work experience are some of the most important questions in this entire interview. Your interviewer is not so much interested in what you've done as in how what you've done has prepared and led you on to the subsequent positions you've held. And he or she is interested in how you reached these decisions—what you considered, why, how you weighed the alternatives, etc. Please go over each of the positions you've held, including the part-time jobs you held prior to assuming a full-time position. Explain as best you can what prompted you to make each choice and repeat the entire question for each of the positions you've held. For each position please explain:

a. What prompted you to change jobs or employers in each case?

b. Explain briefly what your new job entailed.

Opportunity Costs—8

c. If important, please explain why you rejected other job alternatives that were presented to you at the time.

Geographic
Mobility—5

d. If locational considerations factored heavily in your career decision-making, please explain how and why.

Training—9

e. What did you learn in terms of new skills, knowledge, and experience from the job that benefited your career?

Exposure—9
Visibility—9

f. What kinds of contacts did you make with people through your job and how did these benefit your career?

g. Where did the job lead you career-wise, or what new possibilities did the job open up to you?

h. Looking back upon your decision with the benefit of hindsight, how did it work out overall? How was it wise or less than optimum? What would have been better and why?

IV. Strategic Career Considerations

Now as you enter the most important phase of the interview, you continue to focus on the subject of Position Analysis. But now you're evaluating the interviewee's present career position, the specific position that you're considering. Go slowly and carefully. Relate what's said to what you've learned from the other interviews you've made both inside and outside this particular career field. Draw comparisons in your mind and ask the interviewer to comment on the validity of some of them. Reflect. Question. Listen. Compare. Think. Analyze.

Imagine you were in the interviewee's position, had become bored, and wanted to move on to something else. Where could you go within the same career field? Would your developed skills be valuable and therefore transferable outside the field? How much would it "cost" to switch positions or fields? Would this position provide you with good contacts and new job offers, or would you and your talents be positioned outside the mainstream of events, where you might remain undiscovered? In short, at this point in the interview you should do anything and everything that helps you "experience" the interviewee's position. Use your imagination. Get into that position and evaluate its options in accordance with your preferences. Do you feel you have enough flexibility, or do you feel trapped? This is it. You're considering putting one-third of your life on the line, so do your very best.

Position Analysis—9

These questions will require the greatest amount of forethought on your part. However, if your experiences parallel those of most other interviewees, you'll find answering them a very worthwhile learning experience. These questions, all of which refer to your present job position, are designed to give the interviewer an understanding of the career options, flexibility, and possibilities someone in your position has. The interviewer is seriously considering a career position similar to your own, but wants to know what else he or she could do if such a position "just didn't work out."

Let's face it, no matter how carefully individuals investigate and plan their careers, the proof is in the doing. They really cannot know how well they'll like the work until they do it. Because their career is so very important, it's only prudent to investigate the options they would face if they were unable or unwilling to continue in a position such as your own. That's essentially why these questions are being asked. In answering these questions you will probably gain some additional insights into the kinds of things you will want to evaluate when you make your next move into a new position along your own career path. Each of these questions should be answered, but they need not be covered in any particular order. You may just let the discussion find its natural course through these subjects.

Q10: Visibility to Other Potential Employers. It is generally true that individuals whose work brings them into frequent and close contact with individuals and client companies outside their firm often become aware of and are presented with job offers that upgrade their career positions. Management consultants, for example, are often "stolen" by client firms. Would you please comment on how likely it is that someone working in your position will be discovered by other potential employers.

Visibility—9

  a. To whom are you and your work visible, and what kinds of authority do they have? What types of positions can they hire people for or direct them to?
  b. If you care to, please discuss the job offers you've received or are likely to receive in your position.
  c. Is the amount of visibility you have typical of that which others have who occupy positions that the interviewer might consider similar to your position?

Q11: Exposure to Alternative Employment Functions. Until you actually try your hand at a particular kind of work, you just can't know if you'll like it and be able to do it well. Some positions, like that of a

Exposure—9

management consultant, allow you to work on a wide variety of problems, which increases your chances of finding the kind of job functions you like and can perform best. Would you please try to evaluate your present position in terms of the exposure it gives you to the different kinds of work that must be done?

    a. How much variety is there in the job functions you must perform? For example, if you are in sales do you also get directly involved with marketing and management problems, or is your work limited exclusively to sales?

    b. Do you work closely enough with others in other job functions to really understand what their jobs involve? Closely enough to know whether you could and/or would like to do their work?

    c. If you deliberately sought to perform some other work functions outside your present area of responsibility, would your employer approve of this action? Would this benefit you in terms of your career advancement?

Career Mobility—9, 10

Q12: Career Mobility. Let's face it, you might find yourself unwilling or unable to stay in your present career position. What could you or what could the interviewer do if he or she entered your position and then wanted to or had to leave it? Please try to realistically assess the difficulty you would face if you had to leave your present position for reasons of health, personality conflicts, your firm's failure, or because you became bored, etc.

    a. How difficult would it be for you to find similar employment within the same career field?

    b. What other career fields could you enter for which your experience would be relevant, valuable, and paid for by your new employer?

    c. Would changing career fields set you back careerwise? How many years? Have you seen others do this and what were their reasons?

Q13: How Rapidly Is Your Career Field Growing? It is usually a big advantage to be employed in a rapidly growing industry or occupation because it is typically chronically shorthanded. In addition to contributing to greater job security, rapid growth makes it easier for one to move into positions of increased responsibility, higher pay, and greater challenge earlier in one's career. Is your career field growing faster or more slowly than others? How much have your employer's sales increased in recent years, and is this typical of other employers in your industry? Do you know your industry's rate of growth or from whom this information can be gotten? Is your field "crowded" with talent?

Q14: How Does Your Position Rate as a Training Ground? Certain positions are almost better to have been in than to be in. Architects might be wise to spend time working for a renowned master or prestigious firm; physicians in a prestigious hospital; financial people in a large city bank training program; etc. In terms of the training you are given rather than the training you can seek yourself:

    a. How does your present position rate as a training ground?

    b. What positions similar to your own would offer greater advantages in terms of training? Please explain why.

    c. What are the best places for someone who hopes to move ultimately into a position like yours to get his or her initial training? Why?

Q15: Security of Employment. Certain industries such as construction and Wall Street finance have a pronounced cyclical nature—a feast or famine character.

    a. How cyclical is your industry or profession, and how secure is employment in your career field in general?

    b. How does age affect one's employability in your field? Specifically, would it be more difficult for an older than a younger person to find reemployment in your field?

Q16: Outside Income and Fringes. Under this heading, would you please discuss the sources of

Growth—7, 9

Training—9

Job Security—6, 9

Fringe Benefits—9

"income" other than wages and salary that your position allows you to participate in.

   a. Does your position or positions similar to yours provide you with any particularly attractive fringe benefits such as a car, home, club memberships, stock options, bonuses and/or profit-sharing plans, generous expense allowances, legal aid, travel benefits, etc.?

   b. Do you have the opportunity to moonlight in a consulting capacity?

   c. Does being in your position make you aware of and give you access to special investment situations such as those a real estate broker may discover while working?

Geographic Mobility—5   **Q17:** Geographic Mobility. Where else could you pursue your work?

   a. Is your industry or profession geographically concentrated? Where?

   b. Into how small a city could you move and still pursue your career, and how would such a move affect:

      1. Your career potential?

      2. The nature of your work?

      3. Your income?

Self-Employment—9   **Q18:** Opportunities for Self-Employment. How difficult is it for people in your field to go into business for themselves?

   a. How much money is needed?

   b. What else (i.e. skills, experience, established customers, etc.) must they have?

   c. Have you known people who've tried? How have they fared?

   d. Please explain your thinking, attitudes, and plans as regards self-employment.

Minorities—9   **Q19:** Employment Opportunities for Women and Minorities.

   a. Realistically and off the record, how much of a

Women—9, 13   disadvantage do women, Blacks, Jews, Puerto Ricans, and other minorities have in your field:

      1. In the past?

      2. At present?

       3. And what do you expect in this regard in
          the future? Why?
    b. What percentage of the positions similar to
       your own at your present place of employment
       are currently filled by:
          1. Women?
          2. Minorities?

At this point Lee decides to drop real estate brokerage from further consideration. He dislikes the cyclical nature of this business because of the job
and income insecurity it causes. It doesn't help that the field is overcrowed,
and he decides he wouldn't like the kind of people contact involved. Usually,
it's a one-time relationship with most clients. On the other hand, he prefers to
deal with people long enough to get to know them in greater depth and in a
continuing relationship. This leaves only five of the ten original career fields
still open for consideration.

V. Life-Style Considerations

Many of the considerations we discussed in Part I are touched upon in the
course of answering these questions that reveal how the nature of our work
infringes on, and thereby affects, our life outside of work. The answers to
these questions clearly document the need to integrate our career decisions
with our other important life decisions such as marriage and where we choose
to live.

These questions are designed to reveal how your
work affects your life-style and the amount of time
you have left to devote to your family and other non-
career interests. The person interviewing you is
trying to understand how your work affects you and
your life-style off the job. Again, you need not answer these questions in the order they appear here.

Travel—3

Q20: Travel Obligations. How much work-related
travel is generally associated with your type of
work? Is your travel:
    a. Overnight or for longer periods of time?
    b. Can it be planned well in advance?
    c. Must you sometimes remain out of town over
       the weekend? How often?
    d. Do you find the amount of travel you do objec-
       tionable? Do others in your field frequently ob-
       ject to it? Does your family object?

e. Do the travel obligations diminish or increase as your career progresses? Also please explain how much traveling you had to do earlier in your career.

f. Can someone in your career field control the amount of traveling he or she must do? Can it be eliminated completely?

g. Can you honestly say that the amount of traveling you do is just about enough to make the trips an interesting break in your routine?

Civic And Social Obligations—3

Q21: Civic and Social Obligations. How frequently must you represent your firm or profession in a social capacity after normal working hours?

a. Is this expected or demanded of you?

b. How do you view these activities?

Leisure Time—4

Q22: Vacation Time. How much vacation time does your job offer you?

a. How much flexibility do you have in choosing when you take off on a daily, seasonal, and extended period (weeks at a time) basis?

b. How much vacation time have you taken during the last two years and the last five years?

Pressure—3

Q23: Seasonal and Deadline Pressure.

a. Is there a pronounced seasonal pressure associated with your work as, for example, in the fields of retail merchandising and tax accounting?

b. How severe is deadline pressure in your field, and what is the nature of the deadlines you must meet?

Flexible Time Schedule—3, 4

Q24: Flexibility of Hours and Dress. How much flexibility do you and others in your field enjoy as regards:

a. The hours you work (9 A.M. to 5 P.M., etc)?

b. Where you work (at home and/or in your office)?

c. What you wear while you are working?

Homework—3

Q25: Homework. Are you able to confine your work to your place of work?

Work Freaks—4

a. Do you find it difficult to avoid carrying your work-related problems and projects home with you in mind, in spirit, or tangibly to continue working and/or thinking about them after you leave your place of work?
b. How many hours do you work each day and each week on the average?

Tent Dwellers—5

Q26: Moving Residences. Must someone in your career field expect to be moved about during his or her career?
a. How often?
b. During which stages of his or her career?
c. How far and where?
d. Can he or she avoid moving? Would refusing to move adversely affect one's career potential?

Family Life—3, 4

Q27: Effects on Family Ties.
a. Explain how and to what extent you feel your work has interfered with your family ties.
b. How do your spouse and children feel about your career, and how do they evaluate its impact upon:
  1. Themselves?
  2. You?
  3. Your life together as a family?
c. Has it ever been suggested that your type of work is particularly hard on family and other personal relationships? Is it?

Lee now strikes three more fields from his list. He writes off public accounting because of a combination of objections to the nature of the work and when it must be done. Accounting, he learns, involves working with data much more than with people—at least at the beginning of your career, and that's what's so unusual about accounting. The nature of public accountants' work changes dramatically around the seventh year if they're working in a large accounting firm. Although you begin with rather dull and tedious bookkeeping-like number pushing, you may end up in a broad conceptual decision-making capacity in which you function as a quasi-consultant. Lee doesn't relish the early work, but he really balks at the thought of missing most of the ski season, which coincides rather well with the peak of the accounting season.

Lee rejects the stock brokerage position because it is too inflexible and insecure. His being tied to the trading hours would clash directly with his strong preference for a flexible time schedule. Lee objects not only to the insecurity of the brokerage business but also to the inability to do very much to control it. It's just not for him.

Finally, Lee drops the idea of becoming a clinical psychologist because he fears he would be unable to detach himself from his patients. He's almost certain he would bring his patients' problems home with him, to the ruin of his own personal life. He recalls how involved he became with the people he met in the hospital when he had appendicitis and last year when he broke his ankle. That leaves only banking and life insurance still on his list.

VI. Personality and Talent Requirements

This and the following two sections are designed to pull together, organize, and summarize the information about the nature of the work. Much of this information will have already come out in the process of answering the strategic and life-style questions. The difference now lies in our focus, which is directed specifically at the kind of personality and talents it is advantageous to have in this line of work.

At this point we would like to concentrate our attention on the kinds of personality and talent traits it is advantageous to bring to your kind of work. The list of these factors that appears below has been drawn up solely to help you formulate your answer. It should be considered complete; it is only suggestive and serves primarily as a safeguard against overlooking important requirements. You may prefer to formulate your initial response without referring to this list at all. When you do refer to the list, please comment only on those traits that are particularly advantageous or disadvantageous in your line of work.

Identity-Match—3

Training—9

Q28: In your estimation, what are the talents and personality traits that are most likely to generate success and fulfillment in your field? Are there any personality traits that you consider particularly incompatible with your type of work? For example, are any of the following particularly advantageous or disadvantageous?

1. Verbal skills
   a. Writing ability
   b. Speaking ability
2. Mathematical skills
   a. A logical mind

    b. Technical competence in the use of mathematical formulae and methods

3. Analytical skills
4. Ability to deal with people and in what capacity; please explain in detail.
5. Managerial ability
6. Administrative ability
7. Supervisory ability
8. Organizational ability
9. Decision-making ability, decisiveness
10. Ability to assume and bear risks
11. Ability to work quickly, quickmindedness
12. Ability to function well under pressure, calmness
13. Ability to negotiate
14. Ability to debate
15. Sales and promotional ability
16. Persuasiveness
17. Persistence, determination, and tenacity
18. Aggressiveness or go-getterism
19. Courage
20. Ability to self-start and work responsibly with little or no supervision
21. Thoroughness
22. Foresight
23. Ability to plan, budget, or forecast
24. Memory skills: ability to retain and recall facts
25. Attention to details
26. Ability to do routine, tedious, or repetitive work
27. Willingness to work long hours, weekends, and odd hours
28. Imagination
29. Creativeness
30. Intuitive insight
31. Political insight and savvy
32. Shrewdness
33. Tactfulness
34. Patience, a great deal of self-control
35. A service orientation
36. A keen awareness of changing moods, tastes, fashions, trends, etc.—an ear-to-the-ground type of awareness
37. Perceptiveness

38. Manual dexterity
39. Physical stamina

VII. Advantages and Disadvantages of Your Type of Work

Q29: By now you will have already discussed many of the pluses and minuses of your line of work. Would you please bring these together in summary form by indicating what you and others in your field find to be the special advantages and disadvantages of your line of work?

VIII. Your Job and Your Personality: Why Are You Right for Each Other?

If you have covered this already, you may be brief. The interviewer is trying to understand how and why you might feel that you and your job are right for each other.

Identity-Match—3   **Q30:** Please try to explain how and why your job fits:
a. Your personality
b. Your economic needs
c. Your life goals
d. And generally fulfills you as a person

IX. What Would You Do Differently?

At this point we would like to learn from the interviewee's mistakes and experiences. If possible, we would also like to discover career fields we may have overlooked that require talents similar to those needed in the fields we're considering. Unfortunately, people often discover the career field they feel they should have been in after they're no longer willing or able to enter it. In effect, we're searching for additional career field ideas at this point.

These questions are designed to help the interviewer learn from your experiences and perhaps discover other career fields that he or she should consider.

Q31: Imagine for a moment that you were given a fresh start in the game of life. With the benefit of the wisdom, knowledge, and experience you've gleaned from your years, what would you do differently, and why, in:
a. Your career?

    b. Your family?

    c. Your choice of a location?

    d. Your life-style?

    e. What other changes would you make?

Q.32: Are there any mistakes you feel you could have avoided with the aid of better planning and counsel?

Q33: If you know people in other fields in which you feel you also would have been successful and fulfilled if you had received the required training, please identify these fields and explain why they appear attractive to you.

X. How Would You Advise a Young Person like me to Prepare for a Career in Your Field?

Q34: What type of educational program should I pursue?

Identity-Match—3

Q35: How and where can I find part-time and summer jobs that might indicate whether or not I would enjoy a career in your field?

Q36: In your estimation, how good are the future career opportunities within your field?

    a. Do you foresee any big changes or developments occurring in the future?

Growth—9

    b. What are they, and how will they affect career opportunities in the future?

    c. How rapidly is your career field growing now? How rapidly do you believe it will grow in the future? Why?

Supplier
Competition—7

    d. At present, is there an oversupply or undersupply of people entering your field?

    e. Do you know the addresses of any trade or professional organizations I could write to for additional information on present career opportunities within your field?

Q37: Assuming I chose to enter your career field, how would you advise me to advance myself most effectively within your career field?

Q38: Finally, do you have any particular advice that you would like to share with me as I start out in life? This advice or bit of philosophy need not relate directly or even indirectly to the problems of career decision-making.

XI. The End

In concluding the interview, you should try to get the names of several more people in the field whom you could ask for an interview. You should also get the interviewee's permission to call back if questions come up as you go over what you've learned. By this time you probably will have already been talking for several hours, and it will be time to politely thank the interviewee and excuse yourself.

> **Q39:** Finally, because each individual as well as each career position is somewhat different, it is suggested that I talk with at least five people in your career field before I make my final decision. Consequently, would you please consider whether you would be willing to give me the names and phone numbers of several more people in your career field whom I could ask for an interview? It would be most helpful if you could give me the names of people who are working in somewhat different capacities than your own (a different sized firm, different clientele, etc.), and perhaps you could choose people at different stages along their career path (five, ten, fifteen years of experience, etc.). Of course, I want you to realize that your giving me their names does not obligate them. I will call them, explain my request, send them the questions, and only then will I ask them if they are willing to make an interview.

> **Q40:** Thank you. Thank you very much for this generous gift of your time. I hope you too have benefited from these questions. May I please call you if I come across a few more questions in going over what we've discussed?

You will be almost certain to get several referrals because the interviewee will realize that those he or she refers will also have something to gain through your interview. Answering these questions forces the interviewee to make an assessment of his or her career position, which is something each of us would be wise to do periodically. The covering letter, which introduces the booklet containing the extra set of questions to be given to interviewees, explains this to prospective interviewees. Making them aware that they can also benefit from answering these questions greatly increases their willingness to participate more completely and seriously. Both parties should benefit about equally from the interview. It should not be difficult to get referrals and subsequently referrals from these referrals, and so on, until you have made at least five or as many interviews as you feel you want in any field.

Lee's interviews are over now, and only banking and life insurance sales remain on his list of potential career fields. He now constructs the list shown in Table 11–1 to help him make his final decision. This list reproduces all of his mandatory, strongly preferred, and preferred career characteristics in summary form. The checks in the two separate career field columns indicate that the field offers these corresponding characteristics; a plus after a check signifies that the field meets that requirement more satisfactorily than the other field. Table 11–1 reveals that both banking and life insurance satisfy all seven of his

TABLE 11-1
LEE WADE'S FINAL CAREER SHOPPING LIST

A. MANDATORY CAREER CHARACTERISTICS	Banking	Life Insurance
1. Freedom from close supervision.	✓	✓ +
2. Flexible time schedule.	✓	✓ +
3. A comfortable income.	✓	✓
4. A permanent home.	✓	✓
5. Working with people.	✓	✓
6. Variety, change, freshness in the work.	✓	✓
7. Hot summers.	✓	✓

B. STRONGLY PREFERRED CAREER CHARACTERISTICS		
1. Run my own show.		✓
2. Adjustable income.		✓
3. Permanent working relationships with people.	✓	✓
4. Manageable size of community.	✓	✓

C. PREFERRED CAREER CHARACTERISTICS		
1. Tangibly helping people.	✓	✓
2. Frequent little victories.	✓	✓
3. $50,000 in 1976 dollars.	✓	✓ +
4. Six weeks of annual vacation time.		✓
5. Ideal climate and location.	✓	✓
6. Some work-associated travel.	✓	✓

Key
✓ = Career offers this characteristic.

✓ + = Career offers this characteristic more satisfactorily than the other careers that also offer it.

mandatory career characteristics. As is evidenced by the pluses, however, life insurance better meets his requirements of a flexible time schedule and freedom from close supervision.

We see from Table 11–1 that banking does not meet two of Lee's strongly preferred and one of his preferred career characteristics. Life insurance sales, on the other hand, meets all of his career characteristics and is also better than banking on three of the characteristics that banking also meets (the three pluses). Lee decides to sell executive life insurance. In this capacity he will be contacting businesses, professional people, and wealthy individuals to sell them employee pension-fund programs, life insurance, and estate planning services. He will work strictly on a commission basis in this field, which means that he will essentially be in business for himself. He can therefore adjust his income by working harder and earning more commissions. And he will be able to make his own vacation schedule. These three characterisitics—running his own show, being able to adjust his income, and having six weeks of vacation—would be very difficult or impossible for him to expect to achieve in the field of banking.

Lee also likes the position as a sales representative of executive life insurance and pension plans because of the strategic advantages it offers. He will be dealing directly with a very broad range of businesses and executives, which will provide him with excellent visibility and exposure. If he finds he doesn't like his job, he'll be in a very good position to discover what he might like and who can hire him for such a position. He will be developing general skills—ability to deal with people, analytical problem-solving skills, sales ability—that are transferable to many fields, and thus he'll also have considerable mobility among career fields. In short, Lee's choice affords him a good deal of flexibility in his career planning. If things don't work out in the life insurance business, he will still have many other available career options.

Lee followed up the chain of referrals he developed from the first insurance sales representative he interviewed, made a total of eight interviews, and visited four insurance agencies. He still has a long list of referrals he has not yet called. It's time, he decides, to move on instead to the next step in The Career Game.

The Job Search

Lee now calls the insurance people he has interviewed to explain his reasoning and inform them of his decision. He asks them to evaluate his decision and to advise him on where and how to apply for a summer job that will serve as a good background for insurance sales as well as give him a foretaste of it. Ultimately he accepts a summer position with one of the agencies he visited earlier, finds he likes the business, and decides to pursue his original plan.

In his senior year, Lee contacts the insurance people he interviewed to enlist their help in getting good job offers. Later he calls on some of them to evaluate the offers he gets. It's very important to keep in touch with these people. They will be among your most valuable contacts in the industry or profession you enter. You haven't forgotten the value of people power have you? Be good to all your friends, and don't overlook those people who helped set you up. They'll want to know how their "protégé" is doing. Remember them periodically with a call, a card perhaps at Christmas, etc.

We'll have a few more marketing ideas for you in Part III, but you're already basically prepared to begin playing The Career Game right now. How's your case of graduation shock now? Any better?

PART III

MARKETING YOURSELF; ESSAYS; AND NOTES

When we wish to explain or predict human behavior, it is important to remember that what people believe is true is more relevant than what is in fact true. People base their decisions, and therefore act, on the basis of what they believe the facts are.

Charles Guy Moore

*Never lend money to someone who really
needs it.*

Rule 1: The Bankers' Code

MARKETING YOURSELF: A PSYCHOLOGICAL APPROACH
  Know What You Want and Be Able to Explain Why You Want It
  Project Yourself as Their Problem-Solver
  The Continuous Job-Hunting Strategy

THE CONVENTIONAL JOB-FINDING SERVICES:
AN EVALUATION AND DESCRIPTION
  As a Rule, Avoid the Conventional Job-Finding Apparatus
  How and When to Use the Conventional Job-Finding Apparatus
  The Professional Matchmakers
  Other Sources of Career and Job Information

CHAPTER TWELVE

MARKETING YOURSELF

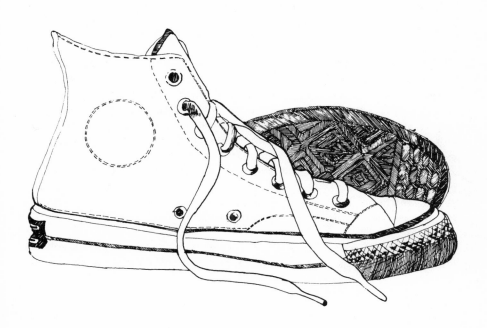

When you're finally ready to look for a job, you'll have three important advantages working for you:

1. You'll know what kind of job you want and why you want to do that kind of work.
2. You'll know how to conduct yourself in an interview.
3. And you'll understand how markets, like the one you'll be selling your services in, function.

This self-knowledge and better understanding of your circumstances will cause you to stand out from the rest of the crowd of job hunters in the minds of the people who interview you for a job. Consequently, yours will be one of the memorable faces in the largely anonymous sea of job candidates whom employers will have interviewed.

MARKETING YOURSELF: A PSYCHOLOGICAL APPROACH

As in all of the previous steps, our approach to this final step of securing employment also relies heavily on the application of the powerful tools of "psychology." Among the most important decisions others will make in your life will be decisions to hire you for jobs you want. If you want to increase the probability that others will hire you for such positions, first you must understand what might make them want to hire you; then you must convince them that you can provide it. When you're being interviewed for a job, you're selling confidence in your potential to do the job—that is, in effect you're selling belief in yourself. What could make your interviewer believe in your ability to do the job and convince him or her that you will be the right person to meet his or her employer's needs?

Earlier we noted that until you've worked at a job for some time, you can't really know if you'll like it and be able to do it well. The person interviewing you confronts parallel risks and uncertainties in considering you for a job. When people hire you, they hire you to accomplish a specific task for them, not to help you develop or learn. But the person who hires you has no sure way of knowing in advance if you'll work out in the job. If you've had previous work experience of a similar nature, your interviewer will at least have those tangible work records on which to formulate expectations about your potential performance in the opening that is available. But if like most new college graduates you haven't held a full-time job before, your interviewer will have much less to go on; consequently, the three advantages listed above will take on increased significance.

It's true that your interviewers can survey your record as a student, but one's grades are often an unreliable predictor of one's performance in a job.

For one thing, most jobs require cooperating with other employees and these skills are not tested in the classroom where most work is done independently of others. In any case, the one thing that will call attention to you, make you memorable, and leave a favorable impression will be your sense of yourself and what you want to accomplish. In addition to projecting this sense of self, you should seek to reveal an understanding of your potential employers' problems and demonstrate specifically how you are qualified and prepared to work on and solve them. This combination is unbeatable. On the one hand, it demonstrates that you have sound reasons for wanting the job and that you are therefore more likely to stay with it. On the other hand, this approach gives your potential employers logical reasons to hire you because you understand their problems and can bring some needed talents to be applied towards solving them. This, in a nutshell, is the approach we recommend you use during job interviews. Your reasons must be honest however, and they will be if you've followed the other steps in our recommended program.

Know What You Want and Be Able to Explain Why You Want It

Everyone is impressed by people who know what they want and are able to explain clearly why they want it. Finding this sense of direction among college students is doubly impressive. Many interviewers point out that it's rare to find a student who even understands what their firm or industry really does, let alone what he or she wants to do for their firm. The employers who hire recent college graduates believe that they must keep doing so in order to assure themselves of a continuous supply of executive talent. But they conceive of themselves as being in a big numbers game in which they're hiring many in the expectation that only a few, whom they can't identify in advance, will work out. You will really impress your interviewers by demonstrating that you've done some serious research and planning before meeting them.

Project Yourself as Their Problem-Solver

Furthermore, when you reveal to your interviewers that you understand their problems and then go on to explain how you can contribute to solving them, you'll have become a serious candidate in their eyes. If you convey confidence but not arrogance regarding your understanding of and ability to meet your potential employers' needs, it will make sense for them to give further consideration to your candidacy. This will typically mean that you will be invited to visit the location at which you would be working, where you will meet your prospective boss and the rest of the team you would be working with.

The same techniques should be used in these subsequent interviews. In this case, however, you will be able to ask more specific questions for which you will be able to get more comprehensive answers. These are the interviews that really matter because only your future boss will have the authority to hire you. In most instances, the interviewers who come on campus are from their employers' personnel departments. These people act as filters in the job market. It is their function to prescreen all prospective candidates, only the most promising of whom are invited back to be interviewed by those who have the authority to actually hire candidates. Thus, the first interviews are important, but their importance is limited. They can only get you to the door of the man or woman who can hire you.

One rather sensitive word of caution is in order here. The people who work in the personnel department are sometimes held in low esteem by the firm's other employees. There are a variety of reasons why this may be so, but it is not very important that we discuss them here.[1] The important thing is to caution you against expressing an *excessively* strong affinity for your first interviewer during your subsequent interviews. Although it is perhaps unlikely, should your potential boss have an ax to grind with the personnel department or the specific individual who first interviewed you, your expression of fondness for that person may work to your detriment with the person who has the real power to hire you. Let this be your first practical lesson in "organizational politics." When you're ignorant regarding the internal political situation, always try to maintain a neutral stance and, if you must, defer to those whom you know to be powerful.

The Continuous Job-Hunting Strategy
The first principle of our continuous job-hunting strategy involves maintaining an *upward focus* upon the positions into which you hope to be promoted. Your attention should always be directed toward identifying and developing the skills needed to function effectively in these roles. Our strategy's second principle involves maintaining an *outward focus* that is directed upon similar position openings among potential employers. This strategy is implemented by using the principles spelled out earlier in Chapters Nine, Ten, and Eleven. Once you have secured your initial career position, you should rely on visibility, exposure, and the other strategic principles of Position Analysis to keep your name and your work ever present in the minds of other employers who might need your talents. This is how you should seek to maintain a sufficient inventory of attractive career options open to you in case you find that you want to or must change career positions. Indeed your whole career focus should be centered around these strategic principles that will generate the career mobility needed to provide you with the only really effective career insurance obtainable anywhere. By adhering to these principles and following the Minimax Option Approach outlined in Chapter Ten, you should never have to fall back on the less effective and often humiliating mechanisms of the conventional job market (discussed in the next section).

These then are our job hunting recommendations:

1. When you seek your first job as well as all subsequent jobs, know what you want and be able to clearly articulate why you want it.
2. Always know what your prospective employer's problems are and explain how you will be effective in helping to solve them.
3. Once you have secured your first job, never wait until you are unemployed to begin looking for another job. Think and plan ahead by using the strategic principles of Position Analysis and the Minimax Option Approach to keep potential employers coming to you with attractive job offers.
4. Avoid relying on the conventional job market mechanism to find employment and generally use them only as outlined in the next section.

That's our advice: simple, concise, and effective. Use it. It will work if you've done your homework.

THE CONVENTIONAL JOB-FINDING SERVICES: AN EVALUATION AND DESCRIPTION

Although we do not recommend that you rely on them, at some point in your career circumstances may force you to fall back on the services of the conventional job market. Consequently, a few words of description and some advice on how to intelligently evaluate and select from this group of services is in order.

As a Rule, Avoid the Conventional Job-Finding Apparatus

There are three very good reasons why you should avoid depending on the conventional job-finding organizations, instruments, and procedures such as employment agencies, resumes, broadcast letters, help wanted ads, etc.:

1. They may make you a beggar.
2. They may erode and destroy your self-confidence and esteem.
3. And they may reduce your status to that of a paper person and number.

Moreover, you should *never* be unemployed when you look for a job because most people do not want to hire the unemployed. Bankers won't lend money to companies that need it for their survival. They prefer to lend to companies that are doing well and can be expected to do even better if they get a little of their bank's money. Likewise, most people don't like to hire others who really need a job. Desperate job hunters are suspect.

"How have they fallen into such desperate straits? Doesn't almost every really good employee already *have* a job? If they're so improvident, what kind of employees would they make? If we hire them and they don't work out, how will we be able to muster the heart to fire them and knowingly return them to such desperate straits?'' These are examples of the thoughts that pass—consciously or unconsciously—through potential employers heads when they consider hiring those who are desperate for a job.

The hiring situation is somewhat similar to making a marriage. You can't throw yourself upon the other person. The other person has enough heavy burdens without accepting you as a helpless soul who is dependent upon him or her for your survival. You must enter a job as you enter a marriage—with your dignity intact. That bit about groveling on bended knee belongs somewhere back there in the Middle Ages with the other conditions of serfdom.

When you wait until you need and must have a job, the ''psychology'' involved in trying to find a job is turned against you. People like to be winners, and they like to avoid unnecessary responsibility. When you go to others for a job, *you win if they give you one.* By way of contrast, if you organize it so that others come to you with job offers while you're still employed, then *you make them winners by accepting their job offer.* And since you've already got a job, you must also believe you're winning if you voluntarily give up your old job for the one they offer you. Those who offer you a job under such circumstances will also not feel they are assuming undue responsibility for you; since you are already employed, your action in accepting their job offer has been taken from a position of strength, not one of weakness and necessity.

If, on the other hand, you wait until you're unemployed to look for your next job and then you rely on the conventional job-finding mechanisms, you may be reduced to the humiliating state of a paper person and become one of the thousands of resume people, almost all of whom overflow off crowded desks and end in the circular file. And, alas, your self-esteem will go up the flue as your ashes settle to the bottom. Somewhere else you'll be case number 106 in file number 3 and elsewhere prospect number 7 in next Wednesday's list of candidates to be screened and classified for possible job openings that may become available in the weeks and months ahead. And your M.B.A. from Columbia plus some luck may land you a part-time job driving taxis. Unfortunately, none of this is folklore. I have seen it happen, and I know people it has happened to. As their self-confidence flags, so does their ability to be an effective problem-solver/decision-maker. Thus their unfitness for the work they desire is likely to be confirmed by the deterioration of their psychological state.

How and When to Use the Conventional Job-Finding Apparatus
If you follow our program, you may only have to rely on the conventional job market when you seek your first job. Even in this case, however, you may be able to avoid it by utilizing the contacts you make during the interviewing stage of your career search, as Lee Wade was able to do. Otherwise, it makes good sense to keep your name and qualifications before the specialized employ-

ment agencies and others who are likely to become aware of position open-ings that you might find attractive. These agencies can be especially helpful in keeping you informed about what you're worth in the marketplace. This is something you should always know in order to make sure that your employer's wage is a fair one and to be sure that you are able to conduct intelligent wage negotiations with others who may want to hire you.

If and when you use these agencies, however, you should already be employed and, second, you should contact them well in advance of the time you even feel that you might want or need a new job. You will be relying on them in this case not to find you a job, but rather to find you a better job. Thus the psychological edge will remain with you. As an already employed candi-date, you'll be operating from a position of strength; and the agency will also be more eager and enthusiastic about marketing you because its clients will know that you are coming to them by choice, not out of necessity and perhaps without any real interest in their jobs. Everyone views you as a more attractive candidate if you already have a job.

These then are the circumstances under which you should consider using the conventional job-finding mechanisms.

1. When you seek a job for the very first time and perhaps have few other alternatives.
2. When you're already employed and must not therefore rely on these agencies for a job, but only for a better job if they can find one for you.

The Professional Matchmakers

The cast of professional matchmakers is indeed diverse. Nevertheless, should you ever consider using any of these or other matchmaking organizations, your first question should always be the same: Who pays their bills? The answer to this question will help to indicate the *degree* to which the matchmaking agency is likely to serve your interests.

Let's face it. Every organization must look out for its own interests first. That's the first rule of survival; those who fail to heed this rule die and cease to be of further consequence. Matchmakers—all matchmakers of every type and description—occupy positions that are inherently rife with conflict of interests. The parties involved in any matchmaking situation have selfish interests to protect, and these interests are typically in conflict with those of the other party to the prospective match. The matchmaker is inescapably caught in the middle.

As was demonstrated in Chapter Seven, the settlement of the employee's wage rate is a classical example of a conflict-of-interest situation in which the interests of the two parties are diametrically opposed. The employer wishes to minimize the wage rate that the employee wishes to maximize, and the matchmaking agency must appear to favor, or at a minimum be neutral to, its clients on both sides of this labor market. However, since they are continually engaged in labor market negotiations, job-finding agencies are better informed about the true price of labor than their clients on either side. While they cannot reveal obvious favoritism to either side, matchmakers can exercise subtle favoritism for either party provided the other party remains unaware of it. Knowing which party pays for the agency's matchmaking services will reveal which party it is probably most interested in pleasing. If a firm repeatedly hires an agency to locate employees for it, the agency's primary allegiance must be to that firm. It follows that the subtle preferences such an agency might exercise are most likely to fall on the employer's scale when the wage negotiation balance is struck.

It so happens that most of the agencies that place college graduates collect their fees from the employer. It is also true that the allegiance of agencies that collect their fees from job hunters is nevertheless also more closely tied to employers because they depend upon employers for the supply of the job openings they sell. And finally it must be noted that because they are in the job market more often, employers are almost always better informed about job market conditions and salaries than the job hunters with whom they negotiate. Thus, any way you look at it, the job hunter is almost always the least informed of the parties and the party most likely to be taken advantage of in these matchmaking situations. This will be true regardless of the type of agency used and regardless of who pays the fee.

Perhaps you're frowning about now and saying, "So what's been the point of all this? I don't need to be depressed over circumstances about which I can do very little anyway." It's sometimes wise to get a little depressed if it will spare you a greater depression in the long run. Perhaps from now on you will realize the weakness of your position whenever you face matchmakers, whatever sort they are. Perhaps you won't let their smiles and pleasantries mislead you. They have good positions that offer the strategic advantages of visibility, growth, exposure, and so forth, and they also have just as many and probably more dead-end jobs. Their livelihood depends on filling all of them: that's their business. It's strictly up to you to make sure that you won't be put into one of the career closet jobs they *must* fill with somebody.

Your business is marketing yourself intelligently and to do this you must fully understand your own circumstances. If you use the services of a matchmaker (and there are some good matchmakers), don't naively assume as so many job hunters do that the matchmaker will be looking out for your interests. Looking out for your interests is your business, not the matchmaker's business; base your assumptions on that reality and act accordingly. Expect that your matchmaker, for purposes of survival, will tend to favor the employer, if anyone. If you can't force your agency into a position of straightforward neutrality, find another agency. Again, if you've done your homework, you'll know how to identify a promising position and an agency won't be able to push you into one of the dead-end positions it must fill.

The type of matchmaker you should choose will depend upon your area of career specialization and the stage you have reached in your career development. There are private employment agencies that specialize in every grade and classification of labor. You must discover which ones specialize in people with your qualifications, training, level of experience, and field of specialization. You should not have to pay an agency a fee until and unless it places you in a job you accept, and even then the employer may be the one who pays the fee. These are the matchmakers you would use until you were well along in your career development, at which time you may become of interest to firms that specialize in searching for and recruiting executives for specific high-level positions. These executive search firms are also called "executive recruiters," "headhunters," and a variety of other colorful names like "flesh peddlers."

Two main characteristics differentiate executive recruiters from the other matchmakers: (1) they take the initiative in searching for candidates and are generally not interested in being solicited by candidates, particularly unemployed candidates; (2) they recruit personnel for positions in middle management and above. Consequently, it is unlikely that you will be of interest to these firms until you're in your thirties. At that time, however, you should find out which of these firms specialize in your field, get one of your colleagues to "whisper in their ears about you," or devise some other effective plan to make your presence known to them. Executive search firms maintain contacts who work in their fields of specialization. These are the people they call on for advice on whom to interview for the job openings they have. Thus doing a superior job and maintaining your visibility are the keys that will maximize your chances of being tapped by one of these firms that often have truly outstanding positions to offer their candidates.

Career counselors are a third group of matchmakers you might encounter, especially if you later attempt to transfer into another career field. But beware. Many of the firms in this category of matchmakers have a reputation for promising the moon and charging fees of up to thousands of dollars for consultations and counseling services that often lead to no jobs at all in the end. Carefully scrutinize the promises they will make *in writing* and investigate their previous record of success with their former clients. Ask them what percentage of their previous clients they actually found jobs for and what kind of jobs -they found them?

Other Sources of Career and Job Information
There are many other valuable sources of career and job information. Industry, trade, and professional associations and groups have established exchanges and clearing houses to facilitate the flow of job and employment information between candidates and employers. Many of these are free to the job hunter, as are those provided by the employment agencies that have been established by most levels of government. The federal government, through its many publications such as the *Occupational Outlook for College Graduates, Occupational Outlook Handbook,* and *Dictionary of Occupational Titles,* also offers a broad range of worthwhile career information. Your guidance counselors and local libraries should have these and a whole battery of other publications that may interest you as a career searcher and job hunter. Although these printed sources, in comparison with our recommended sources, provide career information that is less detailed, more outdated, and not designed to meet your individual needs, they may nevertheless serve as a valuable source of career ideas during the earlier stages of your search for a suitable career.

Much, much more might be said regarding the pitfalls of conventional job-finding procedures, but this would take us beyond the principal focus of this book. By the definitions of others, we at the Institute are also among the so-called "creative minority" that seeks to avoid reliance upon the conventional job-market aparatus.[2] Our experiences have confirmed the wisdom of the creative minority's observations, which have undoubtedly affected our thoughts and positions on these matters. Because our space is limited, we specifically recommend that you consult two of these authors directly. The subject of the job hunt is more central to their concerns and thus receives more comprehensive treatment from them. Their stance in both cases is some-what different from ours and may in certain instances be more appropriate to your immediate needs. Among the many worthwhile publications that place a special emphasis upon the job hunt, the following two books are especially popular among young readers: Richard Nelson Bolles, *What Color Is Your Parachute?* (Ten Speed Press, $3.95 in paperback); and Richard K. Irish, *Go Hire Yourself an Employer* (Anchor Press, $2.95 in paperback).

We have not been capable of distinguishing
the prohibited from the lawful. We have
infringed natural law. We have thus
committed the supreme sin, the sin that is
always punished. The dogmas of scientific
religion and industrial morals have fallen
under the onslaught of biological reality. Life
always gives an identical answer when
asked to trespass on forbidden ground. It
weakens. And civilizations collapse.

Alexis Carrel

CHAPTER THIRTEEN

WHAT DIFFERENCE DOES WOMEN'S LIBERATION MAKE? AN ESSAY

This chapter, which is for both men and women, is *my* chapter. I've tried to sustain objectivity within the main body of the text by refraining from interjecting my personal views and by tending to state rather than interpret the facts that have been presented. This chapter, while also analytical, is much more editorial in nature and has therefore been termed an essay. America is in the midst of a blurring whirlwind of unparalleled change. This chapter addresses those changes that are centrally linked to the changing role of women in our society. These are the changes that concern me most; I view them as the most important developments of our time.

While others might place these matters outside the purview of career planning, I would not. I would not because, as was demonstrated throughout Part I, your career decision will place constraints on your other major life decisions such as your choice of a life-style, where you will be able to work and live, and the viability of your marriage. Since your career decision will inevitably generate these important effects on the rest of your life, these other considerations should also be integrated into your career decision-making. Insofar as this chapter is concerned with similar effects—among others, how you and your spouse will share the responsibility of raising your children— these issues are germane, indeed central, to comprehensive career decision-making.

THE ROLES OF WOMEN: AN EVALUATION

Those of us who are witnessing the changes being introduced by the present women's liberation movement are just too close to them to be very objective. As a society we're still feeling these changes—often without a sense of humor—and reacting emotionally; it could hardly be otherwise. No matter what's said, it will irritate, it will be incomplete, it will not be given or received with full objectivity. Our discussion will be less emotional perhaps because we shall limit ourselves to an inspection of women in their roles as productive resources. As a person, a man, and even in my role as an economist, I find it both unnatural and cold to think of women as resources, as instruments of production. Somehow the term *labor,* which is used by economists to refer to human beings in their capacity as resources, is far less personal than the term *women.* Nevertheless, quite a few important realizations can be gained from this admittedly limited perspective. And, paradoxically, this approach may ultimately bring us to a warmer, more humanistic view of our circumstances during this difficult time of transition.

Why Role Typing Is Undesirable
By persuasion, I am a Jeffersonian liberal: I make the value judgment that the individual's freedom is paramount to everything else. I view placing people in

roles, based on their sex or any other criterion, as undesirable because this constitutes an infringement upon their right to choose for themselves. The problem, therefore, is not that women have a bum role in our society—some women may actually prefer the role society expects of them. Rather, the problem is that women have any expected role at all in our society. That is, the sexual roles themselves are the problem—society should not assign or expect roles of anyone, any woman, any man, any person. The various splinter groups that make up the women's liberation movement also agree that the elimination of sexual role typing represents a common objective sought by all of them.

Once we've agreed that the elimination of sexual role typing is desirable, we must investigate what's involved in making the transition to that state. Moreover, if we advocate and hope to promote social change, we must show why it's necessary, that is, we must show why present arrangements are no longer consistent with present realities. This can be accomplished by comparing the circumstances in which our traditional sexual roles developed with those that exist now. This comparison will help us: (1) demonstrate why change is required which will enable us to better sell our case; (2) identify what's likely to go wrong during the transition so that we can avoid these mistakes; and (3) discover the alternatives that are likely to make the transition as quick and painless as possible.

The History of Sexual Roles

Our presently outmoded sexual roles originated at a time when brute force was an advantage in most wage-earning occupational pursuits and being a housewife was more than a full-time occupation. At that time, our sexual work roles represented a sane way to distribute the labors that had to be done. Most men labored ten or more hours each day at backbreaking physical tasks. Women were also working very hard at home behind wood stoves cooking foods from scratch; making, washing, and mending their family's clothes; bearing and raising children; and often helping out in the fields as well. It was completely beside the point that it was considered socially unacceptable for women to work outside their homes; they didn't have the time. That was how our labors were divided at the time our traditional sexual work roles made sense.

Gradually, technology began to eliminate the backbreaking element from most of men's work, and their work week was cut to 40 hours. Pumps, vacuum cleaners, modern stoves, store-bought clothes, processed foods, refrigeration, and a whole host of other technological aids greatly lightened and shortened the housewife's workload. Then in the crisis atmosphere of World War II, in which labor was desperately needed, it became socially acceptable and even patriotic for large numbers of women to enter the work force. But, when the war was over, these women stayed on in the work force, and affluent parents began to send more of their daughters to college. Finally, more effective contraceptives gave women greater control over their career and family planning. Then when they found they couldn't gain equal access to employment opportunities and equal pay for equal work, women successfully organized to gain them through legislation. This is where we are now—in the midst of a host of legal hassles, with men and women rubbing each other raw, without pleasure. And the lot of many working women has actually deteriorated through all of this.

The position of many working women has worsened because while it has become socially acceptable for them to fill the traditional roles of men, it has not yet become socially acceptable for men to fill the traditional roles of women. Consequently, "liberation" for many married women has meant assuming new roles that were formerly male roles without being relieved from their traditional female roles. This realization must lead us to either of two conclusions, both of which are partially correct in most cases. Women's liberation alone has placed an unfair double yoke of two jobs on most married women who also work outside their homes. Second, the traditional roles of women are not being filled as satisfactorily as they used to be because many women are now working full-time in what used to be men's roles. Although the first conclusion identifies a significant sexual inequity, the conclusion that the traditional roles of women are being filled less satisfactorily seems potentially far more dangerous. By our actions, we seem to have assumed that the traditional services of women are unimportant (at least less important than the services they're providing in their new roles) or that their services can be satisfactorily replaced by technological aides. Let's see if these assumptions can withstand careful scrutiny.

How Important Are the Traditional Services of Women?

It is a hallmark of the affluent that they lose sight of what's most important. If you were to ask an American and a Bengali, "What's most important in life?" the American might give any of a score of answers. The Bengali would answer, "Food." The Bengali would be right. Likewise, as a society we seem to have lost sight of the extreme importance of the services that women have traditionally provided. It's ironic that "women's work," to which we foolishly attach about as much social prestige as we attach to dogcatching, includes some of the most basic services necessary to our very survival.

When we view women as resources, their traditional services can be functionally separated into the three categories of child bearing, cooking, and homemaking. We shall include child raising and all household duties except cooking under the homemaking category. Although most vital and necessary of all, the child-bearing function is of the least importance to our discussion. Women have not yet abandoned this role, and the rather remote possibility that they might need concern us little, for if this happens, all our many problems will be abruptly and permanently resolved. Thus, while the threat posed by large numbers of women abandoning their roles as child bearers could hardly go unnoticed, does their abandonment of the roles of cook and home-maker pose any threats that have gone unheralded? Cooking and homemaking do seem like dull roles—doubly so because our culture has conditioned us to view them as dull—but let's see how important they are and how satisfactory our substitutes for women in these functions really are.

The dietary changes that have resulted from women entering the organized work force represent only the most recent adulterations of the natural diet of human beings. In our most primitive state, before our ancestors had even invented hunting tools, we must have foraged on raw, uncooked vegetables, nuts, berries, and very little meat. Somewhat later we became hunters and adjusted to eating more meat. Although our basic biological needs have not changed in the millions of years since then, technology beginning with the discovery of fire has continually changed our diet. Recent technological changes have altered our diet in two basic ways: improved transportation and refrigeration have greatly expanded the variety of foods that are available throughout the year; and additional processing, chemical additives, and the other chemicals involved in food production have drastically altered the quality of our foods. The changing work role of women has also played a central role in these dietary changes.

As more and more women entered the work force, the food industry lost little time in catering to the needs of these women with two jobs. Working women were soon offered an ever-broadening array of highly processed, time-saving "convenience foods." The food industry, like any other industry, was and still is concerned primarily with profits, which are defined as the difference between the per unit sales price and costs. Profits can be raised by producing products that are in high demand and can therefore be sold at higher prices, or profits can be increased by lowering costs.

Processed foods were in high demand by working women and others who were convenience-minded. Likewise, sweet foods that appealed to the consumers' tastes despite their adverse dietary affects were also in high demand and could be sold at profitable prices. Meanwhile, nutritious foods were causing annoying problems on the cost side of the profit equation because the bugs and molds just loved them. Consequently, the food industry avoided nutritious foods or processed much of the nutritional value out of such foods in order to cut the spoilage costs caused by these gourmet vermin. Chemicals were added to further retard spoilage, and still more chemicals were added to give foods taste and eye appeal. Dramatic changes like these that have occurred in our diet reveal the dangers of specialization as perhaps nothing else can.

Paradoxically, specialization, which results in an increasingly more complex world in the aggregate, is disarmingly simplifying in its separate applications. In many instances the specialist's concentration becomes narrowed upon a single objective, the calculus of which does not include other effects that may be of extreme importance as, for example, in the production of the food we eat. As a specialist, the food producer is concerned with yield alone, the food processor with food that sells and doesn't spoil, and neither of these specialists is concerned about the nutritional value of the consumer's food supply. Moreover, each of these specialists employs still other specialists to work on the individual problems they face. The farmer has some chemical specialists working on fertilizers, others on pesticides, and still others on herbicides and so forth. More specialists are at work on hormones, growth stimulants, and whatever additional feed additives are needed to augment the single yield that counts, be it pounds of beef, the percent of butterfat in milk, dozens of eggs, the color of the chicken's skin, etc.

In the production of our most basic necessity, therefore, our specialized focus has become myopically narrowed upon the individual trees to the neglect of the nutritional forest. There is no specialist who can understand all these separate pieces, assemble them, or fathom the consequences of their interaction with each other. We have our antibiotics, vaccines, and improved methods of treating the sick and injured to thank for our increased longevity, not the foods most of us are eating. Many of you probably believe that our food supply is basically sound. The facts outlined below have changed my mind: I hope they'll also cause you to reconsider your eating habits. I grew up on the land, served as the president of my local 4-H Club, and someday hope to write a book on the subject of specialization, diet, and the extent of special interest control of the Food and Drug Administration. At this point, I'll just state a few of the more important reasons that have recently compelled me to resort to growing all my own food organically.

1. As of 1972, the average American was already consuming in excess of one-fifth of an ounce of food additives per day; and chemical additive production, which stood at 253 percent of its 1955 level, was projected to continue to increase rapidly.[1] These chemicals, which are used as stabilizers, preservatives, antioxidants, extenders, tenderizers, emulsifiers, bleaches, sweeteners, conditioners, colors, and flavors, etc. are tested by the producers themselves. "Dr. Jack Schubert, professor of radiation health at the University of Pittsburgh, in a speech before the Federal Bar Association's Food and Drug Law Committee November 24, 1969, stated that industry testing 'cannot be trusted,' because firms 'withhold data' and do not look for things they do not want to find."[2] Among the chemical additives that were "tested" in this manner, served to the public as "safe," and later found to be hazardous are: cyclamate, agene, dulcin, butter yellow, oil of calumus, safrole, and DES. Nevertheless, testing still is conducted by the producers, not by independent third parties.[3]

2. No doubt you too have heard the public service announcement that cautions us not to mix cleaning agents as this can produce poisonous chemical reactions. A total of 3,000 chemical additives—1,000 added directly and 2,000 added indirectly through processing, packaging, and other procedures—are now entering our foods and the Food and Drug Administration is accepting scores of new additives each year.[4] Even if we wanted to, it would be economically infeasible to test for all the possibly poisonous chemical reactions that could result from the interactions of these 3,000 additives with each other because there are 2^{3000}—trillions of possibly harmful interactions. *Thus, we inevitably become human guinea pigs when we eat these chemicals.*

3. Dr. Benjamin Fiengold has proven that many hyperactive children can be cured by putting them on an additive-free diet.[5] It is practically impossible to find a pediatric medicine that does not have an artificial color or flavor, however, and the ingestion of a single cherry-flavored cough lozenge has sent such children back into a hyperactive state for two weeks.[6]

4. Our first Food and Drug Law was enacted in 1906 after more than a quarter of a century of Congressional debate. Dr. Harvey W. Wiley, one of the leaders in this cause, became its first administrator, only to resign six years later in 1912 because from the very beginning the letter as well as the spirit of the law had been flagrantly violated and he was made powerless to enforce its provisions. In 1929 he published his well-documented account of these events: *The History of a Crime Against the Food Law.*[7] This book's subtitle summarizes its contents: "The Amazing Story of the National Food and Drugs Law Intended to Protect the Health of the People—Perverted to Protect Adulteration of Foods and Drugs." The Department of Agriculture refused to publish the painstaking research conducted by Dr. Wiley's bureau on the harmful effects of preservatives such as benzoic acid and benzoates and more than a dozen other such reports; and today some of these and related substances remain in our food supply.[8]

5. As further testimony to the Food and Drug Administration's (FDA) ongoing conflict of interest problems, "more than a thousand chemicals added to our foods have never been tested for their potentialities of causing cancer, genetic damage or birth defects."[9] Moreover, the FDA has not even required that certain food additives be listed on food labels despite the fact that some of these unlabeled chemical additives have been banned in numerous West European countries and blacklisted by the World Health Organization.[10]

6. The U.S. Department of Agriculture now recommends that apples, which my grandfather sprayed three times annually, be sprayed a minimum of twelve times annually.[11] My neighbor, who is a "progressive," "scientific," strawberry grower, relies on and regularly uses six different herbicides, pesticides, and fungicides to bring his strawberries to market. Unlike ap-

ples, this crop cannot be peeled. Systemic poisons, which enter the plant and become part of its leaves, stems, and fruit, are now widely used on many crops. When these systemic poisons are improperly used, there is absolutely no way to get them out of the fruits and vegetables we eat because they are present in every one of these plants' cells. While these systemic poisons and other pesticides are theoretically regulated, the agency charged with enforcing these regulations in the state of Pennsylvania makes no routine checks of any kind for pesticide residues on fruits and vegetables. Its director, Mr. Joseph Brenan, told me that they are not equipped to do this and that they spend their time instead checking grade sizes of apples, etc.[12]

7. There is a fundamental conflict of interest between food producers and food consumers. The producer sprays to reduce the risk of crop failure, thus increasing the consumer's risk of food poisoning. Many of these poisons are routinely sprayed on the foods we will eat before they are even shown to be "necessary." This is done in order to "just be on the *safe* side" and completely eliminate the risk of a *poor quality* harvest.[13] Everyone who is familiar with modern agriculture is aware that pesticides and other farm chemicals are misused in violation of both the letter as well as the spirit of the law. The extent of these violations is unknown, but violations can only be encouraged by the existing lack of concern for their enforcement.

8. Consequently, I see no way for food consumers to really be on the safe side except if they read labels carefully and avoid all chemical additives. If you have or can rent some land, you might consider growing your own healthful food. Legal changes—especially as regards routine testing procedures—are desperately needed. Our legislators will not confront these powerful chemical, food-processing, and agricultural interests, however, unless the public demands it.

Insofar as they have facilitated the entry of more women into the organized work force, technological change and specialization have played a key role in these dietary changes. Since 1970, Americans have been spending more money for additive-rich processed, convenience, snack, and franchised foods than for fresh foods.[14] Isn't it time we got back to basics and listened to the Bengali? Food is basic: it's the most important thing in life. Can you afford to wait for, and do you really need to await, the proof that may come only after decades of debate in order to realize that a daily ration of one-fifth of an ounce of chemical additives represent a ridiculously reckless and unnecessary threat to your health? Certainly all of us can avoid processed and overly sweet and salted foods. Whatever solution we reach, logic requires that we return to the viewpoint that the food we eat is our most basic necessity. Food selection based on America's present principles of convenience, taste, and eye appeal is clearly absurd. Cooking is very important, and we miss our old-fashioned cooks more than we ever realized we might. When we look at the role of homemaker, we find similar evidence of how much these traditional services of women are presently missed.

By definition we included the two quite different services of child raising and all the household services except cooking under the category of home-making. Throughout the remainder of this discussion, we shall focus solely on the child-raising role. The household services included under the category of homemaking have been largely replaced by machines, just as machines have eliminated the physical element from most of men's work. Vacuum cleaners, washers, dryers, oil furnaces, sewing machines, etc. seem to be adequate substitutes for this category of women's traditional services. It is ironic and sad, however, that machine substitution has progressed to the point that we now find it necessary to build special machines to help us get the physical exercise we need to keep fit. How degrading it is to enter one of New York City's "health clubs" and behold your brothers and sisters running, pushing, and pulling on a maze of stainless steel contrivances in the windowless light. But, alas, this is yet another problem; perhaps gardening could solve it too.

Finding adequate substitutes for the traditional child-raising function of women is quite a different matter than building machine substitutes for their other homemaking services. In this regard, it might again be helpful to develop a historical perspective. From our most primitive state up until the advent of the industrial revolution, most children spent most of their days living and working with both of their parents. Initially, most families lived off the land; then later they farmed it. There were no clocks to regulate them, and weather conditions provided many occasions on which parents and children had little else to do but play and relate with one another. The factory whistle that ushered in the industrial revolution and subjected people to the tyranny of the clock was no less easily accepted in England than it is today in the developing nations.

Children lost at least their father to the factory and its rigid schedule for most of the day. When he returned home exhausted, he probably growled at them and collapsed for too short a night of sleep. The recent acceptance of women into the work force has now robbed many children of their mothers as well as their fathers. In many families both parents now come home tired, snap at their children and each other, eat their highly processed convenience foods, and pass out relating to their color TV sets. Many of them welcome their kids leaving the house so that they can get some peace and quiet. Of course, it can be much better as well as worse than this, but it stands to reason that if both parents are working, they'll have less time and less energy to spend on their children. It cannot be otherwise.

Since around 1940, therefore, an increasingly larger percentage of our families have chosen to devote more of their time to earning money and less time to child raising. Since our children have been getting less attention, parent-child relationships as well as our children's development, values, and future behavior as adults are affected. We might well ask if we've used our time wisely? Have Americans acted responsibly toward their children, or have they been wrong to trade additional time for more money? Let's see if our social statistics can help us answer these questions.

Earlier we learned that during the period 1941 to 1972, the average American's real income (after adjustment for inflation) increased by 109 percent.[15] We also learned that the average industrial work week was 40.6 hours both in 1941 and in 1972.[16] And we saw that whereas the percentage of working women with no children under the age of eighteen increased by 36.6 percent, those working women with children under the age of six increased by 134.6 percent during the period 1950 to 1972.[17] That is, despite the fact that our real income more than doubled, we continued to work just as hard and a much, much larger percentage of our women—especially those with infant children—entered the organized work force. This tremendous increase in real wealth is reflected in a number of significant ways. The percentage of families living in substandard housing declined from 48.6 percent in 1940 to 7.4 percent in 1970.[18] The percentage of persons twenty to twenty-four years old with at least four years of high school education climbed from 26.8 percent in 1940 to 82.7 percent in 1972.[19] The percentage of eighteen- to twenty-four-year-olds in college jumped from 7.3 to 23.2 percent during this period.[20] And the percentage of total personal income spent on food dropped from 29.1 percent in 1940 to 19.8 percent in 1972.[21] Clearly Americans became better housed, much better educated, and no longer needed to spend as large a percentage of their paychecks on the bare necessities of life. We became, as Professor Galbraith has termed us, the *affluent society.*

However, during this same interval of time in which America, which was already the world's most wealthy nation, more than redoubled its material wealth, some surprising social changes occurred. By 1972 the rates per 100,000 of population for violent crimes stood at the following percentages of their 1940 levels: murder, 135 percent; robbery, 336 percent; aggravated assault, 381 percent; and forcible rape, 406 percent.[22] And lest you assume we're talking only about city problems, these increases in violent crimes occurred across the board in American communities of every size category. In 1972 the rates per 100,000 of population for violent crimes by community size stood at the following percentages of their 1960 levels: under 10,000, 427 percent (the largest increase for any size of community); 10,000 to 25,000, 349 percent; 25,000 to 50,000, 381 percent; 50,000 to 100,00, 310 percent; 100,000 to 250,000, 326 percent; and over 250,000 in population , 340 percent.[23] Furthermore, in 1972 deaths per 100,000 of population from cirrhosis of the liver, which usually results from alcholism, were 173 percent of their level in 1940.[24]

And both the legal and illegal drug cultures had shot up from virtually nothing in 1940 to multibillion-dollar businesses in 1972. *Simplistic arguments that attribute crime and social malaise to poverty, overcrowding, and ignorance, therefore cannot explain these developments.*

In attempting to interpret these figures we must consider the possibility that they may be directly related to America's relative neglect of its children. Social values and mores are learned from parents and peers. Since 1940, parents have had less time and energy to spend passing these values on to their daughters and sons. Peer group influence has increased in significance while parental influence has declined. Insofar as our children have been raised with less parental input, we have moved somewhat closer to the kibbutz system with the very important difference that we have not replaced our parents with full-time professional child raisers. It is fully possible, as well as consistent with our statistics on divorce, that our young people are experiencing greater difficulty in being intimate, in committing themselves, in finding fulfillment in deep one-to-one relationships as Dr. Bruno Bettleheim has found among kibbutz children.[25] Dr. Herbert Kendin's conclusions based on extensive research conducted during the sixties and early seventies and published in his most recent book, *The Age of Sensation,* present a very sobering, if not frightening, portrait of the psychological outlook of our young people today.[26] There are so many possible consequences that might result from less parental attention.

Are our children finding it more difficult to love others because many of them have felt unloved and therefore don't really love themselves, which is where loving really begins? That is, do more of them feel they're a burden, feel unloved, unworthy of love, or just plain alone in a world in which they feel nobody cares? Do they conclude, therefore, that it's also foolish to care? How many of our young people are pushed by loneliness and relative emotional emptiness into untenable marriages? How does our family life change when both parents are working, and how does this affect our children's conception of and expectations about marriage? What happens to children whose parents both work when the family moves and they are cut off from their peers on whom they rely heavily for personal contact and involvement? What happens to our children, to ourselves, and how we interact with one another when accelerating technological change makes change itself the only permanent element in our physical environment?[27] What happens to the way human beings view themselves, and through themselves other human beings, under circumstances like these?

While it's nearly impossible to identify and prove the specific significance of social statistics like these, it is clear that our society has not been blessed as fully with happiness as with affluence. Would we not be kidding ourselves to pretend that our reduced time commitment to our children was not probably largely responsible for the deterioration we've witnessed in these social indicators? Can our society afford the masochistic consequences that might be the result of such a pretense? Individuals are the separate reeds of which the social basket is made up; its strength depends on theirs, and we must redirect our attention to their more careful cultivation. We must again heed the Bengali and get back to basics. How? What changes can be undone? What potentially adverse future changes can be avoided?

Few will wish to obstruct technological change or impede the development of larger markets because these developments are cost-saving, and will thus continue to augment our real wealth. Technological change and larger markets will therefore be part of the reality with which we'll have to cope in the future. Among other things, this will probably mean that more of us will be transferred from location to location by our employers as more and more firms and institutions become national and international in scope. Faced then with the almost certain prospect of even less permanence in our lives tomorrow, doesn't it appear that we could benefit more from closer human contact than from still more material wealth in the future? People may be the only possible source of permanence in tomorrow's environment. Isn't it time we opted once for people instead of more material wealth?

Women's, Men's, and Children's Liberation Are Inseparable
Our arguments now bring us logically to the need for men's liberation. We've seen that the traditional services of women are absolutely essential to our physical health and emotional happiness. This is why the widely held view that women represent our most important untapped natural resource is both untrue and ridiculous. It's untrue because it implies that women have traditionally produced little of value, have been mostly idle, or have spent their energy on tasks of small importance. It's ridiculous because the facts clearly reveal that many women are already working two jobs. If women are to escape the double yoke of two jobs that women's liberation alone is bringing them, it must become just as acceptable for men to assume the traditional roles of women as it has become for women to assume the traditional roles of men. The peril to us all lies in the reality that wives are abandoning their traditional roles before husbands have become prepared to assume them. We can give the primary responsibility of raising happy families to either sex; or we can devise some formula whereby it can be shared; but it's just plain foolhardy to assume that this traditional role of women has lost any of its significance. This role must again be filled if we are to liberate our children from the neglect they now experience. Women have not been our drones—their services have always been of at least equal importance. Forcing our daughters and sons to raise themselves will not produce the results sought by any of us.

Once both men and women have become liberated, deciding who will act as the primary homemaker can become a matter of personality, training, and

Stereo-typing.

individual preference. We have no idea how many men might prefer to accept the role of homemaker if society could accept them in it. But as long as men view accepting such a role as a threat to their masculinity, women by and large will also remain unliberated. If you think about it, you already know a number of families that would probably be better off if the parents switched roles. There may be just as many men as women who are miscast in our stereotyped sexual roles. Some men may prefer working with children; some of them may have wives who could earn more money for the family because they are better trained, more aggressive, etc.; and a few of these husbands might find the responsibilities of homemaking more challenging and rewarding.

The comparisons that are drawn between career work and being a house-wife are usually less than fair. They typically pit the position of a woman who is well along in her career with one who has screaming infant children to care for. No mention is made of what career women, or career men for that matter, must go through to get what are considered glamorous positions and how few of them ever make it. These comparisons also overlook the fact that the housewife has the advantages of a flexible schedule, can visit and chat with her friends frequently, has no boss, no politics to play, and that her efforts will be remembered whereas those of the career woman will be forgotten almost the day she leaves her job.

Mention is also never made of the challenge involved in being a good homemaker. Being a moderate success in one's career is almost a certainty if you just apply yourself. Not so if you're a homemaker. You're dealing with a far more complex product when you're trying to raise healthy, well-adjusted children. There are so many subtle judgments to make—you can be too strict as well as too lenient, too protective or not protective enough, too this and too that *ad nauseum.* If your life depended on you're doing a satisfactory job, wouldn't you consider it a safer bet to be a career person rather than a homemaker?

Unfortunately our distorted sense of values is not limited to the importance we've attached to "women's work." Parallels that are easier to track and identify exist in the field of education. Most of us respond to social pressure and by and large swallow our society's values. In our competitive society that means that the more gifted will aspire to and successfully occupy the positions that are considered prestigious. When we kid ourselves about the importance of the role of homemaker, we're being just as foolish as we've been in slighting the importance of teaching. Do you realize that if you attempt to write a textbook for college students your publisher will ask you to use a ninth-grade vocabularly and to avoid three-syllable words wherever possible! If you're in college, you've just come out of our homes and schools. How do you feel about America's commitment to children and education? Have we become, or are we becoming, so concerned about present gratifications that we're losing the will and discipline needed to provide for our children's and our own future?

It seems that it is time to elevate the prestige of the roles of both homemaker and teacher. We need to tell our daughters that the role of homemaker is important and most challenging. We need to make homemaking just as acceptable a role for our sons. What we've done instead is assign a second full-time role to most women, made those who've opted for homemaking feel like cop-outs, and assumed that homemaking is unimportant. The heartbreaking symptoms of our distorted system of values are visible even if we refuse to recognize their origin. Happy people don't commit violent crimes, nor do they rely on alcohol and drugs. Unhappy people, on the other hand, may seek happiness in material wealth; and failing to find it, they may turn to these escapes.

Of course, every society, despite the state of its general health, will have some problems. When a society, such as our own, experiences a period of unparalleled rapid change, however, it's much more likely to lose its perspective. This is really no different from what happens to you and me when our lives turn into a whirlwind of exhausting events. Things happen so fast we hardly have time to catch our breath, and we don't have time to think or reflect. In the whirlwind we lose sight of many details, and the fine points that often connect these events in important simultaneous bonds of causality become especially blurred. Then, as when we make our own career plans, it's time to step outside the whirlwind; objectively evaluate its causes; and ponder and project its probable future course. Isn't it time for us to rest, reflect, and connect?

Some Advice for Men and Women Who Plan to Be Homemakers

I have some personal advice that I would give anyone making a career decision. Question 31 of the interview questionnaire reads as follows: "Imagine for a moment that you were given a fresh start in the game of life. With the benefit of the wisdom, knowledge, and experience you've gleaned from your years, what would you do differently and why?" If I were to answer this question that is designed to help you learn from the most important mistakes of others, I would say that I would begin playing my own game—that is, acting upon my own convictions and doing my own thing—even earlier than I did. One of my few regrets is that I responded to the social pressures of others to the extent that I did for as long as I did. To answer the second part of this question regarding why I would do this, I would play my own game sooner and more fully because it's really the only honest game I believe we can play. When we play our own game we're being true to ourselves, we feel freer, we are happier, and we generally do a better job because we're being responsible to and for ourselves. This advice is especially to the point for those of you who plan to be homemakers, because in our present world with its often distorted values, you are likely to need a special inner strength of conviction in order to overcome the barbs of those around you. For you it may be equally helpful to focus on the reality that life's just too short and irreversible to play anyone's game but your own.

Those of you who choose to be homemakers should realize that you have a very necessary, important, potentially challenging and rewarding job that many have done very poorly in the past. Don't rely on how it was done in your parents' home. Get several good books on each of the subjects of nutrition, child psychology, and child rearing and study them carefully. Approach your duties with imagination so as to stimulate both your children and yourself. Make an effort to keep abreast of what's going on in the world, especially that of your spouse, so that you can continue to relate to him or her on that important aspect of his or her life. Finally, realize that your products are your family's health, emotional happiness, and the stimulation of your children to want to understand, learn about, love, and enjoy their world. Since there's nothing more important that anyone could be charged with, be proud and politely straighten out any fuzzy-headed thinker who believes otherwise. When a society ignores the development of its youth, it has written its suicide note and it cannot be otherwise.

SOME PRACTICAL ADVICE FOR WOMEN WHO PLAN TO ENTER THE ORGANIZED WORK FORCE

Nothing I've said should be interpreted as meaning that women belong in the home. All of us deserve to find as much happiness as we possibly can in this world, which means that we should do our own thing. Even those women and men who choose to opt for the full-time homemaking role will probably want to enter the work force for several periods during their lives. If for no other reason, this experience would help make them aware of and sensitive to the pressures faced by their spouses and others in the organized work force. Such exposure would also enable them to develop a more realistic perspective regarding what they are missing by working at home, which might significantly affect their attitudes toward homemaking and their effectiveness in this role.

Because we are in a transitionary period in which sexual roles are in the process of being ripped down, circumstances are continually changing and this makes it difficult to give advice of lasting value. The best and most timely advice on how to deal with the immediate problems of working women can be obtained directly from the women you interview in positions similar to those you're interested in. In addition, I'd like to offer some advice to women on how I sincerely believe they might improve their positions. It's important, however, that you understand my position and my approach.

My approach is pragmatic, that is, I'm interested in results, not rhetoric. This approach is designed to help women as individuals, not as members of an organization. I do not advocate confrontation, therefore, because I cannot possibly imagine how it could be generally successful if used by single individuals in dealing with those they intend to work with. My approach begins by looking behind the situation in an attempt to gain an analytical understanding of the attitudes, forces, feelings, or whatever that cause, set up, or determine the situation. Once these are understood, it may only be necessary to unlock the window rather than knock it out in order to cool off. This approach has the added advantage that it minimizes the probability that you'll get cut by your own flying glass. Let's analyze the position of women in 1976, and let's be very honest about it.

If you're not a woman, try to imagine for a while that you are. If you're realistic, concerned about your position, and wish to improve it, you must face some unpleasant realities. These are among the more important realities that affect your position as a woman:

1. Men have most of the power in our society: they control almost everything. This is the basic reality the women's movement is working to overcome.

2. Most people, which includes most men, fear change. One of the prime reasons given for the fact that incumbent Presidents almost always win reelection is the fact that people at least know what to expect from the incumbent. They're afraid to change Presidents because the change might be for the worse. For the same reasons, many men and some women also fear women's liberation. Many of their reasons are vague, undefined, and very individualistic. However, they all boil down basically to fear. A general fear of the unknown, of change, and—only in the case of some men—a fear of the loss of their particular position.

3. Although women make up more than half of society, they are not prepared at present to assume an equal role in its direction. This is a plain and obvious truth that reflects more than anything else the past as well as the present position that society has kept women in. The majority of women alive today are not prepared by tradition, preparation, or experience to assume the roles men now hold. Many women are not even presently inclined to assume these roles, which is one of the realities women's consciousness-raising groups are working hard to overcome.

If these are the most important present realities, what can be concluded from them? Among other things:

1. The assumption of an equal amount of power and responsibility by women will require time. It will be a process rather than an event. Large numbers of women really only first entered the work force in the 1940s. Today they already make up 40 percent of it. The self-image and aspirations of young women have changed and are now leading them into every possible line of endeavor. Their brothers accept this far better than their fathers. A certain amount of patience is required during this period of transition.

2. Since men have the bulk of the power, women are consequently in a relatively poor bargaining position. Power, therefore, is what women need to overcome the by-your-leave relationship they presently have vis-à-vis men in general. Weaker nations gain power by aligning with each other and with those nations that are already powerful. The experiences of women are already, and will continue to be, parallel. Through collectively joining together, women have become legally entitled to the equality that has always been their moral right. While absolutely essential, especially in these early stages, women will need more than this collective power base in order to gain the ultimate equality they seek.

Power within organizations lies in the hands of the individuals who direct them. In the final analysis, this type of individual power is shared through individual alliances with those who have it to share. The collective type of power has already proven much more effective in getting women on the team than it has in getting them on the first string. Ultimately, therefore, real power will be shared only by those women who can successfully form alliances, as individuals, with the men who are presently in a position to share meaningful power with whomever they elect to share it with. This is why women will have to rely increasingly on cooperation rather than confrontation in the future.

As a practical matter, a man's bad will can stop a woman's advance in scores of ways it would be difficult to prove were discriminatory. Legal remedies, especially in individual suits, are too slow, expensive, and unpleasant. Can you imagine working for a boss you had beaten in court or, for that matter, seeking a position elsewhere after you had won such a case? Women have had many male sympathizers in the past: this has proved to be not only a successful tradition but a far more intelligent individual approach.

3. Fear very often blocks women's access to the power they need in order to enjoy equality of opportunity. I am convinced that some women haven't moved ahead faster because their actions have intimidated men to the point that many men have decided it's only sensible and even fair to fight back. Since men have had the power, their blocks have often been successful; and this has left these women face to face with a new, still higher wall.

While almost all the demands of the women's liberationists are fully justified, their expectations are frequently unrealistic in the context of human nature. The result is frequently still-higher walls. Perhaps there's no other way for a movement to initially be taken seriously. In any case, however, this is not a very successful approach with people you hope to work with. Perhaps I can make this point without involving women at all.

As I write this book, my time is about equally divided between Jonestown, Pennsylvania (population 900), and New York City (population 8,000,000). The difference in population size between these communities, however, is dwarfed by the much, much larger difference in the mentality of my neighbors in both places. It is literally a case of having your feet in two different worlds. The very same approaches, arguments, and customs that are effective with my friends in New York are often most ineffective with my friends around Jonestown. Sometimes I act very foolishly when I forget that if I am dealing with these country people, I simple must take their background into consideration. They're different. They're different, and they're beautiful in different ways. But are they scared of things they don't understand and haven't experienced—big cities, Blacks, Jews? Not all of them, but many of them.

Well, I used to moralize and fight with these people about their contemptible attitudes towards Blacks and Jews, but it got me nowhere. I only became isolated. So I experimented with laughter and drew some comic comparisons instead. At least I stayed in communication with them, never retreating from my position, but making it more understandable and palatable to them. Gradually my identity shifted from that of an outsider, whom they could ignore, to that of a part-time insider whose differentness was at least communicated and tolerated. They know I don't share their fears and prejudices, and I've even managed to change some of their attitudes, but only because I changed my techniques to accommodate them. From these experiences I've learned the importance of investigating the backgrounds of differences and the value of patience, understanding, humor, and the maintenance of a dialogue in overcoming such differences.

I believe that women's liberationists could likewise learn from their own experiences. Most of them must have fathers and uncles who are male chauvinists. These are the very people the movement must cope with. How are you doing with them? Are they the malicious bastards who are oppressing women, or are they simply the loving dads and uncles who are innocently and unthinkingly passing on the attitudes of their fathers and grandmothers? What is their intent? How can you change them, how much, how fast, and what price is it worth? Must we not sometimes bridle our impetuous drive for unreasonably rapid social change lest we act masochistically as well as sadistically? Who is the enemy, the oppressor? Your father? Men? A man? Me? Society? The acquiescent women who preceded you on this earth? Do we need guilty parties or a consciousness-raising party?

In Part I we detailed how "we become our environment" and I am, of course, a reforming male chauvinist. Let me tell you what it's like to be progressing through that metamorphosis. You wake up one day and you say, "Women really do have a point. They're right. I'm on their side. Right on!" You're more than a little proud and perhaps even self-righteous about being so aware, fair, and otherwise enlightened and good. Good guys like you deserve to be acknowledged and thanked for their support. But instead they jump all over you as they quite correctly point out that "You've got a long way to go, brother."

If you endure these criticisms, you try harder and harder. After a while you begin to realize the extent of your male chauvinism—how instinctive and pervasive it really is. Ultimately, you actually do become sensitized and begin to ask yourself, "Am I being chauvinistic?" It's just like changing the counterproductive attitudes and habits you become aware of through psychoanalysis. You become aware of them intellectually years before you're able to fully incorporate them emotionally. Unconsciously, through your actions, you fear that your lingering chauvinism, like your shadow, will follow you around the rest of your life—a source of embarrassment, nagging evidence of your imperfectness, and a tattletale of your age.

In summary, I believe it is primarily fear you must deal with—fear, a general feeling of awkwardness, embarrassment, uneasiness, and guilt. Believe me, as a reforming chauvinist it's very difficult to deal with the changing role of women. How do you expect it would be to adjust if you've had two, three, or four more decades of chauvinism behind you than I had? It's probably much smarter to work hardest on influencing younger men who can adjust more easily and who will be able to change many more attitudes during their lifetime. But whatever you do, don't push to the point of building higher walls as I once did in Pennsylvania. Bearing in mind everything that I have said (lest I be misunderstood), consider the following general techniques that I believe will help women overcome the fear that blocks them from the power that might gain them equality of opportunity.

1. *Expect to Be Feared.* Try not to react personally to the responses this produces unless you're sure such responses are directed at you personally. If you find yourself in what was until recently a man's world, expect that you may be treated initially more as a symbol than as a person. Regardless of what many of these men may say and do, with a symbol of a woman on what they consider their turf, they may feel threatened and resentful of your presence or be just plain intimidated, nervous, and uncomfortable because you're there.
2. *Don't Remain Isolated.* Fear is dissolved by communication and exposure, through which you will lose your status as a symbol and become a person. Without demeaning yourself or your sex, remain sensitive to the feelings of the men with whom you're working. Go about correcting their chauvinisms in a firm but understanding manner, not because you owe it to them but because such a manner will best serve your own interests. If you're a person who can employ humor tactfully, use this technique to lessen the fear and the distance that separates you from them.
3. *Be Consistent about Chauvinism.* Reject chauvinism's "positive" benefits as well as its negative ones. Arrangements must always be mutually beneficial, otherwise they will be viewed as exploitation by one of the parties and they won't be respected. If you survey men about their attitudes on women's liberation, you frequently get the complaint, "Women want to have their cake and eat it too. They want equal pay, but they don't volunteer to share the cost of dinner, theater tickets, etc." They're right; that's exploitation. Availing yourself of the "positive" benefits of chauvinism won't gain you respect or the internal feeling of independence you need to be emotionally liberated. Undoubtedly the most irrational move that has

been made by the women's movement has been to allow it to gain the connotation—and indeed sometimes even depict it explicitly—of being something very one-sided from which men have almost nothing to gain and a lot to lose. That's a rather unintelligent way to go about promoting anything and especially so in this case, given the existing sexual balance of power. We've seen that men's liberation is itself dependent upon women's liberation, yet who has been loudly proclaiming this reality?

4. *Form Sincere, Mutually Beneficial Alliances with Men.* Although this technique is explained here in the context of a woman to man relationship, it should be used by men and women alike in any relationships they have with others. This technique, which is based on the human need and desire to feel needed and wanted, is an especially effective way to become an "individual" in the eyes of the men (or women) who may fear you. This two-step procedure should be used whenever you have a sincere need for advice or help with a problem. First approach one of your male colleagues with a sincere request for advice and guidance on a matter you're sure he can provide these on. Second, return later with proof that you've profited from his guidance and ask him to check your application of the knowledge you've gotten from him. Then thank him, identify your areas of expertise, and offer to help him in these areas if he should ever need it.

By this technique you've made him a proud teacher, yourself a grateful pupil (as well as a person), and you've formed a potential partnership. Now he too is interested in your success because he has invested in your development. And your competence will have increased in two ways in his eyes. You've learned from him, and you've demonstrated good judgment and wisdom by seeking his advice. Partnerships like this are what hold an organization together, make people friends as well as business colleagues, give them a sense of importance and a feeling that they matter. Form a lot of these alliances. If you have these kinds of partnerships with men, these men will also help you receive fair treatment from your employer.

As has so often been the case, what we've been discussing in this chapter reverts back to our humanness, takes us back to where we began in Chapter Three. Point 4 above is not a cynical trick to help us use other people, but simply an acknowledgement of a human psychological reality. Each of us needs to feel needed and appreciated, needs to feel that we make a difference in the lives of others. Remembering and applying this simple fact will enrich your life as well as the lives of those whom you allow to help you. It's very much like good and beautiful sex itself. It's giving, it's taking, and it's sharing with someone all at the same time. There are too few opportunities like these in our lives, no matter how many fortune places in our path. Please, don't deny yourself the benefits and pleasures of the powerful tools of "psychology."

NOTE ONE

HOW TO WRITE YOUR RESUME

Resumes offer classic examples of the limitations of conventional job-finding mechanisms and attest to the degradation one is subject to as a paper person. The paper people who appear on resumes are intangible, faceless, without dignity or personality, and devoid of a sense of humor. They are utterly defenseless in the clutches of the typically overwhelmed paper shufflers whose survival often depends upon eliminating as many of them as they can as quickly as they can. An indication of just how carefully resumes are evaluated is suggested by reading one of the most successful books on job changing: its very first suggestions are that you use colored and odd-sized paper in order to capture the reader's attention, and it promises greatly improved results if you use these and other gimmicks.[1]

Nevertheless, a resume is sometimes required, and you must learn how to write one. But do remember the inherent limitations of resumes and try to avoid using them. If you must use a resume, use it only to get into an interview where you can smile, where your eyes can reveal that you have a sense of humor, and you can ask intelligent, memorable questions. In an interview you know how to handle yourself and you can be flexible. On paper your statements are likely to be viewed as too weak or too arrogant, too long or too general, etc., and thus even if you are one of the lucky paper people who gets read, you still won't be able to really explain and present yourself.

What to Remember When You Write Your Resume

1. *Resumes are never hired.* The objective in writing a resume is to create just enough interest to gain you an invitation to a personal interview where the job will be offered to you if it's going to be offered to you at all. Your resume, like a piece of bait, can only be helpful in getting your employer to bite, not in actually landing the job. All you want to do with your resume is hook your prospective employer's interest.

2. *Determine what facts about you are relevant.* Your first task in writing a more effective resume is to ascertain the needs of your prospective employer. Ask yourself what the holder of the job must be able to do. Then determine how your training, achievements, and experiences indicate that you are prepared or ultimately capable of handling such work.

3. *Project only your relevant abilities.* Keep your resume short—no more

than one page—and include only those things about you that will be relevant to your employer. Bear in mind that those who read your resume are likely to be looking for excuses to eliminate it. The more superfluous material you include, the harder it will be to find the relevant points and the greater will be their temptation to discard it. As they skim over your resume, they will be more impressed by an uninterrupted string of relevant points than by the same number of relevant points interrupted by superfluous material that is likely to irritate them and reveal poor judgment on your part. Decide therefore, what kind of picture you want to project and maintain a short, clean focus. In order to do this, you may have to prepare a slightly different resume for each of the jobs you wish to be considered for.

4. *Maintain a light, airy, uncrowded appearance.* Nothing will turn off your readers or make them feel more oppressively overburdened than solid print all over your resume. It's like a book without pictures, a house without windows—the psychological impact is deadening. Avoid it. The organization of your resume is flexible, but it must be logical. Things like your work experiences and education achievements should be listed in reverse chronological order because what you've done most recently will be of greater interest to your readers. Also avoid misspellings, erasures, and smudges because they may insult your reader's feelings of importance. Use good English so as to project your ability to communicate with the written and spoken word.

5. *Specific examples of the things you might want to project on your resume.*
   (a) Ability, experience, and training to deal with people, data, or things as the job requires these. Include part-time work experience.
   (b) Problem-solving and decision-making ability.
   (c) Leadership, responsibility, maturity, self-discipline. Have you held any offices, excelled in sports, etc.?
   (d) Ability to work with others.
   (e) Intelligence. Mention your grade point average if it's good, your average in the subjects of relevance to the job, scholastic awards, and scholarships.

6. *Other information.* The following information is typically included on a resume.
   (a) Personal data. Under this heading list your name, address, telephone number, age, height, weight, and marital status.
   (b) Education. List your degrees, where and when you got them, and your major course of study.
   (c) Other headings might include:
      (1) Occupational goals
      (2) Extracurricular activities
      (3) Work experience

These brief recommendations are specifically designed for students who have had little or no previous work experience. It is suggested that you consult your placement office personnel for additional help in organizing your resume. They will also be able to provide you with additional resume examples from which you will also be able to get helpful ideas. Resumes that you write after you've had some full-time work experience should: (1) project achievement by

---

RESUME

Cynthia May Smith   Home Address (after 6/76)
Williams Hall   421 West Palm Drive
Tulane University   Tampa, FL. 33606
New Orleans, LA. 70119   (813) 362-4453
(504) 865-4011

OCCUPATIONAL GOAL

Career position in accounting or quantitative business research.

EDUCATION

Tulane University, B.A., June 1976 Cum: 3.27 (4.00 maximum)

Major: Accounting
Minor: Mathematics

I received full tuition scholarships while at Tulane.

EXTRA CURRICULAR ACTIVITIES

Accounting Society
Math Club
Big Sister Program

WORK EXPERIENCE

Summer, 1975   Brubaker Accounting Associates, Bosier City, LA. Junior Accountant Trainee.

9/72-6/76   Mansfield Stores Inc., 241 South Street, New Orleans, LA. I have worked part time during the school year and full time during the summer for this firm since I began at Tulane. I was initially employed as a bookkeeper, and I am now working on entry-level accounting work.

1970-1972   Librarian's Assistant, Tampa Public School Number 274.

PERSONAL DATA

Age: 22   Health: Excellent   Marital Status: Single

(Note: This resume projects a studious, quantitatively oriented, introverted type of person who is well suited to working with data in a research capacity.)

revealing some hard facts regarding your career accomplishments that are relevant to your prospective employer's needs; and (2) project capability by presenting evidence that your work experiences have helped you develop valuable skills needed by your prospective employer. Finally, the longer you've worked, the less emphasis you should place on your academic accomplishments, which will be less important than your career achievements.

```
                              RESUME


        Ronald T. Luciotti
        Phi Gamma Delta
        University of California
        Berkeley, CA.  94720
        (415) 397-4635
        Home Address (after 6/76)
        281 Greenwood Road
        Seattle, WA.  9810?
        (206) 624-0200


        OCCUPATIONAL GOAL

                Career in industrial sales


        EDUCATION

                University of California at Berkeley
                Degree:  Bachelor of Science, '76
                Major:  Mechanical Engineering
                Minor:  Psychology
                Grades:  Average to good


        EXTRACURRICULAR ACTIVITIES

                Vice President and Social Chairman, Phi Gamma Delta fraternity
                Captain, swimming team
                Student Council delegate (3 terms)
                Track team


        WORK EXPERIENCE

                Summer, 1975  Salesman, Encyclopedia Britannica, Berkeley, CA.

                Summer, 1974  Sales, Windward China Company, Seattle,WA.

                Summer, 1973  Receptionist/Cashier, Host Resort Hotel,
                              Beaver Falls, PA.

                Summers       Counselor and swimming instructor, Camp Onita,
                1970-1972     Moscow, OR.


        PERSONAL DATA

                Age:  22  Height: 6'1"  Weight:  190  Marital Status: Single


        (Note:  This resume projects a well-rounded, people-oriented, extro-
        verted type of person with a technical background that is ideal for
        industrial sales, despite his lackluster grade point average.)
```

NOTE TWO

WHAT YOU CAN DO WHEN THE JOB MARKET IS A DISASTER AREA AS IN 1976

When the job market is in a shambles, despite your very best efforts you may be unable to find work in your chosen career field. Even if this happens and you are forced to accept a bread-and-butter type of job just to tide you over until better times, you will probably still be able to be a little choosy about what you accept. With a little imagination and forethought, you may even be able to turn disaster to your advantage, perfect your people skills instead of just marking time in the unemployment lines, get a better fix on your proper career niche, and even make a lot of sympathetic and potentially helpful friends in your career field. No, we're not going to suggest that you go out and "streak" around in your career field. That's not how we recommend that you use exposure, visibility, and mobility to land a better job.

Eight percent unemployment among a workforce of 93 million means that nearly eight million people are out of work, and that really does seem like the proportions of a disaster. But before we throw up our hands in hopelessness, let's look at that statement from a different perspective and review some additional facts as well. If we turn our first statement around it reads: 92 percent employed and 85 million people with paychecks to spend. That's a lot of people and buying power. An army of salespeople is needed to convince those 85 million people to part with their paychecks. Many salespeople work strictly on a commission basis but, in any case, there's one thing that all salespeople must develop—people skills. Furthermore, there are still a lot of employed people working in your career field, and they are still buying the professional and other products and services they need. Let's see if we can assemble these facts in an imaginative way that might help you further your long-run career objectives as well as satisfy your immediate need for bread and butter on the table.

Let's assume for a moment that you are employed in a sales position selling some product or service to the professionals who work in your chosen career field. From your perspective as a person who hopes to find a job in this career field, what advantages does such a sales position offer? Clearly, such a job offers you *exposure* to a wide range of potential employers, insight into the variety of subspecializations practiced in your field, and a firsthand knowledge and understanding of the broad range of working environments in which you might later pursue your career. This exposure would certainly enable you to get a better fix on the career niche you feel would be ideal for you. In addition to making you *visible* to many of your potential employers, such a position would enable you to form friendships with dozens of colleagues in your field. And finally, such a job would enable you to develop and perfect those all-important *people skills* that will stand you in good stead no matter what kind of work you pursue later in life. (Please note that sales jobs are by no means merely bread-and-butter jobs in most instances. They are only being considered as such in this example in which we are implicitly assuming that you are not interested in selling as a career.) Thus it is clear that a sales job that brings you in contact with those who are working in your career field would be far superior to just any temporary bread-and-butter job. But what are your chances of landing such a job?

Although you may not realize it, you would be a rather attractive candidate for the sales position we've just outlined. First of all, you already understand a great deal about your field and you have a sincere interest in it. This understanding and your interest would give you an immediate rapport with those on whom you would be calling. Because of your background, you might have more insight into the problems and needs of these people than would most of the other candidates who might be interested in such a sales position. Thus, potentially you might be a more effective sales representative. And if you're willing to work primarily or exclusively on a commission basis, employers would risk little by giving you a try even though most of them would correctly assume that you would not stick with the job for very long. You might find it easiest to get a job representing a supplier who has not yet entered the particular area you live in, because this would not cause any conflicts with the firm's already established sales representatives. Yes, you definitely would be an attractive, low-risk candidate. With a little imagination you might "create" your own bread-and-butter job with much much more promise than your other alternatives—for example, driving a taxi, doing secretarial work, tending bar or waiting on tables in the local watering hole.

Thus, we see that the strategic principles of Position Analysis can help us out even in a pinch when our options have been reduced to merely choosing between bread-and-butter jobs. If you can't get a sales job in your career field, you should nevertheless consider sales positions in other fields. Any sales position will enable you to develop your people skills and keep in contact with others through whom you may learn of something better.

NOTE THREE

HOW TO MEASURE PROFITABILITY AND GROWTH RATES

The one thing that is always needed to go into business is money. With enough money, any business can buy or lease the buildings and equipment, pay for the materials, and hire the human talents needed to produce and market its products. The one thing that is always sought from a business is profits. Since most investors are interested in maximizing the amount of profits they earn from their investments, investors will tend to put their money into those businesses that they believe will return the most profits.

Profits are defined as the total dollar sales of the business less all the costs incurred in producing its products and selling them to its customers. Profits, however, must be related to the amount of money that is risked in the business venture and to the length of time the money is invested in the business. The term *profitability,* otherwise known as the *profit rate* (always expressed on an annual basis), does precisely this. It relates annual profits after taxes (also called "net income after taxes") to the amount of money the firm's owners have invested in the firm (also called "total shareholders' equity"). By doing this, that is by calculating a profit rate, a universal standard is created that can be used to compare and rank the attractiveness of all business ventures. The higher an industry's or a firm's profit rate, the greater the return per dollar invested in that industry or firm and thus the more content investors will be to keep their money invested in such ventures and to invest still more money in them.

From your point of view as a potential employee, the higher a firm's profit rate, the more assurance you have that the firm will continue in business and thus continue to need your labor services and be willing and able to pay you well for them. Furthermore, the more profitable a firm is, the more likely it is to grow, and that means improved prospects for earlier promotion and advancement because your status as one of the firm's most experienced employees will advance more rapidly.

Profitability or the profit rate is measured as follows:

$$\text{Profitability or the profit rate} = \frac{\text{Net income after taxes}}{\text{Total shareholders' equity}}$$

If you are considering employment with a publicly held company, these figures will be published in its annual report to its shareholders, which you can get from the person interviewing you or from the company itself.

Finally, in Chapter Six we learned that some industries like the capital goods industries have very good and very bad years whereas other industries like the luxury goods industries have good but not spectacular years every year. The only meaningful way to compare the profitability of firms in different industries, therefore, is to compute average profit rates over a longer period of, for example, five or more years for both firms.

A firm's size is most typically measured in terms of its annual dollar sales. A firm's rate of growth is computed very simply by expressing its year-to-year change in sales as a percentage of its previous year's sales.

$$\text{Annual rate of growth} = \frac{\text{This year's sales} - \text{last year's sales}}{\text{Last year's sales}}$$

These figures can also be obtained from a publicly held corporation's annual reports to its stockholders. Privately held companies (those not required to publish their financial information because they have few shareholders) may also reveal their growth rates, but you will have no way of verifying the accuracy of the figures given you. If you could get information on the rate of growth of the specific division of the company you would be working for or information on the rate at which people are being added to the division in which you would be employed, this more specific information would be even more indicative of your future employment prospects than the firm's overall growth rate.

The rates at which selected industries are growing, projections of the demand for labor in various occupations, data on the number of graduates entering certain career fields, and training, apprenticeship, and some salary information by occupations can also be obtained from the U.S. Department of Labor. If you desire any information along these lines, you are asked to address a letter listing your specific requests and requirements to: Division of Occupational Outlook, Bureau of Labor Statistics, 441 G Street N.W., Washington, D.C. 20212.

- THE CAREER GAME
- CAREER STRATEGY TAPE LIBRARY
- PROFESSIONAL SEMINARS
- COLLEGE SEMINAR WORKSHOPS
- CAREER ADVANCEMENT SEMINARS
- SYNDICATED COLLEGE NEWSPAPER COLUMNS

NOTE FOUR

WHAT IS THE NATIONAL INSTITUTE OF CAREER PLANNING?

The National Institute of Career Planning is a private research organization founded in 1973 to develop and distribute career decision-making and advancement materials. Its products consist of: seventy hour-long career information audio cassette tapes (available in many high school and college guidance departments); books and pamphlets; video tapes; a syndicated column of career advice for college newspapers; professional seminars for high school and college guidance personnel; career advancement seminars held in New York City to help aspiring professionals plan their future promotions; and career decision-making seminar workshops for college students. These seminar workshops last several days and are held in various regional centers within the United States and Canada—usually during periods of college recess.

The Institute is represented on a regional basis by professionals in the fields of guidance and counseling and other qualified educational personnel. Individuals interested in learning more about the Institute's programs should address their inquiries to: NICP, 521 Fifth Avenue, New York, NY 10017.

The Impact of Commuting and Overtime on Workday Leisure Time
The Impact of Commuting and Overtime on Weekly Leisure Time
How Does Vacation Time Affect Annual Leisure Time?
The Leisure/Work Index: A Monitor of the Balance in Your Life

THE IMPACT OF COMMUTING, OVERTIME, AND VACATION TIME ON YOUR TIME MONEY

*When you can measure what you are
speaking about, and express it in numbers,
you know something about it . . .*

                    Lord Kelvin

This appendix focuses on the balance between the time you spend working on your career and the time you have left to spend on your non-career pursuits. The seven detailed tables that are presented demonstrate precisely how commuting time, overtime, and vacation time affect your leisure/work balance on a workday, weekly, and an annual basis.

The Impact of Commuting and Overtime on Workday Leisure Time

Conceptually, our total time income can be broken down into five categories or classifications based on how we spend it. These five categories are:

1. Sleeping time
2. Personal maintenance time—eating, grooming, errands
3. Working time
4. Commuting time—getting to and from work
5. Leisure Time

Since the first four categories represent mandatory uses of our time, our leisure time can be computed as the residual time income we have left after these necessary activities have been attended to. Several assumptions are required, however, before we can estimate the extent of our potential leisure time.

We shall assume that you sleep and work eight hours each workday (lunch is included in this time). We'll also assume that you spend two and a half hours each workday eating, dressing, and running errands. Finally, we'll include a one-way commute to work of fifteen minutes (a total of thirty minutes per day). At most, these assumptions leave you with 5 hours of leisure time each workday (see Table 4–1).

TABLE 4-1
HOW WE SPEND A WORKDAY

ACTIVITY	TIME (hours)	TIME (percent)
Sleeping	8.0	33.3
Working	8.0	33.3
Eating, grooming, errands[1]	2.5	10.5
Commuting	.5	2.1
Leisure time	5.0	20.8
	24.0	100.0

[1] This activity includes shopping, washing clothes, car and home maintenance, pet care, haircuts, doctor visits, etc.

TABLE 4-2
THE IMPACT OF COMMUTING ON WORKDAY LEISURE TIME

	(Maximum leisure: 5 hours)	
LENGTH OF ONE-WAY COMMUTE (*minutes*)	LEISURE TIME EXPENDED (*percent*)	LEISURE TIME REMAINING (*percent*)
None	−10.0[1]	110.0
5	− 6.7[1]	106.7
10	− 3.3[1]	103.3
15[2]	None	100.0
20	3.3	96.7
25	6.7	93.3
30	10.0	90.0
35	13.3	86.7
40	16.7	83.3
45	20.0	80.0
50	23.3	76.7
55	26.7	73.3
60	30.0	70.0
65	33.3	66.7
70	36.7	63.3
75	40.0	60.0
80	43.3	56.7
85	46.7	53.3
90	50.0	50.0
95	53.3	46.7
100	56.7	43.3
105	60.0	40.0
110	63.3	36.7
115	66.7	33.3
120	70.0	30.3

[1]These numbers are negative because less than the assumed 15 minutes of one-way commuting time has been spent getting to and from work. The last column on the right indicates that more than 100 percent of the potential leisure time remains in these instances.

[2]Fifteen minutes is the assumed minimum one-way base commute which serves as the standard for all comparisons. People having this commute are defined as having 100 percent of their maximum potential workday leisure time available after commuting.

It is impossible, of course, to make assumptions that are accurate for everyone. Rather low time estimates have been used; those needed by a well-organized, fast-working person. If it takes you longer than two and a half hours to eat, groom yourself, and run errands, you may wish to adjust these figures when you construct your own table. On the other hand, you might consider your more relaxed pace as one of the luxuries you purchase with your leisure time, in which case you need not adjust the table.

Few people, except those who work at home, enjoy less than a fifteen-minute one-way commute, which is why this figure was used as the minimum base commute. Some individuals claim they enjoy part of the time they spend commuting. They may wish to consider the time they spend socializing, playing cards, reading, etc. as part of their leisure time. These fortunate individuals may subtract the minutes they enjoy from their total commuting time. Their case is not typical of most Americans, however, 87 percent of whom drove to work in 1970.[1]

Table 4–2 reveals how your maximum potential workday leisure time of five hours is affected by longer and longer commutes. Similarly, Table 4–3 demonstrates how overtime working hours affect your potential workday leisure time. Both these tables express these effects in terms of the percentage of your leisure time that is spent and the percentage that remains after allowing for commuting and overtime. Table 4–3 can also be used to reveal the combined effects of commuting and overtime on leisure time. If this is your

TABLE 4-3
THE IMPACT OF OVERTIME ON WORKDAY LEISURE TIME

	(Maximum leisure: 5 hours)	
OVERTIME (*minutes*)	LEISURE TIME EXPENDED (*percent*)	LEISURE TIME REMAINING (*percent*)
0	0	100
15	5	95
30	10	90
45	15	85
60	20	80
75	25	75
90	30	70
105	35	65
120	40	60
135	45	55
150	50	50
165	55	45
180	60	40
195	65	35
210	70	30
225	75	25
240	80	20
255	85	15
270	90	10
285	95	5
300	100	0

TABLE 4-4
HOW WE SPEND OUR WEEKENDS

ACTIVITY	TIME (*hours*)	TIME (*percent*)
Sleeping	16	33.3
Major chores[1]	6	12.5
Meals, grooming, errands[2]	6	12.5
Leisure time	20	41.7
Total	48	100.0

[1]This activity includes lawn and garden work, painting and repairing your home, bill paying, servicing the car, washing and cleaning, and shopping for major items. Six hours is an average figure. Some weekends you may work all day on your home, others not at all, etc.

[2]This activity includes one-half hour each day for each of the following: get up, dress, and groom; breakfast; lunch; and miscellaneous items such as minor errands and pet care. Also includes one hour each day for dinner. Total of three hours each day for these activities.

objective, combine your overtime hours with the total time you spend commuting both ways and then subtract 30 minutes for the assumed commute, which you have already accounted for. Find that figure in the left column and read across to see how much of your potential leisure time you have spent in overtime and commuting combined.

The Impact of Commuting and Overtime on Weekly Leisure Time
Some of you may prefer to evaluate your leisure/work decisions on a weekly basis. The additional assumptions needed to do this are discussed below and summarized in Table 4-4. Table 4–5 shows how your weekly leisure time is affected by commuting and overtime combined.

Major household chores are usually done on weekends. Saturday is often the day people do such things as lawn and garden work, paint and repair the house, pay bills, have the car serviced, do the laundry, clean, and shop for clothing, appliances, and furniture. An assumed minimum of six hours each weekend has been set aside for the completion of these tasks. Again, you will have to be well organized to complete all these duties between, for example, 9 A.M. and 3 P.M. on Saturday. Of course, some of these chores can be done during the week; but regardless of how you shuffle these tasks around in the week or over several weeks, your average maximum weekly leisure time remains the same.

TABLE 4-5
THE IMPACT OF COMMUTING AND OVERTIME ON WEEKLY LEISURE TIME

COMMUTING AND OVERTIME (total hours)	LEISURE TIME EXPENDED (percent)	LEISURE TIME REMAINING (percent)
2.5[1]	None	100.0
3	1.1	98.9
4	3.3	96.7
5	5.5	94.5
6	7.7	92.3
7	9.9	90.1
8	12.2	87.8
9	14.4	85.6
10	16.6	83.4
11	18.8	81.2
12	21.1	78.9
13	23.3	76.7
14	25.5	74.5
15	27.7	72.3
16	30.0	70.0
17	32.2	67.8
18	34.4	65.6
19	36.6	63.4
20	38.8	61.2
21	41.1	58.9
22	43.3	56.7
23	45.5	54.5
24	47.7	52.3
25	50.0	50.0
26	52.2	47.8
27	54.4	43.6
28	56.6	43.4
29	58.8	41.2
30	61.1	38.9

[1] Fifteen minutes is the assumed minimum daily one-way base commute which serves as the standard for all comparisons. People having this commute are defined as having 100 percent of their maximum potential leisure time available after commuting. Over a standard five-day week, such individuals would spend a total of 2.5 hours commuting to and from work.

Meals, grooming, and miscellaneous duties, such as pet care, are assumed to require another six hours each weekend. Sixteen hours are spent sleeping, which leaves a maximum weekend leisure time of 20 hours. Of the maximum total leisure time of 45 hours each week, 25 hours (or 56 percent) is available during the week and the remaining 20 hours (or 44 percent) during the weekend. Of course, as with the earlier tables, you may wish to modify these tables if you find these assumptions unsatisfactory for your particular circumstances.

How Does Vacation Time Affect Annual Leisure Time?

Annual vacation time can vary from one week to several months depending on your career and employer. Table 4–6 shows the significance of vacation time to your total annual leisure time. Each week of vacation is assumed to add 40 hours of additional annual leisure time. Two weeks of annual vacation time is considered the minimum against which all comparisons are drawn. Annual work and leisure time in hours and as a percentage of this two-week standard appear in the center columns of Table 4–6.

TABLE 4-6
ANNUAL LEISURE/WORK CALCULATIONS

Definition Assumed Standard is based on:

Annual Leisure Time

Weekday Leisure (52 weeks × 25 hours) 1,300 hours
Weekend Leisure (52 weeks × 20 hours) 1,040 hours
Vacation Leisure (2 weeks × 40 hours) 80 hours

Total Annual Leisure Time	2,420 hours
Total Annual Working Time (50 weeks × 40 hours)	2,000 hours
Standard Leisure/Work Index (2,420/2,000)	1.21 (standard)

ANNUAL LEISURE/WORK CALCULATIONS

VACATION TIME WEEKS	WORKING TIME		LEISURE TIME		LEISURE WORK INDEX
	Hours	Percent of Standard	Hours	Percent of Standard	
0	2,080	104[1]	2,340	96.7	1.125
1	2,040	102[1]	2,380	98.3	1.167
2	2,000	100	2,420	100.0	1.210
3	1,960	98	2,460	101.7	1.255
4	1,920	96	2,500	103.3	1.302
5	1,880	94	2,540	105.0	1.351
6	1,840	92	2,580	106.6	1.402
7	1,800	90	2,620	108.3	1.456
8	1,760	88	2,660	109.9	1.511
9	1,720	86	2,700	111.6	1.570
10	1,680	84	2,740	113.2	1.631
11	1,640	82	2,780	114.9	1.695
12	1,600	80	2,820	116.5	1.763
13	1,560	78	2,860	118.2	1.833
14	1,520	76	2,900	119.8	1.908
15	1,480	74	2,940	121.5	1.986
16	1,440	72	2,980	123.1	2.129

[1] These figures exceed 100 percent because less than the assumed standard two weeks of vacation time has been taken.

TABLE 4-7
IMPACT OF COMMUTING AND OVERTIME ON ANNUAL
HOURS OF LEISURE AND THE LEISURE/WORK INDEX

(Standard Base Assumes 2,000-hour work year and 15-minute Commute)
Numbers In Each Cluster Represent: Annual Hours of Leisure Time
Annual Hours of Work
Leisure/Work Index

LENGTH OF ONE-WAY COMMUTE (*Minutes*)	AVERAGE WEEKLY HOURS OF OVERTIME WORK					
	None	*2*	*4*	*6*	*8*	*10*
15	2,420[1]	2,320	2,220	2,120	2,020	1,920
	2,000[1]	2,100	2,200	2,300	2,400	2,500
	1.21[1]	1.105	1.009	.922	.842	.768
30	2,295	2,195	2,095	1,995	1,895	1,795
	2,000	2,100	2,200	2,300	2,400	2,500
	1.148	1.045	.952	.867	.790	.718
45	2,170	2,070	1,970	1,870	1,770	1,670
	2,000	2,100	2,200	2,300	2,400	2,500
	1.085	.986	.895	.813	.738	.668
60	2,045	1,945	1,845	1,745	1,645	1,545
	2,000	2,100	2,200	2,300	2,400	2,500
	1.023	.926	.837	.759	.685	.618
75	1,920	1,820	1,720	1,620	1,520	1,420
	2,000	2,100	2,200	2,300	2,400	2,500
	.960	.867	.782	.704	.633	.568
90	1,795	1,695	1,595	1,495	1,395	1,295
	2,000	2,100	2,200	2,300	2,400	2,500
	.898	.807	.725	.650	.581	.518
105	1,670	1,570	1,470	1,370	1,270	1,170
	2,000	2,100	2,200	2,300	2,400	2,500
	.835	.748	.668	.596	.529	.468
120	1,545	1,445	1,345	1,235	1,135	1,035
	2,000	2,100	2,200	2,300	2,400	2,500
	.773	.688	.611	.537	.473	.414

[1] These are the figures for the standard which assumes a 15-minute one-way commute, a 40-hour, five-day work week without overtime, and two weeks of annual vacation time.

The Leisure/Work Index: A Monitor of the Balance in Your Life

The leisure/work index is an analytical tool designed to help you monitor the leisure/work balance in your life. It is constructed as follows by expressing your annual leisure hours as a percentage of the time you spend working each year:

$$\text{Leisure/Work Index} = \frac{\text{Annual Hours of Leisure Time}}{\text{Annual Hours of Work}}$$

The leisure/work indexes that appear in Table 4–6 have been computed as a function of annual weeks of vacation time. These calculations are based on a standard forty-hour, five-day work week and a fifteen-minute one-way commute. The standard leisure/work index of 1.21 also assumes two weeks of annual vacation time.

As you experiment with your own leisure/work index, you will discover that it is very sensitive to changes in overtime hours. This sensitivity is due to the fact that overtime hours are subtracted from the numerator and added to the denominator of this index. Likewise, this index is very sensitive to gains in additional vacation time. In this case, your index rises rapidly because the balance in the way you are spending your time income has shifted away from your career to your leisure-time pursuits.

Finally, because most readers will commute more than 15 minutes, the impact of longer commutes is shown in Table 4–7. Separate calculations that reveal the joint effect of overtime and commuting are also provided. The top, middle, and bottom numbers in each commuting/overtime category refer respectively to annual hours of leisure time, annual hours of work, and the leisure/work index that was computed by dividing the top number by the middle number. For example, if you commute 45 minutes one way and work an average of two hours of overtime each week, your annual leisure time is 2,070 hours, you work 2,100 hours annually, and your leisure/work index is 2,070/2,100 or .986. Table 4–7 dramatically demonstrates just how rapidly commuting and overtime can erode the leisure/work balance in your life.

FOOTNOTES

CHAPTER TWO

[1]"Bonehead English," *Time*, Nov. 11, 1974, p. 106.
[2]"Learning Less," *Time*, March 31, 1975, p. 67.
[3]"Too Many A's," *Time*, Nov. 11, 1974, p. 106.
[4]"Too Many A's," *Time*, Nov. 11, 1974, p. 106.

CHAPTER THREE

[1]Maya Pines, *The Brain Changers*, Harcourt Brace Jovanovich, New York, 1973. This book, which is written for a lay audience, was awarded the annual prize of the American Psychological Association. The material that appears in this section has been summarized from Chapter Seven of this book, which is available now in paperback from the New American Library.
[2]Ibid., p. 152.
[3]Maxwell Maltz, *Psycho-Cybernetics*, Essandess Special Editions, New York, 1960. The information in this section is taken from this interesting book.
[4]Ibid., p. 32.
[5]Ibid., pp. 31–32.

CHAPTER FOUR

[1]U.S. Department of Labor, Bureau of Labor Statistics, *Handbook of Labor Statistics 1973*, Bulletin 1790, Washington, 1973, pp. 287, 403–404 (served as the source for the income data).

U.S. Bureau of the Census, *Statistical Abstract of the United States: 1972*, 93rd edition, Washington, 1972, p. 5 (served as the source for the population data).

Figures were constructed by converting both years' gross national product figures into constant 1967 figures, for which the consumer price indexes for all items were used; and then dividing these figures by total population, including armed forces abroad, to get annual per capita income in 1967 dollars for both years from which the percentage increase was computed.

[2]U.S. Department of Labor, Bureau of Labor Statistics, *Handbook of Labor Statistics 1973*, Bulletin 1790, Washington, 1973, p. 31.

[3]Executive Office of the President: Office of Management and Budget, *Social Indicators 1973*, Washington, 1973, p. 142.

CHAPTER FIVE

[1]Larry H. Long, "Migration Differentials by Education and Occupation: Trends and Variations," *Demography*, vol. 10, no. 2, p. 245, Population Association of America, Washington, May 1973.

[2]George Gallup, "City Life Continues to Lose Appeal; Fear for Personal Safety May Be Key Reason," Field Enterprises, Inc., Chicago, 1972.

[3]Mary Bralove, "The New Nomads," *The Wall Street Journal*, August 1, 1973, p. 1.

[4]Ronald G. Shafer, "A Fading Dream," *The Wall Street Journal*, Sept. 3, 1974, p. 1.

[5]Lindley H. Clark, Jr., "Trend Buckers," *The Wall Street Journal*, Dec. 31, 1973, p. 1. Readers interested in documentation of this phenomenon should read this article. Among other things, this report reveals that Arizona's economy continued to grow at an average annual rate of 6.6 percent even during national recessions, whereas Michigan has had the greatest economic instability of any state.

CHAPTER SIX

[1]These are the National Bureau of Economic Research's reference cycle turning points as revised in 1975.

CHAPTER SEVEN

[1]Milton Friedman, *Capitalism and Freedom*, University of Chicago Press, Chicago, 1962, p. 154.

[2]*1975 Pennsylvania Tree Fruit Production Guide*, The Pennsylvania State University, Cooperative Extension Service, University Park, 1975, pp. 42–51, 93.

CHAPTER EIGHT

[1]This statement is supported by the following quote, which is also an indication of how effective legal entry barriers (discussed in Chapter Seven) have been in raising physicians' wages. "The average private in-office physician in Lebanon County made $97,049 in 1972, according to a study released yesterday by the Pennsylvania Department of Health." By way of comparison, the median money income of a family headed by a man was $12,965 in the U.S. in 1973. Lebanon County is a rural area located in central Pennsylvania where this book was completed. Source of this quote: "Co. Physicians' Average Pay Set at $97,000," *Lebanon Daily News*, November 11, 1975, p. 1.

CHAPTER NINE

[1]*The Failure Record through 1965*, Dunn & Bradstreet, New York, 1966.

CHAPTER TWELVE

[1]For more on these matters see Stanley M. Herman, *The People Specialists*, Alfred A. Knopf, New York, 1968.

[2]Richard Nelson Bolles, *What Color Is Your Parachute?*, Ten Speed Press, Berkeley, 1972, p. 37.

CHAPTER THIRTEEN

[1]Gaylord Nelson, *Congressional Record*, 92nd Cong., 2d Sess., February 14, 1972.

[2]Ibid.

[3]"Controlling Additives," *The Washington Post*, January 17, 1973.

[4]Gaylord Nelson, *Congressional Record*, 94th Cong., 1st Sess., March 3, 1975, pp. S.2883–S.2886.

[5]Benjamin Feingold, *Why Your Child Is Hyperactive*, Random House, New York, 1975.

[6]"The Feingold Diet Has Worked Wonders for Jamie," *Prevention*, August 1975, p. 61.

[7]This book can be purchased for $3.00 from the non-profit Lee Foundation for Nutritional Research, 2023 West Wisconsin Avenue, Milwaukee, Wisconsin 53201.

[8]Harvey W. Wiley, *The History of a Crime Against the Food Law*, Lee Foundation for Nutritional Research, Milwaukee, 1955 (reissue date), pp. 61–62.

[9]Beatrice Trum Hunter, *Fact Book on Food Additives*, Keats Publishing, New Canaan, Conn., 1972, p. 2.

[10]Ibid., pp. 99–106.

[11]*1975 Pennsylvania Tree Fruit Production Guide*, The Pennsylvania State University, Cooperative Extension Service, University Park, 1975, pp. 42–51, 93.

[12]This information was obtained directly from Mr. Joseph Brennan, Chief, Pennsylvania Bureau of Foods and Chemistry, December 1975.

[13]The farmers' "safety and risks" are diametrically opposite those of food consumers, however, only in their role as food producers and not even there. Most farmers are now specialists and, consequently, they too eat our commercially grown foods. Farmers also inevitably get a little of these poisons directly as they are applying them. Incidentally, one of the chief advantages of systemic pesticides (those that enter into the plant itself and its fruit) is that those people, such as the pickers, who work with these systemically treated fruits and vegetables are not as likely to be poisoned by these pesticides as by the pesticides that are applied to the plants' surfaces.

[14]"Controlling Additives," *The Washington Post*, January 17, 1973.

[15]U.S. Department of Labor, Bureau of Labor Statistics, *Handbook of Labor Statistics 1973*, Bulletin 1790, Washington, 1973, pp. 287, 403–404 (served as the source for the income data).

U.S. Bureau of the Census, *Statistical Abstract of the United States: 1972*, 93rd edition, Washington, 1972, p. 5 (served as the source for the population data).

Figures were constructed by converting both year's gross national product figures into constant 1967 figures, for which the consumer price indexes for all items were used; and then dividing these figures by total population including armed forces abroad to get annual per capita income in 1967 dollars for both years from which the percentage increase was computed.

[16]U.S. Department of Labor, Bureau of Labor Statistics, *Handbook of Labor Statistics 1973*, Bulletin 1790, Washington, 1973, p. 31.

[17]Executive Office of the President: Office of Management and Budget, *Social Indicators 1973*, U.S. Government Printing Office, Washington, 1973, p. 142, Table 4/13.

[18]Ibid., p. 206, Table 6/1.

[19]Ibid., p. 100, Table 3/2.

[20]Ibid., p. 105, Table 3/13.

[21]Ibid., p. 180, Table 5/12.

[22]Ibid., p. 64, Table 2/1.

[23]Ibid., p. 65, Table 2/3.

[24]Ibid., p. 30, Table 1/6.

[25]Bruno Bettelheim, *The Children of the Dream*, Avon Books, New York, 1970.

[26]Herbert Hendin, *The Age of Sensation*, W. W. Norton & Co., New York, 1975.

[27]For a comprehensive evaluation of the effects of rapid change on human behavior read Alvin Toffler's bestseller, *Future Shock*, Random House, New York, 1970. Available also in paperback from Bantam Books.

NOTE ONE

[1]Robert J. Jameson, *The Professional Job Changing System*, 3rd ed., Performance Dynamics, Verona, N.J., 1974, pp. 150–151.

APPENDIX CHAPTER FOUR

[1]Executive Office of the President: Office of Management and Budget, *Social Indicators 1973*, Washington, 1973, p. 149, Table 4/24.

YOUR CAREER SHOPPING LIST

YOUR CAREER SHOPPING LIST

YOUR CAREER SHOPPING LIST

YOUR CAREER SHOPPING LIST

YOUR CAREER SHOPPING LIST

YOUR CAREER SHOPPING LIST

YOUR CAREER SHOPPING LIST

YOUR CAREER SHOPPING LIST

YOUR CAREER SHOPPING LIST

YOUR CAREER SHOPPING LIST

YOUR CAREER SHOPPING LIST

ABOUT THE AUTHOR

Dr. Moore graduated from Lehigh University, attended universities in Europe and Africa for three years, and completed his graduate studies in Economic Theory at Northwestern University. His professional career spans both education and industry. He has taught on the faculties of four universities, held the post of Senior Economic Analyst at Exxon Corporation, acted as a general economic consultant to industry, and served as the Executive Director of the National Institute of Career Planning since its inception in 1973.

A prolific scholar and author, Dr. Moore has received numerous research grants and delivered and published a variety of professional papers and articles. He is the author of more than 70 published titles alone on the subject of career decision-making, including his most recent analysis of the career prospects of the postwar baby boom generation (born 1946-1965) entitled, *Baby Boom Equals Career Bust,* published by the U.S. Office of Career Education of HEW. Dr. Moore has been interviewed on numerous television and radio talk shows and speaks frequently to college audiences about career opportunities for college graduates and effective job-finding strategies.